MW01033533

THE FATHERS OF THE CHURCH

A NEW TRANSLATION

VOLUME 146

THE FATHERS OF THE CHURCH

A NEW TRANSLATION

ORIGEN

HOMILIES ON PSALMS 36–38

Translated by

MICHAEL HEINTZ

THE CATHOLIC UNIVERSITY OF AMERICA PRESS
Washington, D.C.

Printed in the United States of America

The paper used in this publication meets the minimum requirements of the American National Standards for Information Science--Permanence of Paper for Printed Library Materials, ANSI Z39.48 - 1984.

∞

Cataloging-in-Publication data is available from the Library of Congress.
ISBN 978-0-8132-3649-0

CONTENTS

INDICES

ACKNOWLEDGMENTS

In the design of divine Providence I was privileged to complete work on the final proofs of this volume while on retreat at Tabgha on the northwest shore of the Sea of Galilee, in the land where Origen spent the second half of his life and ministry, and where, a century later, Rufinus for a time lived the monastic life.

This translation began years ago in a doctoral seminar at the University of Notre Dame taught by the late Rowan Greer in his capacity as visiting professor. It was at his prompting and encouragement that I began work on Origen's *Homilies on the Psalms* in Rufinus's translation. I am no less grateful to those seminary professors who first introduced me to the study of the Fathers, in particular Fathers John Farrell, William Palardy, and Laurence McGrath.

I wish to thank my former student and now learned friend, Andrew Chronister, who at an early stage in the production of this volume was of enormous technical assistance, as well as my current students Sean O'Connor and Tomás Villacis, for their generous work in compiling the indices.

I am also deeply indebted to Carole Burnett of the Catholic University of America Press: her sharp eye and sound editorial judgment are equaled only by her generosity and graciousness. Working with her has been a great joy.

Finally, but first in the order of importance, I am most grateful to those who guided my studies at the University of Notre Dame, especially John Cavadini, Brian Daley, Robin Darling Young, Joseph Wawrykow, and Daniel Sheerin. These were my teachers who in various ways had a profound impact on the shape of my mind, and whom I was also soon blessed to join as a colleague in the Theology Department. I am abidingly grateful for their many kindnesses, not least their witness of scholarship at the service of the Church: Οὐκ ἔστιν μαθητὴς ὑπὲρ τὸν διδάσκαλον...ἀρκετὸν τῷ μαθητῇ ἵνα γένηται ὡς ὁ διδάσκαλος αὐτοῦ (Matthew 10.24–25).

ABBREVIATIONS

General Abbreviations

CCL	Corpus Christianorum, Series Latina [Turnhout, 1954–]
CPG	Clavis Patrum Graecorum [ed. M. Geerard, 1974–87]
CPL	Clavis Patrum Latinorum [ed. E. Dekkers, 1995]
CSEL	Corpus Scriptorum Ecclesiasticorum Latinorum [Vienna, 1866–]
GCS	Die griechischen christlichen Schriftsteller der ersten drei Jahrhunderte [Leipzig and Berlin, 1897–]
GK	*Origenes vier Bücher von den Prinzipien* [ed. H. Görgemanns and H. Karpp, 1992]
Lewis and Short	*A Latin Dictionary* [ed. C. Lewis, 1879]
LXX	Septuagint
OLD	*Oxford Latin Dictionary* [ed. P. G. W. Glare, 1982]
PG	J.-P. Migne, Patrologiae Cursus Completus, Series Graeca [Paris, 1857–1866]
PL	J.-P. Migne, Patrologiae Cursus Completus, Series Latina [Paris, 1844–1864]
SC	Sources Chrétiennes [Paris, 1942–]
Souter	*Glossary of Later Latin* [ed. A. Souter, 1949]
TLL	*Thesaurus Linguae Latinae* [Leipzig, 1900–]
VL	Vetus Latina/Old Latin version of the Scriptures
Vlg	Vulgate

Abbreviations of Origen's Works

Comm in Cant	*Commentary on the Canticle of Canticles*
Comm in Jn	*Commentary on the Gospel of John*
Comm in Rom	*Commentary on the Letter to the Romans*
Dial Heracl	*Dialogue with Heraclides*
Ex ad Mart	*Exhortation to Martyrdom*
Hom in Cant	*Homilies on the Canticle of Canticles*
Hom in Ex	*Homilies on the Book of Exodus*
Hom in Ez	*Homilies on the Prophet Ezekiel*
Hom in Gen	*Homilies on the Book of Genesis*
Hom in Jer	*Homilies on the Prophet Jeremiah*
Hom in Jos	*Homilies on Joshua*
Hom in Jud	*Homilies on the Book of Judges*
Hom in Lev	*Homilies on the Book of Leviticus*
Hom in Luc	*Homilies on the Gospel of Luke*
Hom in Num	*Homilies on the Book of Numbers*
Hom in Ps	*Homilies on the Psalms*
Hom in Sam	*Homilies on the Books of Samuel*

SELECT BIBLIOGRAPHY

Text

Origene, Omelie sui Salmi. Biblioteca Patristica 18. Edited by Emanuela Prinzivalli. Florence: Nardini Editore, 1991.

Origène, Homélies sur les Psaumes 36 à 38. Sources Chrétiennes 411. Edited by Emanuela Prinzivalli. With introduction, French translation, and notes by Henri Crouzel and Luc Brésard. Paris: Cerf, 1995.

Studies

Adler, William. "*Ad verbum* or *ad sensum:* The Christianization of a Latin Translation Formula in the Fourth Century." An unpublished paper presented at the meeting of the American Society of Church History, Williamsburg, VA, April 1, 1993.

Bader, Günther. *Psalterium affectuum palaestra: Prolegomena zu einer Theologie des Psalters.* Tübingen: J. C. B. Mohr, 1996.

Barnes, Timothy D. *Constantine and Eusebius.* Cambridge, MA: Harvard University Press, 1981.

Behr, John. *Origen: On First Principles.* Oxford: Oxford University Press, 2018.

———. *The Way to Nicaea.* Crestwood, NY: St Vladimir's Seminary Press, 2001.

Benjamins, Hendrik S. *Eingeordnete Freiheit: Freiheit und Vorsehung bei Origenes.* Leiden: Brill, 1994.

Blaise, Albert. *A Handbook of Christian Latin: Style, Morphology, and Syntax.* Translated by Grant C. Roti. Washington, DC: Georgetown University Press, 1994.

Blosser, Benjamin. *Become Like the Angels: Origen's Doctrine of the Soul.* Washington, DC: The Catholic University of America Press, 2012.

Borkowski, Andrew, and Paul Du Plessis. *Textbook on Roman Law.* 3rd ed. Oxford: Oxford University Press, 2005.

Bostock, David G. "Medical Theory and Theology in Origen." In *Origeniana Tertia,* edited by R. P. C. Hanson and Henri Crouzel, 191–99. Rome: Edizioni dell'Ateneo, 1985.

Bradshaw, Paul, Maxwell Johnson, and Edward Phillips. *The Apostolic Tradition.* Minneapolis, MN: Fortress, 2002.

Brent, Allen. *A Political History of Early Christianity*. London: T&T Clark, 2009.

Burton, Philip. *The Old Latin Gospels: A Study of their Texts and Language*. Oxford: Oxford University Press, 2000.

Butterworth, G. W., trans. and ed. *Origen: On First Principles*. Gloucester, UK: Peter Smith, 1973.

Cadiou, René. *Commentaires inédits des Psaumes: Étude sur les textes d'Origène contenus dans le manuscrit* Vindobonensis 8. Paris: Société d'édition Les Belles Lettres, 1936.

Caloz, Masséo. *Étude sur la LXX origénienne du Psautier: Les relations entre les leçons des Psaumes du Manuscrit Coislin 44, les Fragments des Hexaples et le texte du Psautier Gallican*. Fribourg: Éditions universitaires, 1978.

Carriker, Andrew. *The Library of Eusebius of Caesarea*. Leiden: Brill, 2003.

Cavadini, John. "From Letter to Spirit: The Multiple Senses of Scripture." In *The Oxford Handbook of Early Christian Biblical Interpretation*, edited by Paul M. Blowers and Peter W. Martens, 126–48. Oxford: Oxford University Press, 2019.

Cerrato, J. A. *Hippolytus Between East and West: The Commentaries and the Provenance of the Corpus*. Oxford: Oxford University Press, 2002.

Chadwick, Henry. *Origen: Contra Celsum*. Cambridge: Cambridge University Press, 1953.

———. *The Sentences of Sextus: A Contribution to the History of Early Christian Ethics*. Cambridge: Cambridge University Press, 1959.

Chiesa, Paolo. "*Ad verbum* o *ad sensum*? Modelli e coscienza metodologica della traduzione tra tarda antichità e alto medioevo." *Medioevo e Rinascimento* 1 (1987): 1–51.

Clark, Elizabeth A. *The Origenist Controversy: The Cultural Construction of an Early Christian Debate*. Princeton: Princeton University Press, 1992.

Consolino, Franca Ela. "Le prefazioni di Girolamo e Rufino alle loro traduzioni di Origene." In *Origeniana Quinta*, edited by Robert J. Daly, 92–98. Leuven: Peeters, Leuven University Press, 1992.

Coppa, Giovanni. *Settantaquattro omelie du libro dei Salmi*. Turin: Pauline, 1993.

Crouzel, Henri. *Origen*. Translated by A. S. Worrall. San Francisco: Harper and Row, 1989.

———. *Origène et la connaissance mystique*. Bruges: Desclée de Brouwer, 1961.

———. *Origène et la philosophie*. Paris: Aubier, 1962.

———. "Quand le Fils transmet le Royaume à son Père: L'interprétation d'Origène." *Studia Missionalia* 33 (1984): 359–84.

———. *Théologie de l'image de Dieu chez Origène*. Paris: Aubier, 1956.

Dal Covolo, Enrico. "Note sulla dottrina origeniana della morte." In *Origeniana Quinta*, edited by Robert J. Daly, 430–37. Leuven: Peeters, Leuven University Press, 1992.

Daley, Brian. "Is Patristic Exegesis Still Usable? Reflections on Early Christian Interpretation of the Psalms." *Communio* 29 (2002): 185–216.

———. "Origen's *De Principiis:* A Guide to the Principles of Christian Scriptural Interpretation." In *Vetera et Nova: Patristic Studies in Honor of Thomas Patrick Halton,* edited by John Petruccione, 3–21. Washington, DC: The Catholic University of America Press, 1998.

Daniélou, Jean. *The Angels and their Mission according to the Fathers of the Church.* Translated by David Heimann. Westminster, MD: The Newman Press, 1957. Reprinted, Allen, TX: Christian Classics, 1987.

———. *The Bible and the Liturgy.* Notre Dame, IN: University of Notre Dame Press, 1966.

———. *From Shadows to Reality: Studies in the Biblical Typology of the Fathers.* Translated by Wulstan Hibberd. London: Burns and Oates, 1960.

———. *Gospel Message and Hellenistic Culture.* Translated by John Austin Baker. Philadelphia: Westminster, 1973.

———. *Origen.* Translated by Walter Mitchell. New York: Sheed and Ward, 1955.

Dawson, David. "Allegorical Reading and the Embodiment of the Soul in Origen." In *Christian Origins: Theology, Rhetoric, and Community,* edited by Lewis Ayres and Gareth Jones, 26–43. London: Routledge, 1998.

———. *Christian Figural Reading and the Fashioning of Identity.* Berkeley: University of California Press, 2002.

de Lange, Nicholas. *Origen and the Jews: Studies in Jewish-Christian Relations in Third-century Palestine.* University of Cambridge Oriental Publications 25. Cambridge: Cambridge University Press, 1976.

de Lubac, Henri. *History and Spirit: The Understanding of Scripture According to Origen.* Translated by Anne Englund Nash. San Francisco: Ignatius, 2007.

———. "Tripartite Anthropology." In de Lubac, *Theology in History,* translated by Anne Englund Nash, 117–200. San Francisco: Ignatius, 1996.

Devreesse, Robert. *Les anciens commentateurs grecs de Psaumes* [*Studi et Testi* 264]. Rome: Biblioteca Apostolica Vaticana, 1970.

Dihle, Albrecht. *The Theory of Will in Classical Antiquity.* Berkeley: University of California Press, 1982.

Dively Lauro, Elizabeth Ann. *The Soul and the Spirit of Scripture within Origen's Exegesis.* Boston: Brill, 2005.

Dorival, Gilles. "Aperçu sur l'histoire des chaînes exégétiques grecques sur le psautier (V–XIV siècles)." *Studia Patristica* 15 (1984): 146–69.

———. *Les chaînes exégétiques grecques sur les Psaumes: Contribution à l'étude d'une forme littéraire.* 4 vols. Leuven: Peeters, 1986.

———. *Le Psautier chez les Pères.* Strasbourg: Centre d'analyse et de documentation patristiques, 1994.

Drewery, Benjamin. *Origen and the Doctrine of Grace.* London: Epworth Press, 1960.

Edwards, Mark J. "Christ or Plato?" In *Christian Origins: Theology, Rhetoric, and Community,* edited by Lewis Ayres and Gareth Jones, 11–25. London: Routledge, 1998.

———. *Origen against Plato.* Aldershot: Ashgate, 2002.

Fischer, Balthasar. *Die Psalmen als Stimme der Kirche: Gesammelte Studien zur christlichen Psalmenfrömmigkeit.* Trier: Paulinus, 1982.

Flynn, William. "Liturgical Music." In *The Oxford History of Christian Worship,* edited by Geoffrey Wainwright and Karen Westerfield Tucker, 769–92. Oxford: Oxford University Press, 2006.

Frede, Michael. *A Free Will: Origins of the Notion in Ancient Thought.* Berkeley: University of California Press, 2011.

———. "Origen's Treatise *Against Celsus.*" In *Apologetics in the Roman Empire: Pagans, Jews, and Christians,* edited by Mark Edwards, Martin Goodman, and Simon Price, in association with Christopher Rowland, 131–55. Oxford: Oxford University Press, 1999.

Godin, André. *Érasme lecteur d'Origène.* Geneva: Librairie Droz, 1982.

Gögler, Rolf. "Inkarnationsglaube und Bibeltheologie bei Origenes." *Theologische Quartalschrift* 165 (1985): 82–94.

Grafton, Anthony, and Megan Williams. *Christianity and the Transformation of the Book: Origen, Eusebius, and the Library of Caesarea.* Cambridge, MA: Belknap, 2006.

Grant, Robert. "More Fragments of Origen?" *Vigiliae Christianae* 2 (1948): 243–47.

Grappone, Antonio. "Annotazioni sulla cronologia delle Omelie di Origene." *Augustinianum* 41 (2001): 27–58.

———. *Omelie origeniane nella traduzione di Rufino. Un confronto con i testi greci.* Rome: Institutum Patristicum Augustinianum, 2007.

Hadot, Ilsetraut. *Arts libéraux et philosophie dans la pensée antique.* Paris: Études Augustiniennes, 1984.

Hadot, Pierre. *What is Ancient Philosophy?* Translated by Michael Chase. Cambridge, MA: Harvard University Press, 2002.

Hale Williams, Megan. *The Monk and the Book: Jerome and the Making of Christian Scholarship.* Chicago: University of Chicago Press, 2006.

Hällström, Gunnar af. *Fides Simpliciorum according to Origen of Alexandria.* Helsinki: Societas Scientiarum Fennica, 1984.

Hammond Bammel, Caroline. "The Last Ten Years of Rufinus' Life and the Date of his Move South to Aquileia." *Journal of Theological Studies* n.s. 28 (1977): 372–429.

———. *Der Römerbriefkommentar des Origenes: Kritische Ausgabe der Übersetzung Rufins, Buch 1–3.* Freiburg: Herder, 1990.

Hanson, R. P. C. *Allegory and Event: A Study of the Sources and Significance of Origen's Interpretation of Scripture.* Louisville, KY: Westminster John Knox, 2002.

Harl, Marguerite. *Origène et la fonction révélatrice du Verbe incarné.* Paris: Éditions du Seuil, 1958.

Harnack, Adolf. *Geschichte der altchristlichen Litteratur bis Eusebius.* 4 vols. Leipzig: J. C. Hinrichs, 1958.

Heine, Ronald. *The Commentary of Origen on the Gospel of St. Matthew.* 2 vols. Oxford: Oxford University Press, 2018.

———. "Epinoiai." In *The Westminster Handbook to Origen,* edited by John A. McGuckin, 93–95. Louisville, KY: Westminster John Knox, 2004.

———. *Gregory of Nyssa's Treatise on the Inscriptions of the Psalms.* Oxford: Clarendon, 1995.

———, trans. Origen. *Homilies on Genesis and Exodus.* Fathers of the Church 71. Washington, DC: The Catholic University of America Press, 1982.

———. "Origen on the Christological Significance of Psalm 45 (44)." *Consensus* 23 (1997): 21–37.

———. *Origen: Scholarship in the Service of the Church.* New York: Oxford University Press, 2011.

Hennessey, Lawrence. "Origen of Alexandria: The Fate of the Soul and Body After Death." *Second Century* 8 (1991): 163–78.

———. "A Philosophical Issue in Origen's Eschatology: The Three Senses of Incorporeality." In *Origeniana Quinta,* edited by Robert J. Daly, 373–80. Leuven: Peeters, Leuven University Press, 1992.

Hurtado, Larry. *The Earliest Christian Artifacts: Manuscripts and Christian Origins.* Grand Rapids, MI: Eerdmans, 2006.

James, Mark Randall. *Learning the Language of Scripture: Origen, Wisdom, and the Logic of Interpretation.* Leiden: Brill, 2021.

Janson, Tore. *Latin Prose Prefaces: Studies in Literary Conventions.* Stockholm: Almqvist and Wiksell, 1964.

Jülicher, Adolf. *Itala: Das Neue Testament in altlateinischer Überlieferung.* 4 vols. Berlin: De Gruyter, 1954.

Kelly, J. N. D. *Jerome: His Life, Writings, and Controversies.* Peabody, MA: Hendrickson, 1998.

King, J. Christopher. *Origen on the Song of Songs as the Spirit of Scripture: The Bridegroom's Perfect Marriage Song.* Oxford: Oxford University Press, 2005.

Klosterman, Erich, and Ernst Benz. *Origenes Matthäuserklärung II: Die lateinische Übersetzung der Commentariorum Series* [= *Die griechischen christlichen Schriftsteller der ersten drei Jahrhunderte 44: Origenes Werke XI*]. Revised edition by Ursula Treu. Berlin: Akademie Verlag, 1976.

Kolbet, Paul. "Athanasius, the Psalms, and the Reformation of the Self." *Harvard Theological Review* 99 (2006): 85–101.

Latko, Ernest. *Origen's Concept of Penance.* Quebec: Laval, 1949.

Le Boulluec, Alain. "La polémique contre les hérésies dans les *Homélies sur les Psaumes* d'Origène." *Adamantius* 20 (2014): 256–74.

Leclercq, Jean. *The Love of Learning and the Desire for God: A Study of Monastic Culture.* Translated by Catharine Misrahi. New York: Fordham University Press, 1961.

———. "Nouveaux témoins sur Origène au XIIe siècle." *Medieval Studies* 15 (1953): 104–6.

———. "Origène au XIIe siècle." *Irénikon* 24 (1951): 425–39.

Lewy, Hans. *Sobria Ebrietas: Untersuchungen zur Geschichte der antiken Mystik.* Giessen: Verlag von Alfred Töpelmann, 1929.

Louth, Andrew. *The Origins of the Christian Mystical Tradition: Plato to Denys.* Oxford: Clarendon, 1981.

Marcovich, Miroslav. *Iustini Martyris Dialogus cum Tryphone.* Berlin: De Gruyter, 1997.

Martens, Peter W. *Origen and Scripture: The Contours of the Exegetical Life.* New York: Oxford University Press, 2014.

Marti, Heinrich. *Übersetzer der Augustin-Zeit.* Munich: Wilhelm-Fink, 1974.

Matter, E. Ann. *The Voice of My Beloved: The Song of Songs in Western Medieval Christianity.* Philadelphia: University of Pennsylvania Press, 1990.

Maur, H. J. auf der. *Das Psalmenverständnis des Ambrosius von Mailand: Ein Beitrag zum Deutungshintergrund der Psalmenverwendung im Gottesdienst der Alten Kirche.* Leiden: Brill, 1977.

McGuckin, John Anthony. "Caesarea Maritima as Origen Knew It." In *Origeniana Quinta,* edited by Robert J. Daly, 3–25. Leuven: Peeters, Leuven University Press, 1992.

———. "Origen's Use of the Psalms in the Treatise *On First Principles.*" In *Meditations of the Heart: The Psalms in Early Christian Thought and Practice. Essays in Honour of Andrew Louth,* edited by A. Andreopoulos, A. Casiday, and C. Harrison, 97–118. Turnhout: Brepols, 2011.

McKinnon, James. *Music in Early Christian Literature.* Cambridge: Cambridge University Press, 1986.

Merlo, Francesca, and J. Gribomont. *Il Salterio di Rufino.* Vatican City: Libreria Vaticana, 1972.

Metzger, Bruce. *The Canon of the New Testament: Its Origin, Development, and Significance.* Oxford: Clarendon, 1987.

Miranda, Americo. "La nozione di 'corpo spirituale' in Origene e nella tradizione antiochena." *Gregorianum* 84 (2003): 295–314.

Mitchell, Margaret. "'Problems and Solutions' in Early Christian Biblical Interpretation: A Telling Case from Origen's Newly-Discovered Greek Homilies on the Psalms (*Codex Monacensis Graecus* 314)." In *Adamantius* 22 (2016): 40–55.

Mohrmann, Christine. "*Praedicare–Tractare–Sermo.*" *Maison-Dieu* 39 (1954): 97–107.

Monaci Castagno, Adele. "Contesto liturgico e cronologia della predicazione origeniana alla luce della nuove *Omelie sui Salmi.*" In *Adamantius* 20 (2014): 238–55.

———. *Origene predicatore e il suo pubblico.* Turin: Franco Angeli, 1987.

———. "Origen the Scholar and Pastor." In *Preacher and Audience: Studies in Early Christian and Byzantine Homiletics,* edited by Mary B. Cunningham and Pauline Allen, 65–87. Leiden: Brill, 1998.

Morgan, Teresa. *Literate Education in the Hellenistic and Roman Worlds.* Cambridge: Cambridge University Press, 1998.

Mühlenberg, Ekkehard. *Psalmenkommentare aus der Katenenüberlieferung.* 3 vols. Berlin: De Gruyter, 1975–1978.

———. "Zur Überlieferung des Psalmenkommentars von Origenes." In *Texte und Textkritik,* edited by Jürgen Dummer, 441–51. Berlin: Akademie Verlag, 1987.

Murphy, Francis X. *Rufinus of Aquileia (345–411): His Life and Works.* Washington, DC: The Catholic University of America Press, 1945.

Nautin, Pierre. *Le Dossier d'Hippolyte et de Méliton.* Paris: Cerf, 1953.

———. "L'homélie d'Hippolyte sur le psautier et les oeuvres de Josipe." *Revue de l'histoire des religions* 179.2 (1971): 137–79.

———. *Origène: Sa vie et son oeuvre.* Paris: Beauchesne, 1977.

Neuschäfer, Bernhard. *Origenes als Philologe.* 2 vols. Basel: Friedrich Reinhardt, 1987.

Noce, Carla. *Vestis Varia: L'imagine della veste nell'opera di Origene.* Rome: Augustinianum, 2003.

Notley, R. Steven, and Zev Safrai. *Eusebius,* Onomasticon: *The Place Names of Divine Scripture, including the Latin edition of Jerome.* Boston: Brill, 2005.

Nussbaum, Martha C. *The Therapy of Desire: Theory and Practice in Hellenistic Ethics.* Princeton: Princeton University Press, 1994.

O'Cleirig, P. "*Topoi* of Invention in Origen's Homilies." In *Origeniana Sexta,* edited by Gilles Dorival and Alain Le Boulluec, 277–87. Leuven: Peeters, Leuven University Press, 1995.

Olivar, Alejandro. *La predicación cristiana antigua.* Barcelona: Herder, 1991.

Opelt, Ilona. "Origene visto da san Girolamo." *Augustinianum* 26 (1985): 217–22.

Pace, Nicolà. *Ricerche sulla Traduzione di Rufino del* De principiis *di Origene.* Florence: La Nuova Italia Editrice, 1990.

Peri, Vittorio. *Omelie origeniane sui Salmi: Contributo all'identificazione della testo latino.* Rome: Vatican, 1980.

Perrone, Lorenzo. "Discovering Origen's Lost *Homilies on the Psalms.*" *Auctores Nostri* 15 (2015): 19–46.

———. "'I cuori e I reni': Note sull'interpretazione origeniana de Sal 7,10." *Adamantius* 22 (2016): 87–104.

———. *Il cuore indurito del Faraone: Origene e il problema del libero arbitrio.* Genoa: Marietti, 1992.

———. "The Dating of the New Homilies on the Psalms in the Munich Codex: The Ultimate Origen?" *Proche-Orient Chrétien* 67 (2017): 243–51.

———. "Origenes alt und neu: Die Psalmenhomilien in der neuentdeckten Münchner Handschrift." *Zeitschrift für Antikes Christentum* 17 (2013): 193–214.

———. "*Origenes redivivus:* La découverte des *Homélies sur les Psaumes* dans le Cod. Gr. 314 de Munich." *Revue des études augustiniennes et patristiques* 59 (2013): 55–93.

Perrone, Lorenzo, with Marina Molin Pradel, Emanuela Prinzivalli, and Antonio Cacciari. *Die neuen Psalmenhomilien: Eine kritische Edition des Codex Monacensis Graecus 314.* GCS n.f. 19, Origenes XIII. Berlin: DeGruyter, 2015.

Pitra, Jean Baptiste. *Analecta Sacra spicilegio Solesmensi parata.* 8 vols. Farnborough, UK: Gregg, 1966.

Pizzolato, Luigi, and Marco Rizzi, eds. *Origene: Maestro de vita spirituale.* Milan: Università Cattolica del Sacro Cuore, 2001.

Poschmann, Bernhard. *Penance and the Anointing of the Sick.* Translated by Francis Courtney. New York: Herder and Herder, 1964.

Preuschen, Erwin. *Palladius und Rufinus: Ein Beitrag zur Quellenkunde des ältesten Mönchtums: Texte und Untersuchungen.* Giessen: J. Rickersche, 1897.

Prinzivalli, Emanuela. "La tradizione manoscritta e le edizioni della *Omelie sui Salmi* di Origene tradotte da Rufino." *Vetera Christianorum* 31 (1994): 155–69.

Rahner, Karl. *Theological Investigations XV: Penance in the Early Church.* Translated by Lionel Swain. New York: Crossroad, 1982.

Rondeau, Marie-Josèphe. *Les commentaires patristiques du Psautier (IIIe–Ve siècle).* 2 vols. Rome: Institutum Studiorum Orientalium, 1982–1985.

———. "L'Élucidation des interlocuteurs des Psaumes et le développement dogmatique (III/e–V/e siècle)." In *Liturgie und Dichtung,* edited by Hansjakob Becker and Reiner Kaczynski, 509–77. Sankt Ottilien: EOS Verlag, 1983.

———. "Les polémiques d'Hippolyte et de Filastre de Brescia concernant le psautier." *Revue de l'histoire des religions* 171 (1967): 1–51.

Russell, Norman. *The Doctrine of Divinization in Greek Patristic Thought.* Oxford: Oxford University Press, 2004.

Scheck, Thomas. "Law." In *The Westminster Handbook to Origen,* edited by John A. McGuckin, 138–40. Louisville, KY: Westminster John Knox, 2004.

Schenker, Adrian. *Psalmen in den Hexapla: Erste kritische und vollständige Ausgabe der hexaplarischen Fragmente auf dem Rande der Handschriften Ottobonianus graecus 398 zu den Ps 24–32.* Vatican City: Biblioteca apostolica vaticana, 1982.

Sheerin, Daniel. "Rhetorical and Hermeneutic *Synkrisis* in Patristic Typology." In *Vetera et Nova: Patristic Studies in Honor of Thomas Patrick Halton,* edited by John Petruccione, 22–39. Washington, DC: The Catholic University of America Press, 1998.

———. "The Role of Prayer in Origen's Homilies." In *Origen of Alexandria: His World and His Legacy,* edited by Charles Kannengiesser and William L. Petersen, 200–214. Notre Dame, IN: University of Notre Dame Press, 1988.

Silvas, Anna. "Rufinus' Translation Techniques in the *Regula Basili.*" *Antichthon* 37 (2003): 71–93.

Simonetti, Manlio. "Leggendo le *Omelie sui Salmi* di Origene." *Adamantius* 22 (2016): 454–80.

———. *Origene esegeta e la sua tradizione.* Brescia: Morcelliana, 2004.

Sinkiewicz, Robert. *Evagrius of Pontus: The Greek Ascetic Corpus.* Oxford: Oxford University Press, 2003.

Stewart-Sykes, Alistair. *Hippolytus: On the Apostolic Tradition.* Crestwood, NY: St Vladimir's Seminary Press, 2001.

Stough, Charlotte. "Stoic Determinism and Moral Responsibility." In *The Stoics,* edited by John M. Rist, 203–30. Berkeley: University of California Press, 1978.

Thomas, Matthew. "Origen on Paul's Authorship of Hebrews." In *New Testament Studies* 65 (2019): 598–609.

Torjesen, Karen Jo. "'Body,' 'Soul,' and 'Spirit' in Origen's Theory of Exegesis." *Anglican Theological Review* 67 (1985): 17–30.

———. *Hermeneutical Procedure and Theological Method in Origen's Exegesis.* Berlin: De Gruyter, 1986.

———. "Influence of Rhetoric on Origen's Old Testament Homilies." In *Origeniana Sexta,* edited by Gilles Dorival and Alain Le Boulluec, 13–26. Leuven: Peeters, Leuven University Press, 1995.

———. "Origen's Interpretation of the Psalms." *Studia Patristica* 17 (1982): 944–58.

Trigg, Joseph W. *Origen.* New York and London: Routledge, 1998.

———. "Origen and Origenism in the 1990s." *Religious Studies Review* 22 (1996): 301–8.

———, trans. Origen. *Homilies on the Psalms: Codex Monacensis Graecus 314.* Fathers of the Church 141. Washington, DC: The Catholic University of America Press, 2020.

Vessey, Mark. "Jerome and Rufinus." In *The Cambridge History of Early Christian Literature,* edited by Frances Young, Lewis Ayres, and Andrew Louth, 318–27. Cambridge: Cambridge University Press, 2004.

Viciano, Alberto, *"Homeron ex Homerou Saphenizein:* Principios Hermenéuticos de Teodoreto de Ciro en su Comentario a las Epístolas Paulinas." *Scripta Theologica* 21 (1989): 13–61.

Wagner, M. Monica. *Rufinus the Translator: A Study of his Theory and his Practice as Illustrated in his Version of the* Apologetica *of St. Gregory Nazianzen.* Washington, DC: The Catholic University of America Press, 1945.

Williams, A. N. *The Divine Sense: The Intellect in Patristic Theology.* Cambridge: Cambridge University Press, 2007.

Williams, Rowan. *Arius: Heresy and Tradition.* Grand Rapids, MI: Eerdmans, 2002.

———. "Origen: Between Orthodoxy and Heresy." In *Origeniana Septima,* edited by Wolfgang A. Bienert and Uwe Kühneweg, 3–14. Leuven: Peeters, Leuven University Press, 1999.

Winkelmann, Friedhelm. "Einige Bemerkungen zu den Aussagen des Rufinus von Aquileia und des Hieronymus über ihre Übersetzungstheorie und -Methode." In *Kyriakon: Festschrift Johannes Quasten.* 2 vols. Edited by Patrick Granfield and Josef Jungmann. Munster/Westfalia: Aschendorff, 1970.

Wolinski, Joseph. "Le recours aux *epinoiai* du Christ dans le Commentaire sur Jean d'Origène." In *Origeniana Sexta,* edited by Gilles Dorival and Alain Le Boulluec, 465–92. Leuven: Peeters, Leuven University Press, 1995.

Young, Frances. *Biblical Exegesis and the Formation of Christian Culture.* Cambridge: Cambridge University Press, 1997.

INTRODUCTION

INTRODUCTION

The Nine *Homilies on Psalms 36–38*

There are extant, in the Latin translation of Rufinus of Aquileia,[1] nine homilies on Psalms 36–38 by Origen:[2] five on Psalm 36,[3] two on Psalm 37, and two on Psalm 38. There are also some 58 Greek fragments culled from later *catenae;* most of these, however, are no more than a few lines in length. In 1991, Emanuela Prinzivalli published the first critical edition of these homilies (including the Greek fragments) in the series Biblioteca Patristica,[4] which renders obsolete the earlier edition

1. CPG 1428.

2. This is their numbering in the LXX and Vulgate; they are numbered as Psalms 37–39 in the Hebrew psalter.

3. In 2012, a remarkable discovery was made. While cataloguing manuscripts, Marina Pradel discovered in an early twelfth-century manuscript from the collection of the Staatsbibliothek in Munich (*Codex Monacensis Graecus* 314), a cache of twenty-nine homilies of Origen preserved in Greek; among the newly discovered homilies are the first four homilies on Psalm 36, translated here from the Latin of Rufinus. On the discovery, see Lorenzo Perrone, "Origenes alt und neu: Die Psalmenhomilien in der neuentdeckten Münchner Handschrift," in *Zeitschrift für Antikes Christentum* 17 (2013): 193–214; "*Origenes redivivus:* La découverte des *Homélies sur les Psaumes* dans le Cod. Gr. 314 de Munich," in *Revue des études augustiniennes et patristiques* 59 (2013): 55–93; "Discovering Origen's Lost Homilies on the Psalms," in *Auctores Nostri* 15 (2015):19–46; and for the critical edition of the twenty-nine homilies, see Lorenzo Perrone, Marina Molin Pradel, Emanuela Prinzivalli, and Antonio Cacciari, *Die neuen Psalmenhomilien: Eine kritische Edition des Codex Monacensis Graecus 314* (Berlin: DeGruyter, 2015) [GCS n.f. 19, Origenes XIII]; for the critical edition, Emanuela Prinzivalli edited the four homilies on Psalm 36. For the English translation and an excellent introduction, see Joseph W. Trigg, *Homilies on the Psalms: Codex Monacensis Graecus 314*, Fathers of the Church 141 (Washington, DC: The Catholic University of America Press, 2020).

4. *Origene, Omelie sui Salmi,* ed. and trans. Emanuela Prinzivalli, Biblioteca Patristica 18 (Florence: Nardini Editore, 1991).

of Charles Delarue (Paris, 1733), reprinted by J.-P. Migne in his Patrologia Graeca 12, and which itself was used as the *textus receptus* for her critical edition.[5] This was followed in 1995 by a reprint of her edition (without *apparatus criticus*) in the series Sources Chrétiennes.[6] This is no mean contribution; for while the editors of Die griechischen christlichen Schriftsteller have produced critical editions of almost all of Origen's major works, neither his *Commentary on Romans*[7] nor his *Homilies on Psalms 36–38* had appeared in that corpus; thus the edition of these homilies commonly available to scholars was that found in Migne, PG 12. Finally, while the 1991 edition of Prinzivalli is accompanied by an Italian translation, and the 1995 Sources Chrétiennes edition includes the French translation of Henri Crouzel and Luc Brésard, until now there has been no English translation of these homilies.

According to Jerome,[8] Origen's works devoted to the Scriptures can be classified in three categories: τόμοι (*volumina*), σχόλια (*excerpta*), and ὁμίλιαι (*homiliae, tractatus*).[9] The lengthy commentaries (*volumina*), which Jerome suggests offer the greatest witness to Origen's genius, tend to be denser and to include extended discussion of the text of a particular scriptural book. Scholia are (to speak anachronistically) short es-

5. According to Prinzivalli, the *editio princeps* was published by J. Merlin in 1512; Erasmus is numbered among the editors of the text prior to Delarue; see Prinzivalli, *Origene, Omelie sui Salmi* (1991), 19.

6. *Origène, Homélies sur les Psaumes 36 à 38*, ed. Emanuela Prinzivalli, trans. with intro. and notes by Henri Crouzel and Luc Brésard, Sources Chrétiennes 411 (Paris: Cerf, 1995).

7. Now partially remedied by Caroline P. Hammond Bammel's *Der Römerbriefkommentar des Origenes: Kritische Ausgabe der Übersetzung Rufins, Buch 1–3* (Freiburg: Herder, 1990).

8. In the preface to his translation of the *Hom in Ez* [SC 352.30–32], Jerome writes: *ut scias Origenis opuscula in omnem scripturam esse triplicia. Primum eius opus Excerpta, quae graece* σχόλια *nuncupantur, in quibus ea quae sibi videbantur obscura aut habere aliquid difficultatis, summatim breviterque perstrinxit. Secundum homileticum genus, de quo et praesens interpretatio est. Tertium quod ipse inscripsit* τόμους, *nos volumina possumus nuncupare, in quo opere tota ingenii sui vela spirantibus ventis dedit et recedens a terra in medium pelagus aufugit.*

9. Also referred to elsewhere as σημειώσεις ("observations" or "remarks"), a seemingly equivalent term; so Pierre Nautin, *Origène: Sa vie et son oeuvre* (Paris: Beauchesne, 1977), 372–73.

says or "notes" (often, though not exclusively, philological in character) relative to particularly problematic passages of the text. The homilies are transcripts of sermons Origen delivered to the community at Caesarea, in some cases later polished or redacted by the preacher. Eusebius indicates that Origen late in life allowed ταχυγράφοι (*notarii*, stenographers) to make transcriptions of his homilies,[10] and a number of these homilies are extant, preserved largely in the translations of Jerome and Rufinus.

Jerome's *Letter* 33 to Paula,[11] written c. 385 AD, provides a catalogue of Origen's works known to him. What may have been one of Origen's first ventures into exegesis, a *Commentary on Psalms 1–25*, which he composed around 222–225 at Alexandria, survives only in fragments.[12] P. Nautin has suggested that there was also a second, more ambitious *Commentary* on the Psalms begun at Caesarea[13] as well as a set of *Excerpta in (totum) psalterium* (later used rather freely by Jerome in his own *Excerpta de psalterio*),[14] both now extant in fragments.[15] Jerome's

10. *Historia ecclesiastica* 6.36.1 [SC 41.138]: ὑπὲρ τὰ ἑξήκοντά φασιν ἔτη τὸν Ὠριγένην γενόμενον, ἅτε δὴ μεγίστην ἤδη συλλεξάμενον ἐκ τῆς μακρᾶς παρασκευῆς ἕξιν, τὰς ἐπὶ τοῦ κοινοῦ λεγομένας αὐτῷ διαλέξεις ταχυγράφοις μεταλαβεῖν ἐπιτρέψαι, οὐ πρότερόν ποτε τοῦτο γενέσθαι συγκεχωρηκότα. For Eusebius as intellectual heir to Origen, see T. D. Barnes, *Constantine and Eusebius* (Cambridge: Harvard University Press, 1981), 93–105.

11. CSEL 54.253–259. Ilona Opelt, "Origene visto da san Girolamo," in *Augustinianum* 26 (1985): 217–22, has questioned the authenticity (at least in its present form) of *Ep.* 33. This view has not gained wide acceptance.

12. Cf. Eusebius, *Historia ecclesiastica* 6.24.2 [SC 41.123–125]; Cf. Joseph W. Trigg, *Origen* (New York and London: Routledge, 1998), 69–72; on the text and date, see Pierre Nautin, *Origène*, 262–75, 371. Jerome, *Ep.* 33.4 [CSEL 54.255–256], classifies them as *Excerpta* (σχόλια), and (inaccurately, in the view of modern scholarship) suggests they treat Psalms 1–15; Eusebius uses neither of the terms σχόλια and τόμοι in reference to Origen's treatment of Psalms 1–25, but mentions them at the same time as he is discussing what we know are his *Commentaries* on John, Genesis, and Leviticus, in reference to which he writes explicitly of τόμοι πέντε.

13. Presumably the one Jerome lists in *Ep.* 33.4 [CSEL 54.256], beginning "*Rursum in psalmo primo librum I ...*," and as distinct from what precedes as "*Excerpta in psalmos a primo usque ad quintum decimum,*" the latter being a reference to the Alexandrian *Commentary*.

14. Edited by G. Morin and printed in CCL 72.163–245.

15. Nautin, *Origène: Sa vie et son oeuvre*, 275–79, 282–92, suggests another

list also includes some 120 homilies on 63 different Psalms, including the nine on Psalms 36–38 extant in the translation of Rufinus.[16] These nine homilies (four of which are found in Greek in the Munich Codex) are among the only homilies of Origen on the Psalms to have survived antiquity.[17] In fact, with the exception of various fragments of different authors culled from the later *catenae* (the value of which is not unquestioned), these homilies may be among the earliest extant Christian treatment of the Psalms in themselves.[18]

Dating the *Homilies on the Psalms*

When were these homilies preached? Eusebius claims that Origen allowed stenographers to transcribe his preaching only after his sixtieth year: ὑπὲρ τὰ ἑξήκοντά φασιν ἔτη τὸν Ὠριγένην γενόμενον ... τὰς ἐπὶ τοῦ κοινοῦ λεγομένας αὐτῷ διαλέξεις ταχυγράφοις μεταλαβεῖν ἐπιτρέψαι.[19] If this is the case, then all the homilies of Origen that are extant date from no earlier than around 245 AD, a good decade or so after Origen's ar-

---

attempt at a Psalm commentary undertaken by Origen at Caesarea and also extant only in fragments, in addition to the *Excerpta.*

16. CSEL 54.257–258.

17. Unless one accepts the intriguing argument, though far from universally accepted, of Vittorio Peri, that Jerome's *Tractatus* on the Psalms are substantially a paraphrase of Origen; see his *Omelie origeniane sui Salmi: Contributo all'identificazione della testo latino* (Rome: Vatican, 1980); and now Giovanni Coppa, *Settantaquattro omelie sul libro dei Salmi: Introduzione, traduzione e note* (Turin: Pauline, 1993).

18. Pierre Nautin has reconstructed what he argues is a homily of Hippolytus on the Psalms, which he has dated as roughly contemporaneous with the Caesarean period of Origen; see *Le Dossier d'Hippolyte et de Méliton* (Paris: Cerf, 1953), 166–83, and "L'homélie d'Hippolyte sur le psautier et les oeuvres de Josipe," in *Revue de l'histoire des religions* (1971): 147–54. For Perrone's assessment of the value of the *catenae* as witnesses, see "Discovering Origen's Lost *Homilies on the Psalms,*" *Auctores Nostri* 15 (2015): 19–46, especially 22–23.

19. *Historia ecclesiastica* 6.36.1 [SC 41.138]. See the full quotation in n. 10 above. The suggestion of J. Christopher King, *Origen on the Song of Songs as the Spirit of Scripture* (Oxford: University Press, 2005), 10, that these διαλέξεις—because they are qualified by Eusebius as "public" (ἐπὶ τοῦ κοινοῦ)—refer not to his preaching but to his public disputations with Jews and heretics, seems unsustainable.

rival in Caesarea (conventionally dated to around 232 AD). Further, there is a piece of internal evidence, found in *Homily* 36.1.2, which may help to determine with greater precision the date of its delivery. In explaining Psalm 36.2 [37.2] (*Sicut fenum cito arescent et sicut holera herbarum cito decident*), Origen refers to Isaiah 40.6 (*Caro fenum et omnis gloria ut flos feni*), which prompts an allusion to the vagaries of political power: "*Vide quis imperavit ante hos triginta annos, quomodo imperium eius effloruit: continuo autem sicut flos feni emarcuit, tunc deinde alius post ipsum, deinde alius atque alius …*"[20] This led Harnack, who accepted Eusebius's assertion that transcriptions began to be taken only after Origen's sixtieth year, to posit this as a reference to Caracalla (r. 211–217 AD), thus placing their delivery around 247 AD.[21]

Pierre Nautin, in attempting to reconstruct a detailed chronology of the life and works of Origen, expressed less confidence in Eusebius's reckoning. Taking Origen's remark as a reference to Septimius Severus (193–211 AD), Nautin suggested an earlier date, 239–242 AD.[22] Further, Nautin attempted a reconstruction of the liturgical cycle of Origen's day in Caesarea, and, on the basis of this reconstruction, proposed that almost all of the homiletic work of Origen now extant was preached over this three-year period, 239–242 AD.[23] Nautin's view, however, has not been without criticism, and there are good reasons to reconsider his reconstruction. Lorenzo Perrone, drawing on the cache of homilies found in the recently discovered Munich Codex, has made a strong case for accepting Eusebius's assertion that it was only in later life that Origen allowed transcription of his preaching.[24] In fact, the case has now been made that the *Homilies on the Psalms*—or at least a good number of them—can be dated to the last years of Origen's life and ministry. Perrone has not been alone in

20. SC 411.62–64.

21. A. Harnack, *Geschichte der altchristlichen Litteratur bis Eusebius* (Leipzig: J. C. Hinrichs, 1958), tome 2, vol. 2, 44.

22. Nautin, *Origène: Sa vie et son oeuvre,* 404–11.

23. Nautin, *Origène: Sa vie et son oeuvre,* 394–405.

24. Perrone, "The Dating of the New *Homilies on the Psalms* in the Munich Codex: The Ultimate Origen?" in *Proche-Orient Chrétien* 67 (2017): 243–51.

suggesting that Nautin's hypotheses were based far more on conjecture than on fact.[25] On the basis of a reference Origen makes in his eighth *Homily* on Psalm 77, correcting his earlier interpretation of Deuteronomy 32.8–9, one that he had offered in his *Contra Celsum* 5.29, Perrone contends that this particular homily must have been delivered only after Origen had completed *Contra Celsum,* and so, along with his *Commentary on Matthew,* is among the last of the works of Origen, perhaps from 247–248. This suggestion may be not insignificant in terms of that particular homily (*Hom in Ps* 77.8.1).[26]

Prinzivalli had taken Origen's passing reference in *Homily* 36.5.4 [27] to a "*pacis tempore*" as a likely reference to the relative calm experienced by the Church during the reign of Philip the Arabian (244–249 AD), and hence further refined the date of delivery to c. 245–249 AD, a date that is consistent with the witness of Eusebius and also roughly contemporaneous with the composition (likely at Athens) of the first five books of his *Commentary on the Canticle.*[28] There is good reason to believe that many, if not all, of the homilies discovered in the Munich Codex (including the four found in Rufinus's Latin translation) may date from the very end of Origen's ministry in Caesarea and may represent, in Perrone's words, "the ultimate Origen."

Psalmody in Early Christian Life

Evidence for the use of psalmody in early Christian life is scant, though it is clear from the manuscript evidence that

25. Cf., among others, Adele Monaci Castagno, *La biografia di Origene fra storia e agiografia* (Rimini: Pazzini, 2004); and now eadem, "Contesto liturgico e cronologia della predicazione origeniana alla luce delle nuove *Omelie sui Salmi,*" in *Adamantius* 20 (2014): 238–55.

26. Cf. Perrone, "Discovering Origen's Lost Homilies," 24–25, 449–51. For a rehearsal of this question of dating in relation to the *Commentary on Matthew,* see Ronald Heine, *The Commentary of Origen on the Gospel of St Matthew* (Oxford: Oxford University Press, 2018), vol. 1, 24–28; see also idem, *Origen: Scholarship in the Service of the Church* (New York: Oxford University Press, 2011), 219–21.

27. SC 411.234.

28. Prinzivalli, *Origene, Omelie sui Salmi* (1991), 17; Crouzel seems to concur, SC 411.234, n. 2.

the Psalms were treasured in Christian circles.[29] In Acts (1.20; 13.33–35) the Psalms are understood as prophetic and are employed in support of the apostolic kerygma: the mystery of Christ is prefigured in the Psalms. In 1 Corinthians 14.26, the term ψαλμός is used, but apparently as a generic reference to hymnody, rather than to a specific text of Scripture. In the Pauline literature, there are two references to Psalms. In Ephesians 5.19, within a passage that is paraenetic, the author encourages his audience to employ psalms, hymns, and spiritual odes in their common life and worship: λαλοῦντες ἑαυτοῖς ἐν ψαλμοῖς καὶ ὕμνοις καὶ ᾠδαῖς πνευματικαῖς, ᾄδοντες καὶ ψάλλοντες τῇ καρδίᾳ ὑμῶν τῷ κυρίῳ. In Colossians 3.16, using a strikingly similar and gnomic expression, the author exhorts his readers to use singing as a means of strengthening community life: ἐν πάσῃ σοφίᾳ διδάσκοντες καὶ νουθετοῦντες ἑαυτούς, ψαλμοῖς ὕμνοις ᾠδαῖς πνευματικαῖς ἐν τῇ χάριτι ᾄδοντες ἐν ταῖς καρδίαις ὑμῶν τῷ θεῷ. In both cases there is no definitive evidence that these references to ψαλμοί need mean anything more than some form of singing accompanied by harp or stringed instrument (the original meaning of the term), though the inference may be drawn that the Psalms of the Old Testament played some part in the experience of the first Christians, perhaps as prophetic texts employed in preaching and teaching, but also as a source of hymnody.

There are three post-biblical references to psalmody in Christian life that are contemporaneous with, or even perhaps slightly earlier than, Origen's pastoral activity. The first is found in the so-called *Apostolic Tradition* ascribed in modern times (an ascription now under serious scrutiny) to Hippolytus.[30] Chapter 29, extant only in an Ethiopic version (and

29. See the study of Larry W. Hurtado, *The Earliest Christian Artifacts: Manuscripts and Christian Origins* (Grand Rapids: Eerdmans, 2006), 27–29, who contends that, on the basis of the earliest extant manuscripts (codices of the second and third centuries), the Psalms are rivaled only by the Gospels of Matthew and John (and, interestingly, the *Shepherd of Hermas*) in their popularity.

30. On the vexed questions of authorship, provenance, and date, one may consult the three most recent assessments of the *status quaestionis:* Alistair Stewart-Sykes, *Hippolytus: On the Apostolic Tradition* (Crestwood, NY: St Vladimir Seminary Press, 2001); Paul Bradshaw, Maxwell Johnson, Harold W. Attridge,

found in the later *Testamentum Domini*),[31] is a discussion of what may be an early form of the *lucernarium*, an evening service of thanksgiving for the light, situated around a common, non-eucharistic meal. Having given thanks and having eaten, 29.11 then records, "And when they have risen after the supper and have prayed, the children and the virgins are to say the Psalms."[32] Then the deacon is described as "holding the mixed cup of the oblation, [and he] is to say a Psalm from the ones over which 'Hallelujah' [one of the Hallel Psalms] is written"; a presbyter and the bishop are also then described as saying one of these Psalms, the people responding "Hallelujah."[33] A sharing of the bread then takes place (perhaps something akin to the *antidoron* in the Byzantine liturgy today).

There is also the aforementioned *Homily on the Psalms* attributed to Hippolytus and edited by Nautin.[34] It is clearly apologetic in nature (Valentinus receives explicit mention), and treats issues of authorship of the Psalms, their various titles, and their correct (namely, Christological) interpretation; these issues, in fact, seem to be the author's principal concern. The First and Second Psalms had been read in the assembly (ἀναδράμωμεν ἐπὶ τὴν ἀνάγνωσιν τὴν γεγενημένην. δύο ἡμῖν ἀνεγνώσθησαν ψαλμοί) and form the basis for the author's preaching.[35] What is clear is that the Psalms were both read in the assembly and formed the basis for preaching and teaching.

Tertullian's *De oratione*, probably intended for catechumens, dates from before his move toward Montanism (thus before c. 208 AD). Having provided an explanation of the Lord's Prayer, he addresses related, practical questions. He notes that those more conscientious add an "Alleluia" or a Psalm of sim-

---

and L. Edward Philips, *The Apostolic Tradition* (Minneapolis, MN: Fortress, 2002); and J. A. Cerrato, *Hippolytus Between East and West: The Commentaries and the Provenance of the Corpus* (Oxford: Oxford University Press, 2002).

31. Following the division of the text as found in Bradshaw et al., 158–60; in Stewart-Sykes's edition, it is chapter 25.

32. Bradshaw et al., 156.

33. 29.12–15; Bradshaw et al., 156; cf. Stewart-Sykes, 135–36.

34. For an English translation, see Stewart-Sykes, 175–82. For the Nautin edition see n. 18 above.

35. *Hom in Ps* 18; Nautin, *Le Dossier d'Hippolyte et de Meliton*, 181.

ilar kind when praying; those present with them finish it in response: *Diligentiores in orando subiungere in orationibus alleluia solent et hoc genere psalmos, quorum clausulis respondeant qui simul sunt.*[36] He then argues that the worship "in spirit and truth" taught by Jesus (John 4.23) is accomplished in sincere prayer, brought to God's altar and accompanied by the singing of Psalms: *Hanc de toto corde devotam, fide pastam, veritate curatam, innocentia integram, castitate mundam, agape coronatam cum pompa operum bonorum inter psalmos et hymnos deducere ad Dei altare debemus omnia nobis a Deo impetraturam.*[37] From the witness of Tertullian, then, it can be demonstrated that the Psalms both formed part of the daily prayer of Christians and were sung in the liturgy.

The Psalms were clearly part of Christian life at Caesarea, as they form the basis of Origen's preaching in the nine homilies included in Rufinus's translation. There are two explicit references in these homilies relative to the particular use of psalmody. At one point, in a transitional phrase, Origen mentions that the Psalm had just been read: *Denique iste psalmus qui nunc lectus est, nobis ostendit ut si forte aliquando praevenimur in delictis qualiter nos et cum quo affectu orare oporteat et medico supplicari pro doloribus vel infirmitatibus nostris.*[38] The use of *legere* can certainly bear the implication "to read out loud" (far more common in antiquity than reading silently or privately) or "read publicly."[39] In *Hom in Ps* 36.3.6, in glossing Paul's comment regarding the Corinthians (1 Corinthians 1.5) that they are rich "in every word and in all knowledge," Origen expresses reservations about those who know some texts in the Scriptures but not all of them (they are not rich in *every* word or *all* knowledge), even the hypothetical individual who might be able to "chant the

36. *De oratione* 27 [CCL 1.273].

37. *De oratione* 28.4 [CCL 1.273].

38. *Hom in Ps* 37.1.1 [SC 411.260].

39. *OLD*, s.v. § 8.b; but see also Michael Slusser, "Reading Silently in Antiquity," in *Journal of Biblical Literature* 111 (1992): 499. Cf. a more ambiguous use of *legere* in *Hom in Ps* 36.5.3 [SC 411.232]: *Nos ergo si secundum hoc quod legimus, ore nostro sapientiam et lingua nostra loquatur iudicium et lex Dei sit in cordibus nostris, adipiscemur illud quod sequitur, "Et non supplantabuntur gressus eius."*

entire psalter at will": *et integrum psalterium cum voluerit canit.*[40] This would suggest that the chanting of the Psalms was certainly known to him, but how and when within (or apart from) the liturgical assembly this occurred remains uncertain. One historian of music in Christian liturgy, however, while recognizing the paucity of evidence for pre-Constantinian practice, has observed that in the early centuries, "the public 'reading' of scripture and prayers may have had a musical element (declamation stylized into cantillation). Second, if such chant were sung, it would no doubt have been answered by congregational acclamations such as 'Amen,' 'Maranatha,' and 'Alleluia.'"[41] This latter statement would seem to be confirmed by the earlier witness of both Hippolytus and Tertullian. It was in the fourth century, under the influence of growing urban monasticism, that psalmody came to be a regular feature of the Christian eucharistic liturgy, and that a shift in the manner of its liturgical proclamation occurred: "[f]or much of the fourth century the Psalm was still considered to be a reading, but it changed from a slightly inflected reading to a more melodic chanting."[42] While there are several other texts within Origen's extant corpus that make reference to music, none of them refers explicitly to psalmody and there are actually few specifics to be culled from them.[43] Thus, while the Psalms were employed in Caesarean worship in Origen's time, there is no way of determining, on the basis of the evidence available, whether or not the Psalms were inflected when read, or whether they were chanted or sung.

40. SC 411.150.

41. William T. Flynn, "Liturgical Music," in *The Oxford History of Christian Worship,* ed. Geoffrey Wainwright and Karen Westerfield Tucker (Oxford: Oxford University Press, 2006), 770. For the place of the Psalms in the piety of the early Church, see Balthasar Fischer, *Die Psalmen als Stimme der Kirche: Gesammelte Studien zur christlichen Psalmenfrömmigkeit* (Trier: Paulinus, 1982), esp. 15–36.

42. Flynn, 770.

43. Collected and helpfully annotated by James W. McKinnon, *Music in Early Christian Literature* (Cambridge: Cambridge University Press, 1987), 36–41.

The Translation of Rufinus

As Origen was still in Jerome's good graces at the time of his letter to Paula (385 AD), and Rufinus's work as a translator of Origen did not commence until after Jerome's support for Origen had been reversed (c. 393 AD),[44] Crouzel posits 398 AD as the date of Rufinus's translation of the *Homilies on the Psalms,*[45] thus shortly after his return to Italy. The first of Origen's works Rufinus translated was the *De principiis,* rendered into Latin during the spring and summer of 398 AD.[46] In the subsequent fall he turned his attention to the *Homilies on the Psalms,* the first of Origen's exegetical works to receive his attention as translator. It was between 403 and 410 AD that he translated the other homilies of Origen now extant through his rendering (those on the Pentateuch and Joshua and Judges) as well as the commentaries on Romans and the Canticle, the last of Origen's works to receive his attention.

For some time, the scholarly view was that Rufinus's translations of Origen's works were to be treated with great suspicion. In fact, in the introduction to his translation of *De principiis,* G. W. Butterworth epitomizes this view: "The fact must be faced that we cannot trust him [Rufinus] ... [t]here are not only long additions and omissions, but mistranslations, some deliberate, some perhaps unconscious, paraphrases in which

44. Jerome's break with Rufinus and its context are discussed by J. N. D. Kelly, *Jerome; His Life, Writings, and Controversies* (Peabody, MA: Hendrickson, 1998), 195–209. See also Caroline P. Hammond Bammel, "The Last Ten Years of Rufinus' Life and the Date of his Move South to Aquileia," in *Journal of Theological Studies* n.s. 28 (1977): 372–429, who provisionally dates his translation of *Hom in Ps* to 401 (at p. 394); and now Megan Hale Williams, *The Monk and the Book: Jerome and the Making of Christian Scholarship* (Chicago: University of Chicago Press, 2006), 288–92.

45. SC 411.18. This is consistent with the date suggested by Rufinus's modern biographer, F. X. Murphy; see his *Rufinus of Aquileia (345–411): His Life and Works* (Washington, DC: The Catholic University of America Press, 1945), 234. The same date has been established independently by Franca Ela Consolino, "Le prefazioni di Girolamo e Rufino alle loro traduzioni di Origene," in *Origeniana Quinta,* ed. Robert J. Daly (Leuven: Peeters, Leuven University Press, 1992), 92–98.

46. The following relies on the reconstruction of Consolino, 98.

the point and force of the original is completely lost, and countless minor alterations which must be studied in detail before their cumulative effect can be appreciated."[47] This conventional view of Rufinus, however, has recently been challenged. Nicolà Pace, after a careful comparative study of Rufinus's Latin translation of the *De principiis* and the extant Greek text, has made the case that this conventional view is unduly harsh and misleading.[48] In Pace's view, Rufinus's fundamental concern was to make Origen accessible to a Latin audience. He sometimes lacked nuance and an appropriate Latin vocabulary with which to express Origen's Greek (especially in regard to technical philosophical terminology). The extent, however, to which Rufinus might have altered, truncated, or added to the text to accommodate it to later standards of orthodoxy is by and large limited, Pace argues, to matters of Trinitarian expression. In fact, on the basis of passages that can be compared to extant fragments, Pace suggests that Rufinus's translation is generally reliable in matters of Origen's protology (including, for example, issues of the pre-existence of souls) and eschatology, topics that seem not to have been a doctrinal concern to Rufinus. Pace's conclusions regarding Rufinus's work in rendering *De principiis* can reasonably be applied to his other translations; in fact, Crouzel concurs with Pace's conclusions in regard to the quality of Rufinus's translation of the *Homilies on the Psalms*.[49] Subsequent examination and analysis

47. G. W. Butterworth, trans. and ed., *Origen: On First Principles* (Gloucester, MA: Peter Smith, 1973), xlvii.

48. Nicolà Pace, *Ricerche sulla Traduzione di Rufino del* De principiis *di Origene* (Florence: La Nuova Italia Editrice, 1990). Cf. the helpful and perceptive analysis of Pace's argument offered by Joseph W. Trigg, "Origen and Origenism in the 1990s," *Religious Studies Review* 22 (1996): 301–8, esp. 302–3. Cf. also Annie Jaubert's comments on Rufinus as translator in her edition of Origen's *Hom in Jos*, SC 71.68–82, as well as Ronald Heine's assessment of Rufinus as translator in his translation of Origen, *Homilies on Genesis and Exodus*, Fathers of the Church 71 (Washington, DC: The Catholic University of America Press, 1982), 25–39. For an analysis of Rufinus's technique (relative, however, to another author and work), see Anna Silvas, "Rufinus' Translation Techniques in the *Regula Basili*," in *Antichthon* 37 (2003): 71–93.

49. SC 411.11–12; of course, this is based on conjecture and the few Greek fragments available to him.

of the Greek text of the *Homilies on the Psalms* found in the Munich Codex alongside the Latin translation of Rufinus has led Emanuela Prinzivalli essentially to confirm the assessment of Pace.[50]

Further, research into the theory of translation in antiquity supports a more generous estimation of Rufinus's efforts and intent.[51] There were two principal approaches to translating an ancient text from one tongue to another: *ad verbum,* a literal, word-for-word rendering; and *ad sensum,* an approach that sought to convey the idea or meaning of the text without being bound by a literal formulation and that sought to capture the eloquence of the Greek original (perhaps something akin to what, in contemporary discussion, has been termed "dynamic equivalence"). Cicero was the principal theorist of this approach; for it was his desire and contention that the Greek classics be made available in (and in fact outdone by) Latin translation.[52] In the course of his career, Jerome engaged in numerous translations, but offered no consistent theory of translation. In fact, his views on the matter varied depending upon the context. Initially, he held that translation *ad sensum* was preferable, but that for the text of Scripture, a more literal rendering was desirable; he was, however, hardly consistent in his views, and polemic and his own defensiveness often caused his views—and his presentation of himself—to be shifted.[53]

Scholars, in comparing the translations of Jerome and Rufinus—and due in no small part to Jerome's own self-promotion as the more careful translator—have tended perhaps too summarily to judge Rufinus's translations as paraphrastic and thus at best less than reliable, or at worst deliber-

50. GCS n.f. 19, Origenes XIII, 34–57.

51. An unpublished paper by William Adler, "*Ad verbum* or *ad sensum:* The Christianization of a Latin Translation Formula in the Fourth Century," presented at the American Society of Church History, Williamsburg, Virginia, April 1, 1993; cf. also Paolo Chiesa, "*Ad verbum* o *ad sensum?* Modelli e coscienza metodologica della traduzione tra tarda antichità e alto medioevo," in *Medioevo e Rinascimento* 1 (1987): 1–51; Heinrich Marti, *Übersetzer der Augustin-Zeit* (Munich: Wilhelm-Fink, 1974), 61–72.

52. Adler, 2.

53. Adler, 17–23.

ately deceptive. In the words, however, of one recent defender and promoter of Origen—whose provocative argument seeks to distance Origen from Platonism—"while the translations of Rufinus may be free, they have not been proved to be mendacious,"[54] and, "Rufinus is a discreet translator rather than a dishonest one, and generally his version [of the *De principiis*] shows some traces of the errors laid to Origen's account by his traducers,"[55] thus suggesting that Rufinus cannot be flatly accused of conniving to alter Origen's text in a substantial way (Rufinus himself was convinced that others had maliciously altered the Greek text of Origen).[56] Elizabeth Clark, in her careful study of the recurring Origenist controversies, has demonstrated—and this confirms the research of Pace—that Rufinus found little objectionable in Origen's protology and eschatology (matters that Rufinus viewed as still undefined or unsettled matters of theological speculation).[57] The earlier view that Rufinus willfully altered the text of Origen simply to conform his thought to later standards of orthodoxy may, then, be too simplistic and seems to have given way in contemporary scholarship to a more positive appreciation of Rufinus's efforts, even with an admission that he might have been hampered by a kind of theological or philosophical naïveté; and what might be inferred to be naïveté could quite plausibly be accounted for as a kind of pastoral attentiveness to the particular needs or capacity of his intended reader. In any case, the view of Rufinus as, given the standards of his age, a largely faithful translator, even if at times inclined to moralizing and extrapolation on Origen's words, has been supported by the study of Antonio Grappone.[58] It remains a question whether, despite his self-presentation, Jerome was himself any more theologi-

54. Mark J. Edwards, *Origen against Plato* (Aldershot: Ashgate, 2002), 5.

55. Edwards, 91.

56. Cf. his *De adulteratione librorum Origenis* [CCL 20.1–17], originally appended to his translation of Pamphilus's *Apology*, and forming part of his arsenal against the recriminations of Jerome and others.

57. Elizabeth A. Clark, *The Origenist Controversy: The Cultural Construction of an Early Christian Debate* (Princeton: Princeton University Press, 1992), 166–71.

58. Antonio Grappone, *Omelie origeniane nella traduzione di Rufino. Un confronto con i testi greci* (Rome: Institutum Patristicum Augustinianum, 2007).

cally astute than Rufinus, whose translations have been held suspect by later minds because of his freer style of translation.

Until the discovery of the Munich Codex, the principal, though quite incomplete, source for much of the Greek of Origen's preaching, including the *Homilies on the Psalms,* was the *catenae.* The Greek fragments of these homilies published in Migne[59] and by Cardinal Pitra[60] are taken from what G. Dorival has identified as the earliest Palestinian *catena* on the Psalms, assembled at Caesarea by an otherwise unknown pupil of Procopius of Gaza († c. 538) and preserved in a 9th/10th century manuscript now at Oxford, *Baroccianus Graecus* 235. Dorival contends that this manuscript was the exemplar for the other extant witnesses.[61] This early *catena* also includes glosses taken from Asterius, Athanasius, Basil, Cyril of Alexandria, Didymus, Eusebius, Gregory of Nazianzus, John Chrysostom, Severus, and Theodoret.[62] Dorival's research has revealed the complex textual history of the various *catenae* on the Psalms, including, for example, the likelihood that a later significant witness, *Parisinus Graecus* 139, is a conflation of a later, second Palestinian *catena* with another *catena* that he describes as a paraphrase.[63] While *Baroccianus Graecus* 235, from which the Greek fragments of the *Homilies on the Psalms* have been culled, is an arguably reliable witness to Origen's Greek (and so further demonstrating Rufinus's basic fidelity as a translator), given the existence and influence of *catenae* that are paraphrastic, in general the Greek *catenae* must be treated with some reserve.[64]

59. PG 17.117–36.

60. J. B. Pitra, *Analecta Sacra spicilegio Solesmensi parata,* 8 vols. (Farnborough: Gregg, 1966), vol.3, pp. 13–34.

61. Gilles Dorival, *Les chaînes exégétiques grecques sur les Psaumes: Contribution à l'étude d'une forme littéraire,* 4 vols., vol. 1 (Leuven: Peeters, 1986), 99–127. Cf. also Robert Devreesse, *Les anciens commentateurs grecs de Psaumes,* Studi et Testi 264 (Rome: Biblioteca Apostolica Vaticana, 1970), esp. 14–17; Ekkehard Mühlenberg, *Psalmenkommentare aus der Katenenüberlieferung,* 3 vols., vol. 1 (Berlin: De Gruyter, 1975–1978), 44–45.

62. Dorival, 123.

63. Dorival, 122–24.

64. See CPG 1428; various fragments on the Psalms (also culled from later *catenae*) attributed to Origen can be found in PG 12.1085–1320, 1409–1686, and PG 17.105–149. The Greek fragments of the *Hom in Ps* 36–38 (those known

The Assessment of Erasmus

Erasmus (1466–1536) himself, in a series of brief evaluations of Origen's works,[65] raised questions about the authenticity of the *Homilies on the Psalms* in Rufinus's translation (which Erasmus refers to as *Commentarii in tres Psalmos*).[66] He begins by remarking that "I am of two minds about this work" (*De hoc opere sum ancipiti sententia*), and he notes that the style (*phrasis*) is more like (*propius*) that of Chrysostom, perhaps because of the moral tenor of the homilies. He suggests the possibility that someone other than Rufinus authored the translation, or perhaps that Rufinus, in character, cribbed another's work.[67] Further, he is critical of the translation itself, referring to it variously as clumsy, without feeling, borrowed, and contrived.[68] He does note Rufinus's own remarks about his translation of these homilies, found in the Epilogue he appended to his translation of Origen's *Commentary on Romans*,[69] where he makes clear that, "As for the homilies on Joshua, Judges, and on Psalms thirty-six, thirty-seven, and thirty-eight, I translated them simply as I found them and without much effort."[70] One

prior to the discovery of the Munich manuscript) are published in the appendix of the editions of Prinzivalli, *Origene, Omelie sui Salmi* (1991), 471–91, and Crouzel, SC 411.408–453. As an indication of the daunting task of sifting through the layers of construction in the catenae, see Cordula Bandt, "Origen in the *Catenae* on Psalms," in *Adamantius* 20 (2014): 238–55.

65. Which he calls *Censurae* ("Critiques"); see *Desiderii Erasmi Roterdami Opera Omnia*, ed. Jean Leclercq (Lugduni Batavorum, 1703–4), 8.434. For a summary of Erasmus's assessment, see André Godin, *Érasme lecteur d'Origène* (Geneva: Librarie Droz, 1982), 612–14.

66. In fact, his conclusion is that someone (whether Rufinus or another) has taken a commentary on these Psalms and recast them as homilies: *suspicor enim Ruffinum, aut si quis fuit alius, haec vertisse liberius e commentario perpetuo,* at 8.434.

67. Erasmus 8.434: *Suspicor enim qui scripsit fuisse Latinum, aut si vertit Ruffinus, more suo quod alienum erat fecit suum tractando, hoc est, contaminando.* The use of *contaminare* (*OLD* s.v. § 2b) insinuates the introduction of inferior, foreign material (*aliena*) as well as mere mistranslation.

68. Erasmus 8.434: *Sunt quaedam dure, quaedam frigide interpretata, quaedam aliena et ascititia.*

69. For the text, see CCL 20.276–777.

70. CCL 20.276: *Nam illa quae in Jesum Nave et in Judicum et in tricesimum*

reason for a remark like this might, however, have been apologetic: Rufinus's epilogue was written in 405–406 AD,[71] not long after Jerome's *Apology*[72] against him (401 AD), in which Jerome defends his own alternative translation (now lost) of *De principiis* as having been rendered from the Greek *simpliciter*.[73] Perhaps this was Rufinus's way of defending himself and his earlier translations (c. 398–403 AD).

Erasmus continues his assessment by noting the awkwardness of Rufinus's handling of the Greek text of Psalm 36.1 (μὴ παραζήλου ἐν πονηρευομένοις), found in *Homily* 36.1.1,[74] as well as the choice of *non gentem* (see LXX Deuteronomy 32.21: ἐπ' οὐκ ἔθνει) as applied to Christians in the same context.[75] Erasmus is also perplexed by the halting construction of the preface (*Jam praefatio videtur inanibus et male cohaerentibus sensiculis consarcinata*), which he notes never even offers the name of the original author, and which—even granting that Rufinus had rendered this translation (a premise to which Erasmus seems less than fully committed)—is hardly reflective of Rufinus's otherwise generally fluent prose (*certe natura facundus*). Regardless, the work does not reflect Origen's usual felicity of expression (*modo fateamur operis genium non referre Origenicam felicitatem*).[76]

Rufinus's own words (referred to by Erasmus) about his translation of these homilies, as well as a piece of internal evidence, may offer an explanation of the style of the translations that so provoked Erasmus and which is, at times, noticeably unbalanced. Rufinus himself had noted that, among several other works of Origen, he translated the homilies on the Psalms

---

sextum et tricesimum septimum et tricesimum octavum psalmum scripsimus, simpliciter ut invenimus, et non multo cum labore transtulimus.

71. Consolino, 98.

72. Hale Williams, 294.

73. *Apologia contra Rufinum* 1.7 [CCL 79.6–7]; see Adler, 23, on the apologetic nature of Rufinus's remarks.

74. SC 411.54–56.

75. A criticism, it would seem, here leveled more at the author than the translator; it is interesting that Erasmus's criticisms of the translation are limited to the preface and the first few pages of the first homily; he offers nothing about the text beyond this.

76. Erasmus 8.434.

"simply as I found them and without much effort."[77] For example, in *Hom in Ps* 37.2.1, there is found a lengthy dependent clause without a genuine apodosis:

Licet amici mei et proximi mei contrarii sint et propinqui mei longe se faciant a me, dum ego ipse mei accusator efficior, dum crimina mea nullo me arguente confiteor, dum nolo imitari eos, qui etiam cum in iudiciis arguantur et testibus convincantur et etiam tortoribus arguantur, tegunt tamen mala sua et plus apud eos obtinet commissi pudor quam cruciantis poena.[78]

One would expect Rufinus to have tidied up this irregularity or to have attempted to emend this in his translation. He appears not to have done so, and this may indicate that he can be taken quite literally at his word (*simpliciter ut invenimus, et non multo cum labore transtulimus*). Thus the use of the phrase *simpliciter ut invenimus* may be more than an apologetic aside in response to criticism by Jerome,[79] and may also be an honest admission that he simply spent little time crafting a polished translation.

These irregularities might also be explained by positing that the manuscript with which he worked was perhaps no more than a notarius's copy, a transcript neither reviewed nor edited by Origen himself. This would indeed explain some of the oddities of style: namely, that Rufinus's manuscript was no more than a stenographer's transcript of a *viva voce* delivery and that Rufinus did not take the time or effort to emend the work as he translated.[80] In support of this hypothesis, Michael Frede has identified a similar problem in the text of the *Contra Celsum*.[81] At 1.28, the second sentence is a doublet of the first, leading scholars to conjecture that Origen dictated the

77. CCL 20.276.

78. SC 411.302–304; this is a text not found among the homilies in the Munich manuscript, and thus for which the Greek is not extant.

79. Cf. Adler, 23.

80. On the scriptorium at Caesarea, see Anthony Grafton and Megan Williams, *Christianity and the Transformation of the Book: Origen, Eusebius, and the Library of Caesarea* (Cambridge, MA: Belknap, 2006), 68–70.

81. Michael Frede, "Origen's Treatise *Against Celsus*," in *Apologetics in the Roman Empire: Pagans, Jews, and Christians*, ed. Mark Edwards, Martin Goodman, and Simon Price, with Christopher Rowland (Oxford: Oxford University Press, 1999), 131–55.

preface after having begun 1.28 (Origen himself states this in the preface), and then took up where he left off, reduplicating the sentence where he had paused to compose the preface.[82] Frede suggests that this both explains how Origen could be so prolific a writer, in that he relied on stenographers to whom he could readily and easily dictate, and, further, indicates that Origen might have been less than attentive in proof-reading or revising texts once dictated. As Frede puts it: "And we also see that Origen cannot have proof-read, as it were, at the end—at least not with care—as otherwise he would have deleted the second sentence. It looks as if Origen, having dictated the text, left its further production to others."[83] One cannot posit a pattern on the basis of a singular instance, but it does offer some substantiation to the possibility that the text of the *Homilies on the Psalms* from which Rufinus was working was itself not carefully proof-read or edited by Origen.[84]

The *Preface* of Rufinus

Rufinus's dedicatory preface to his translation of the *Homilies on the Psalms* offers some insight into his understanding of them. The preface is addressed to Apronianus. The Roman senator Turcius Apronianus, his wife Avita, and their daughter Eunomia are mentioned twice by Palladius,[85] who records

82. For the English text, see Henry Chadwick (who notes the difficulty), *Origen: Contra Celsum* (Cambridge: Cambridge University Press, 1953): preface 6 at pp. 5–6, the doublet at pp. 27–28.

83. Frede, "Origen's Treatise *Against Celsus*," 141.

84. It would be worth pursuing, though not here, an examination of the other homilies that Rufinus claimed to have translated *simpliciter ... et non multo cum labore,* those on Joshua and Judges. See the assessment of Annie Jaubert, SC 71.69, who characterizes Rufinus's efforts in translating the *Hom in Jos* as "parfois hâtive" ("sometimes hasty"), but who is convinced of his ultimate fidelity to Origen's thought.

85. *Lausiac History* 41.5 and 54.4 (c. 419–420 AD), in *La Storia Lausiaca,* ed. G. J. M. Bartelink (Milan: Fondazione Lorenzo Valla, 1974), 212 and 246–48; cf. Robert Meyer, *Palladius: The Lausiac History* (Westminster, MD: Newman Press, 1965), 119, 135, and his helpful annotations, 203–4, as well as Erwin Preuschen, *Palladius und Rufinus: Ein Beitrag zur Quellenkunde des ältesten Mönchtums: Texte und Untersuchungen* (Giessen: J. Rickersche, 1897). It was Apronianus who conveyed to Rufinus Jerome's correspondence with Pammachius critical of Rufinus, thus prompting Rufinus's own *Apology against Jerome* (401 AD) [see CCL

that Apronianus was converted by Melania the Elder, his wife's aunt. Apronianus and Avita are also praised by their friend and contemporary Paulinus of Nola in one of his *Carmina.*[86] The entire family had embraced an ascetic life, and Apronianus and his wife had elected to live in continence.[87] In addition to his translation of the *Homilies on the Psalms,* Rufinus also dedicated his translations of the *Homilies* of Basil, Gregory of Nazianzus's *Orations,* and the *Sentences of Sextus* to Apronianus.[88] These works were all undertaken about the time Rufinus had returned to Aquileia from the East, following a brief sojourn at Rome,[89] thus late in 398.[90]

It would seem that it was particularly the moral teaching of both the *Sentences* and the *Homilies on the Psalms,* and his desire to share that teaching with Apronianus, that prompted Rufinus's choice of these works for translation. Further, it is intriguing that in the prefaces he wrote both for the *Sentences* translation and for Origen's *Homilies on the Psalms,* Avita, wife of Apronianus, figures significantly as the principal beneficiary of this moral teaching. In his preface to the *Sentences* translation,[91] Rufinus wrote: *Religiosa filia mea, soror iam in Christo tua,*[92] *poposcerat me ut ei aliquid quod legeret tale conponerem, ubi*

20.37]; on this series of events, see J. N. D. Kelly, *Jerome: His Life, Writings, and Controversies* (Peabody, MA: Hendrickson, 1998), 249–51.

86. *Carmen* 21.60ff (c. 407 AD) [CSEL 30.160–162]; see P. G. Walsh, *The Poems of Paulinus of Nola,* Ancient Christian Writers 40 (Westminster, MD: Newman Press, 1975), 175ff.

87. *Lausiac History* 54.4 (ed. Bartelink, 246–248); see also Hammond Bammel, "The Last Ten Years," 386–87.

88. See CCL 20.255, 259. On the chronology, see Hammond Bammel, "The Last Ten Years," 387.

89. It was at Rome, just prior to his departure for Aquileia, thus c. 397, where he produced his translations of the *Rule* of Basil, the *Apology* of Pamphilus, and the *De principiis,* as well as authoring his own *De adulteratione librorum Origenis;* see Hammond Bammel, "The Last Ten Years," 386.

90. So Hammond Bammel, "The Last Ten Years," 387; cf. Consolino, 96–98.

91. Rufinus, like many of his contemporaries, assumed the *Sentences* to be the teaching of Pope Sixtus (Xystus) II († 258 AD); in all likelihood, they reflect Pythagorean teaching. On this, see Henry Chadwick, *The Sentences of Sextus: A Contribution to the History of Early Christian Ethics* (Cambridge: Cambridge University Press, 1959), esp. 117–19.

92. Hammond Bammel takes this reference as an indication of their recent

neque laboraret in intellegendo et tamen proficeret in legendo, aperto et satis plano sermone.[93] He refers as well to Avita in his preface to his translations of Origen's *Homilies on the Psalms*, writing *Ne forte religiosa filia mea, soror in Christo tua, ingrata sit operi nostro, si id semper laboriosum intellectui suo pro asperitate sentiat quaestionum.*[94] The implication is relatively clear: it was Avita perhaps more than Apronianus who had pressed Rufinus (*poposcerat me*) for the translation of such works, and it is precisely the accessibility of their moral teaching that Rufinus highlights in each preface. While in his translation he characterizes the teaching of the *Sentences* as patent and clear (*aperto et satis plano sermone*), and while he likens this little enchiridion to a small ring (*annulus*) that can be easily carried in hand, its potent teaching is nonetheless directed toward moral perfection (*ut unius versus sententia ad totius possit perfectionem vitae sufficere*).[95] The *Homilies on the Psalms* provide, without much effort on the part of the reader (*absque labore lectoris*), teaching on simplicity of life (*vitae simplicitas*) and moral progress (*profectionem morum*) in language that is clear and straightforward (*sensu lucido et simplici sermone*).[96] This simplicity of language, he contends, makes the teaching of these collected homilies beneficial not only to men, but also to devout women (presumably the likes of Avita and Eunomia),[97] and serves as a source of nourishment even to more simple, less sophisticated souls (*ex quo profectus pervenire non solum ad viros, verum etiam ad religiosas feminas possit et excolere simplices mentes*).[98] Rufinus's decision, then, to translate almost simultaneously these two works stems, it would seem, from Avita's request and the need to make accessible works on moral or spiritual progress and perfection of life in clear, simple language,[99] and likely reflects Rufinus's con-

decision to live in continence; see Hammond Bammel, "The Last Ten Years," 387.

93. CCL 20.259.

94. SC 411.46 [= CCL 20.251].

95. CCL 20.259.

96. SC 411.46 [= CCL 20.251].

97. So Prinzivalli, *Origene, Omelie sui Salmi* (1991), 26–28.

98. SC 411.46 [= CCL 20.251].

99. Both of these works, the *Sentences* and the *Homilies on the Psalms*—as

sciousness of this fact in his self-presentation as translator and authentic expositor of ascetical teaching for a Latin-speaking literary clientele.[100]

Rufinus observes immediately the moral character of these nine homilies (*expositio tota moralis est*)[101] and the fact that they reveal certain principles for a reformed way of life and progress in it (*instituta quaedam vitae emendatioris ostendens … ad emendationem vel profectionem morum*). He describes the translation as providing an example of preaching (*dictio*) that is devoted entirely to improvement and moral progress. He further suggests that the teaching of the homilies might be divided into two aspects or stages, each bipartite: conversion and penance, healing and progress (*nunc conversionis ac paenitentiae, nunc purgationis et profectuum*). The fact that Rufinus seems to view these nine homilies together as a group is significant as well, and his characterization of them as fundamentally moral likely derives from Origen's own comments in the first homily in the series. *Hom in Ps* 36.1 begins by quoting Hebrews 1.1,

well as the fact that Rufinus produced translations of them almost simultaneously—could be characterized as providing for Apronianus and Avita a kind of ascetical-moral handbook or florilegium, as Rufinus himself indicates in his Preface to the *Hom in Ps* [SC 411.46]: *Idcirco tibi eam, Aproniane fili carissime, in novem oratiunculis, quas Graeci* ὁμιλίας *vocant velut in uno corpore digestam in Latinum transtuli, ut intra unum codicem collectam haberes dictionem, quae ad emendationem vel profectionem morum tota respiceret.* On the role of texts in Hellenistic moral philosophy, see Martha C. Nussbaum, *The Therapy of Desire: Theory and Practice in Hellenistic Ethics* (Princeton: Princeton University Press, 1994), esp. 336–38, whose characterization of Stoic views on the nature and importance of texts reveals the fissures between Hellenistic moral philosophy and what Rufinus (arguably reflecting the main contours of the early Christian ascetical enterprise) is undertaking here. On what distinguished the Christian appreciation of the sacred text and its use in the ascetic enterprise vis-à-vis the way texts functioned among their pagan and philosophical forebears and contemporaries, see A. N. Williams, *The Divine Sense: The Intellect in Patristic Theology* (Cambridge: Cambridge University Press, 2007), 12–14.

100. Cf. the verdict of Mark Vessey, "Jerome and Rufinus," in *The Cambridge History of Early Christian Literature*, ed. Frances Young, Lewis Ayres, and Andrew Louth (Cambridge: Cambridge University Press, 2004), 325: "Had they survived, his 'many' letters would doubtless have confirmed his proficiency as a teacher of ascetic piety."

101. SC 411.46 [= CCL 20.251].

and Origen then distinguishes between Scriptures whose purpose is to instruct the reader in mysteries transcending human speech (*ineffabilia sacramenta*), those that teach about Christ and the Incarnation (*de salvatore et de eius adventu*), and those that aim to correct and reform one's manner of life (*mores nostros corrigit et emendat*).[102] He then speaks in reference to Psalm 36: *Incipientes igitur explanationem tricesimi sexti Psalmi, invenimus quod totus Psalmus iste moralis est et velut cura quaedam ac medicina humanae animae datus.*[103] Thus Rufinus is here perhaps simply following Origen's lead in understanding these Psalms as fundamentally moral in tenor.

Origen on Scripture and Anthropology

The *locus classicus* for understanding the relation of Scripture and anthropology in Origen is *De principiis* 4.2.4.[104] While introducing the reader to the proper way to read Scripture and grasp its meaning (φαινομένη ἡμῖν ὁδὸς τοῦ πῶς δεῖ ἐντυγχάνειν ταῖς γραφαῖς καὶ τὸν νοῦν αὐτῶν ἐκλαμβάνειν), he suggests it is necessary that the threefold (τριχῶς) meaning of the Scriptures be copied or inscribed (ἀπογράφεσθαι) on the soul

102. SC 411.50.

103. Ibid.

104. GK 708–710; cf. Karen Jo Torjesen, "'Body,' 'Soul,' and 'Spirit' in Origen's Theory of Exegesis," in *Anglican Theological Review* 67 (1985):17–30, and the classic study of Henri de Lubac, "Tripartite Anthropology," in *Theology in History,* trans. Anne Englund Nash (San Francisco: Ignatius, 1996), 117–200, esp. his treatment of Origen, 130–44. On the overarching purpose of the work vis-à-vis the correct reading of Scripture, see Brian Daley, "Origen's *De Principiis:* A Guide to the Principles of Christian Scriptural Interpretation," in *Vetera et Nova: Patristic Studies in Honor of Thomas Patrick Halton,* ed. John Petruccione (Washington, DC: The Catholic University of America Press, 1998), 3–21; and now as well John Behr's substantial introduction to his two-volume edition of *Origen: On First Principles* (Oxford: Oxford University Press, 2018). On early Christian reading of Scripture and exegetical strategies, see the excellent essay of John Cavadini, "From Letter to Spirit: The Multiple Senses of Scripture," in *The Oxford Handbook of Early Christian Biblical Interpretation,* ed. Paul M. Blowers and Peter W. Martens (Oxford: Oxford University Press, 2019), 126–48; for a recent study of Origen as exegete, see Peter W. Martens, *Origen and Scripture: The Contours of the Exegetical Life* (New York: Oxford University Press, 2014).

of the reader or hearer. In this context, Origen refers to the "flesh" (σάρξ/ *corpus*) of the Scriptures, which nourishes simpler ones (ἁπλούστεροι/ *simpliciores*) with what he calls the "obvious" or "literal interpretation" (πρόχειρον ἐκδοχήν).[105] He then speaks of the individual who is more advanced (ὁ δὲ ἐπὶ ποσὸν ἀναβεβηκώς), who is edified by the "soul" (ψυχή/ *anima*) of the Scriptures. Finally, the one who is perfect (ὁ τέλειος) benefits from the "spiritual law" (πνευματικὸς νόμος/ *spiritalis lex*). This "spiritual law" contains a "shadow" (σκία) of the things to come.[106] This tripartite anthropology (body–soul–spirit) is thus reflected in the very fiber of the Scriptures, ordered by divine goodness toward human salvation. Karen Torjesen, however, while recognizing the relation between anthropology and the sacred text, has shrewdly warned against too facile an understanding of their exact or exclusive correspondence. Basing her research on Origen's practice of preaching,[107] she contends that one must not see these three senses or levels of meaning as each directed to a particular kind of hearer (and so in some sense mimicking or assuming gnostic anthropology), but rather as simultaneously directed toward the pedagogy of the soul among all hearers, regardless of whether they be considered among the *simpliciores* or the more advanced.[108]

Origen's understanding of these three constituents of the human person is itself derived from Scripture: in 1 Thessalonians 5.23, Paul exhorts:

αὐτὸς δὲ ὁ θεὸς τῆς εἰρήνης ἁγιάσαι ὑμᾶς ὁλοτελεῖς καὶ ὁλόκληρον ὑμῶν τὸ πνεῦμα καὶ ἡ ψυχὴ καὶ τὸ σῶμα ἀμέμπτως ἐν τῇ παρουσίᾳ τοῦ κυρίου ἡμῶν Ἰησοῦ Χριστοῦ τηρηθείη [*Ipse autem Deus pacis santificet vos per omnia:*

105. For Origen, the "literal" meaning is just that: the words and their sequence, the text on the page. Modern understandings of "literal" meaning are tied to authorial intention in a way that is not the case for Origen; see Crouzel, *Origen*, 62.

106. Origen quotes Hebrews 10.1; cf. *Hom in Ps* 38.2.2 [SC 411.374–382].

107. Theoretical formulations are hardly ever employed rigidly; it is the mistake of much contemporary history of exegesis to regard such theoretical expressions too seriously.

108. Torjesen, "'Body,' 'Soul,' and 'Spirit,'" 17–30; see also Frances Young, *Biblical Exegesis and the Formation of Christian Culture* (Cambridge: Cambridge University Press, 1997), 242.

ut integer spiritus vester, et anima, et corpus sine querela in adventu Domini nostri Jesu Chrisi servetur].[109]

This expression of the apostolic kerygma, far more than simply the philosophic *koinē* of his day,[110] formed Origen's understanding of the human person. Most obviously, σῶμα or *corpus* refers to the physical dimension of individual human existence, and in Origen (who simply follows Paul), this is to be distinguished from σάρξ or *caro,* which almost always has a pejorative sense. The noun πνεῦμα or *spiritus* refers to the capacity of the individual to share in God's Spirit, though this *spiritus* may, in fact, remain dormant, in a sense, in one who is not engaged in things divine; thus in some it remains only a potentiality. The notion of ψυχή or *anima* (occasionally *animus*)[111] is complex.[112] It has a higher dimension or activity, generally referred to as νοῦς (*mens*), the term common in Platonic usage, and is sometimes expressed in language roughly equivalent to the Stoics' preferred terminology, τὸ ἡγεμονικόν; this is

109. On this, see Edwards, *Origen against Plato,* 135–37; the bulk of the description that follows relies heavily upon the account of Crouzel, *Origen,* 87–90.

110. This, of course, is the thrust of Edwards's argument: Origen is far more a biblical theologian than a mere cipher for the Hellenistic varieties of Platonism.

111. The noun *animus* occurs ten times in the *Homilies on the Psalms:* 36.5.6 [SC 411.246]; 37.1.1 [SC 411.262]; 37.1.5 [SC 411.290]; 37.2.1 [SC 411.300]; 37.2.1 [SC 411.304]; 37.2.3 [SC 411.308]; 38.1.3 [SC 411.338]; 38.1.5 [SC 411.344]; in some cases, it seems no more than an alternative to *anima;* in others, it seems more precisely an expression for *mens* (νοῦς); twice it is linked with *mens: mente et animo,* 38.1.11 [SC 411.366] and 38.2.2 [SC 411.378]. On the ambiguous relationship—at times seemingly synonymous—between *anima* and *mens* in Origen, see *De principiis* 2.8.2 [GK 386] and 2.11.5 [GK 448]. Crouzel consistently renders both *anima* and *animus* as *âme.*

112. For the (faulty) etymology that derives ψυχή from ψύχεσθαι ("to grow cool"), see Origen's discussion in *De principiis* 2.8.3 [GK 390–392]. The words are perhaps cognates, but not as Origen relates them: the relation of the words has more to do with "breathing" and "breath" than "growing cool." See now also the fine work of Benjamin Blosser, *Become Like the Angels: Origen's Doctrine of the Soul* (Washington, DC: The Catholic University of America Press, 2012), who argues that Origen, while working with philosophical precedent, was nonetheless free from any simplistic replication of Middle Platonist psychology and that the most important features of his doctrine of the soul are governed by the Scriptures.

usually rendered by the Latin *principale cordis*[113] or *principalis intellectus.*[114] Origen understands the biblical term καρδία (*cor*) as expressive of, and basically equivalent to, this higher activity or νοῦς;[115] in his *De oratione* he explicitly equates the biblical term καρδία with the Stoic term τὸ ἡγεμονικόν.[116] ψυχή also has a lower dimension or activity, which Origen usually characterizes as σάρξ or *caro,* a tag deriving ultimately from Romans 8.6, τὸ φρόνημα τῆς σαρκός, "the understanding (or wisdom) of the flesh."[117] This is usually found in the Latin as *carnalis sapientia,*[118] *sensus carnalis/ carnis,*[119] or *prudentia carnis.*[120] Crouzel suggests that it is better to understand these higher and lower dimensions less as "component parts" and more like "tendencies": either elevating the soul to things of the Spirit or drawing it downward toward the transient and material (typified as "flesh" or "fleshly"). The soul (or more precisely, its will), Origen provisionally proposes in *De principiis,* functions, as it were, as a kind of "medium" between the flesh and the spirit: *Et si ita est, constat quod huius animae voluntas media quaedam est inter carnem et spiritum, uni sine dubio e duobus serviens et obtemperans.*[121] The life of faith is the life of assimilation to the Spirit, so that, rather than becoming "carnal" or "fleshly" by association with lower things, the soul (including its lower dimension or tendency) might be healed, elevated, and, as it were, permeated by the Spirit.[122] This schema provides the background to

113. As in Rufinus's translation of the *Comm in Cant* 1.2.3; 6; 7 [SC 375.192; 194] and in Jerome's translation of Origen's *Hom in Ez* 3 [PL 25.714C].

114. As found in *Hom in Ps* 36.1.4 [SC 411.82].

115. See Edwards, "Christ or Plato?" 16–18; for *cor* in this sense, see *Hom in Ps* 36.1.2 [SC 411.68]; *Hom in Ps* 36.3.2 [SC 411.132–134]; *Hom in Ps* 36.4.1 [SC 411.184]; *Hom in Ps* 36.5.3 [SC 411.232]. But now also see Lorenzo Perrone, "'I cuori e i reni': Note sull'interpretazione origeniana di Sal 7,10," in *Adamantius* 22 (2016): 87–104.

116. *De oratione* 29.2 [GCS 3.382], in explanation of Leviticus 17.11: [ἡ ψυχὴ τῆς πασῆς σαρκὸς] ἥτις ἐστὶν ὁμονύμως ᾧ ἐγκατοικεῖ σώματι τὸ ἡγεμονικὸν ὃ καλεῖται καρδία.

117. Origen discusses this in *De principiis* 3.4.3–4 [GK 612–618].

118. *Hom in Ps* 36.1.2 [SC 411.68].

119. *Hom in Ps* 37.1.2 [SC 411.280].

120. *Hom in Ps* 38.2.8 [SC 411.396].

121. *De principiis* 3.4.2 [GK 610]; see also *De principiis* 2.8.4 [GK 396].

122. For Origen's speculations on the pre-existent state of the soul, one may

and informs the theology expressed in the nine *Homilies on the Psalms* translated by Rufinus.

The fact that Rufinus follows Origen in characterizing the explanation of these Psalms as "moral" further indicates that their teaching is fundamentally about the progress or pedagogy of the soul and its healing, instruction, and elevation, as is evident from the text of all nine homilies. This also reflects the intersection of anthropology and Scripture, in that for Origen the moral sense refers to the "soul" of the text and corresponds to the ψυχή of the reader.[123] Despite modern reservations about the integrity of the "moral" or "psychic" sense in Origen's practice,[124] the *Homilies on the Psalms* offer, in fact, an explicit example in practice (the act of preaching) of discussion of this very sense (*expositio tota moralis est*).

It has been the more recent scholarly consensus that while

---

refer to his treatment in *De principiis* 2.6–8 [GK 354–398], though not without consulting the reservations expressed by Edwards, *Origen against Plato,* 87–114. There is no indication, even implicit, in the *Homilies on the Psalms* about the pre-existence of souls; rather, they are very much about souls "in the Church"; on this account of the "moral sense," see Edwards, *Origen against Plato,* 136.

123. On this important issue one can consult the seminal work of Henri de Lubac, *History and Spirit: The Understanding of Scripture According to Origen,* trans. Anne Englund Nash (San Francisco: Ignatius, 2007), a more generous account than that found in R. P. C Hanson, *Allegory and Event: A Study of the Sources and Significance of Origen's Interpretation of Scripture* (Louisville: Westminster John Knox, 2002). Jean Daniélou, *Gospel Message and Hellenistic Culture,* trans. John Austin Baker (Philadelphia: Westminster, 1973), while generally sympathetic to Origen's exegesis, contends that specifically Christological typology is the only mode of allegory that is distinctively Christian; other forms of allegory run the risk of becoming flights of fancy. Additionally, the recent studies by Elizabeth Ann Dively Lauro, *The Soul and Spirit of Scripture within Origen's Exegesis* (Boston: Brill, 2005), and J. Christopher King, *Origen on the Song of Songs as the Spirit of the Scripture* (Oxford: Oxford University Press, 2005), both offer helpful analyses of the two higher senses in Origen.

124. See the helpful summary of recent scholarship in Dively Lauro, 15–26; her own work seeks to rehabilitate the psychic (moral) sense and offers an analysis of its role—precisely in its correlation with the pneumatic (spiritual) sense—in Origen's practice. She shrewdly demonstrates how—in a way reflective of his anthropology—Origen employs the psychic (moral) analysis precisely to lead to the pneumatic (spiritual) in a way that becomes mutually self-mediating. So too, in the believer, the soul (and even the body) is to become ordered by and to the spirit. Cf. Dively Lauro, 238–40.

in *De principiis* 4.2.4, Origen enumerates the moral or psychic meaning, correlated to the soul, as discoverable in the text of Scripture, in practice the moral or psychic meaning is never elucidated in itself or in isolation, but only in relation to the spiritual or pneumatic meaning. Further, the moral element is not at all, in the not-undisputed views of Hanson or Daniélou, distinctively Christian, but perhaps more akin to Philonic exegesis.[125] Moreover, Torjesen, in her analysis of Origen's treatment of Psalm 37, has suggested that Origen presents merely the historical sense and does not engage in allegory at all.[126] She characterizes his method in these homilies thus: "In Origen's hand the exegesis of the historical situation of the Psalmist becomes simultaneously an exposition of the soul, the church, and the spiritual life."[127] One should observe that while her characterization is quite correct, the conclusion she draws is insufficient to account for what is occurring in Origen's preaching. Rather, Origen discovers precisely within the "historical" the *moral* meaning of the text. The historical voice of the Psalmist reveals the moral meaning for the reader or hearer of the text. Mark Edwards has rightly contended that for Origen the Incarnation (the reality of the incarnate Word's body, soul, and spirit) is the condition of possibility for the multivalent meaning of the scriptural Word (the Word incarnate in the text—body, soul, and spirit). He has also warned against drawing too fine a distinction between the historical and the moral meaning of the text, arguing that for Origen the moral sense addresses precisely the meaning of the text for one who is *in* the "body" of the Church, the moral (psychic) meaning being found *in* the literal (somatic or bodily) meaning.[128]

125. Dively Lauro, 22, characterizing the (among themselves still differing) views of de Lubac, Hanson, and Daniélou.

126. Karen Jo Torjesen, "Origen's Interpretation of the Psalms," in *Studia Patristica* 17 (1982): 944–58; see also her lengthier study, *Hermeneutical Procedure and Theological Method in Origen's Exegesis* (Berlin: De Gruyter, 1986).

127. Torjesen, "Origen's Interpretation," 945.

128. Edwards, *Origen against Plato,* 136. Cf. also Rolf Gögler, "Inkarnationsglaube und Bibeltheologie bei Origenes," in *Theologische Quartalschrift* 165 (1985): 82–94. One of the intriguing features of Origen's *Comm in Cant* (and

Elizabeth Dively Lauro has made the convincing case that what she calls the two "non-literal" senses, the psychic (moral) and the pneumatic (spiritual), in fact function together in Origen's pastoral pedagogy, making the "eternal focus of the pneumatic sense" accessible by means of the "temporal call to moral purification."[129] That is, the anagogical is accessed precisely through the moral, and moral progress renders the soul more attuned to the Spirit, which is the anthropological *telos* in Origen's system.[130] What becomes obvious to the reader of these homilies (as Rufinus clearly saw, and as Origen himself had apparently asserted) is that these Psalms provide an occasion for a properly moral (psychic) exegesis (*expositio tota moralis est*), since within them one discovers the dynamics of the soul's healing, instruction, and elevation toward the Spirit within the community of the Church.[131]

---

one that deserves more extensive study) is that he explicitly speaks of the spousal relation sung in the text as expressing the relation "Church to Christ" and "soul to the *Logos*": *Spiritalis vero intelligentia, secundum hoc nihilominus quod in praefatione signavimus, vel de ecclesia ad Christum sub sponsae vel sponsi titulo vel de animae cum Verbo Dei coniunctione dirigitur* (*Comm in Cant* 1.1.2 [SC 375.176]). This distinction is maintained elsewhere in his exposition, e.g., at 1.1.4–5 [SC 375.178]; 1.2.23 [SC 375.204]; 1.4.4 [SC 375.222]; 1.5.3 [SC 375.242], though not merely as a means of distinguishing the ecclesial interpretation (as found in Hippolytus) from what might be called the psychic (individual) interpretation. Rather, he seems consciously to avoid expressing the relation as "Church to the *Logos*" or "soul to Christ," perhaps as a means of emphasizing that the soul, "embodied" in the community of the Church, relates to the *Logos* "embodied" in the Incarnate Christ. Cf. the peroration of *Hom in Cant* 1.10 [SC 37bis.98–100], where the two are elided, and the soul is situated (properly) in the Church: *tu melior es omnibus filiabus, tu sponsa, tu ecclesiastica anima, omnibus animabus quae non sunt ecclesiasticae.*

129. Dively Lauro, 238.

130. Cf. *De principiis* 3.6.6–9 [GK 658–667].

131. Jean Daniélou, in discussing the typology of Rahab in Origen's *Homilies on Joshua,* observes that "Origen gives a moral interpretation, which is the application to the individual [soul] of what is true first of all of the Church ... the microcosm of each soul reproduces the macrocosm of the Church"; in *From Shadows to Reality: Studies in the Biblical Typology of the Fathers,* trans. Wulstan Hibberd (London: Burns and Oates, 1960), 252–53.

The Moral Sense in Practice

There are, in fact, a number of instances within these homilies where the moral meaning is adduced by Origen, usually as a complement, though occasionally in juxtaposition, to the literal sense. In *Hom in Ps* 36.3.6, commenting on Psalm 36.16, Origen notes immediately that for the simple, the literal meaning has something useful or beneficial to offer: *secundum litteram continuo etiam simplicioribus quibusque utilis admonitio est, de qua et prius dicendum est.*[132] Before discoursing on its literal meaning (*quid ergo nos doceat littera*), he notes that there is nonetheless a deeper meaning (*profundius aliquid*), "something hidden" (*quid etiam secreti*), also to be pursued. His explanation of this deeper meaning is moral and is cast in terms of the believer living within the Church (*videas autem unum de ecclesia*).[133] For Origen, the moral meaning is very much about the dynamics of living as a member of the Church. This approach is continued in making sense of the very next verse ("the arms of sinners will be broken"), which he observes makes no sense if taken literally (*secundum litteram*), but which is intended, like many passages of the Scriptures, to arouse the dense and sleepy to invest themselves further in rising above the letter to understand the spiritual meaning.[134] This "spiritual meaning" is explained, however, in moral terms. He speaks against the dangers of pride, excoriates the hesitancy to give alms, and observes the diabolical opposition to good works, all of which are presented in terms of the dynamics of communal life. The next verse, too, Origen notes, is problematic when taken literally ("the Lord knows the days of those without blemish"). Uncertain of the possibilities of a literal reckoning, he suggests that each person "makes" a "day" proper to himself (*propriam*

132. SC 411.144–146; on the categories *simplices* or *simpliciores* in Origen's exegesis and preaching, see Gunnar af Hällström, *Fides Simpliciorum according to Origen of Alexandria* (Helsinki: Societas Scientiarum Fennica, 1984).

133. SC 411.146.

134. *Hom in Ps* 36.3.7 [SC 411.152]: *Sunt multa in scripturis ita posita, quae etiam eum qui valde brutus est et stertit, movere possunt, immo cogere ut necesse habeat littera derelicta ad intellectum conscendere spiritalem.*

sibi faciat ipse diem),[135] through integrity in his relations with others, by withdrawal from company hostile to the Church, and through the fraternal charity that is expressed in care for widows, orphans, and those in distress (quoting James 1.27). Here again, the meaning is expressed explicitly and almost exclusively within the context of ecclesial life and in very practical, moral terms.[136]

Verse 21 of Psalm 36 ("The sinner will borrow and not return, but the just one shows mercy and lends") receives similar explanation. Since there is ample evidence that the wicked do in fact borrow (at interest) and return, Origen maintains that this cannot be taken *secundum litteram*.[137] Thus for Origen, the correct explanation requires a particular mode of understanding relative to the text and the logic inherent in it: *si intellegas quis est qui fenerat et quis est qui accepit fenus et requiras quis est peccator qui non redit pecuniam quam sumpsit, intelleges consequentiam* [probably rendering ἀκολουθίαν] *habere quod scriptum est*.[138] The "money" of which the Psalm speaks is, for Origen, the content of sound teaching and preaching, and he contrasts genuine money, expressive of what has been "borrowed" from the Lord and, in turn, "loaned" to his congregants, with the counterfeit coinage produced by heretics. Valentinus, Basilides, and Marcion are mentioned together, and Origen criticizes them as fabricating coinage outside the "mint" of the Church (*extra monetam figurata est, quia extra ecclesiam composita est*). The one who repays his loan with interest is the one who "returns" not only by fidelity to the Word received but also with good

135. *Hom in Ps* 36.3.9 [SC 411.156–158]: *Sed et hoc secundum litteram nescio si possit consequenter exponi … Verum si sacratiorem adhuc sensum in hoc loco perscrutari volumus*. Cf. *Hom in Ps* 38.1.8 [SC 411.358].

136. *Hom in Ps* 36.3.9 [SC 411.156–157]: *Et si quando abicientes mendacium loquimur veritatem cum proximo nostro … similiter et cum retrahimus nos ab his qui oderunt fratres et in tenebris ambulant et in dilectione fratrum permanemus … sed et cum iustitiam custodimus et cum visitantes viduas atque orphanos in tribulatione sua, immaculatos nos custodimus ab hoc saeculo immaculatorum nobis ipsis facimus dies.*

137. *Hom in Ps* 36.3.11 [SC 411.168].

138. SC 411.168; for ἀκολουθία (meaning logic, order, sequence, or coherence) as a technical term in ancient literary culture and in Origen's exegesis, see Bernhard Neuschäfer, *Origenes als Philologe* (Basel: Friedrich Reinhardt, 1987), 244–46.

works.[139] Origen then gives concrete examples of how to "hear" the Word and what it means to "repay with interest": avoiding lewd company, avarice, and rapaciousness, and showing mercy to the weak.[140] Once again, it is precisely life in the Church and the moral obligations to charity incumbent upon its members that are discovered in the Psalm.

In *Hom in Ps* 36.4.3–4, the improbability of the literal sense (*secundum historiam … secundum simplicem intellectum*) of David's words[141] in Psalm 36.25–26 ("I was young and have grown old, and I have not seen the just man abandoned, nor his offspring seeking bread"), compels Origen to distinguish the several ages of the "inner man," and thus he can discuss the dynamics of moral growth and spiritual maturity, contrasting the difficulties that not infrequently afflict the just individual's "outer man," with the internal stability that is the mark of the spiritually mature "inner man."[142] This, too, is related to life in the Church, as Origen discusses the various meanings of the term "presbyter," explicitly referring to those who hold this office in the community: rather than merely indicating seniority, the title is meant to convey internal spiritual maturity.[143] Here, too, the insufficiency of the literal sense prompts Origen to seek out the Psalm's teaching in terms of moral progress and maturity, as he had done in the previous homily. Later he reprises the interpretation he had offered in an earlier homily regard-

139. SC 411.170.

140. SC 411.172: *Ad impudica rursum devolveris scorta et effectus peccator … ut cupiditati tuae satisfacias invadis quae aliena sunt … Non solum, inquit fenerat iustus, hoc est non solum praedicat verbum, hoc est non solum docet imperitos, verum etiam miseratur infirmos.*

141. Origen here simply assumes Davidic authorship of the Psalm.

142. SC 411.202–216. This distinction, rooted in Ephesians 3.16, between the "inner" and the "outer" man is introduced elsewhere in the homilies as well; cf. *Hom in Ps* 36.1.4 [SC 411.74–76], *Hom in Ps* 36.3.4 [SC 411.140], *Hom in Ps* 36.4.1 [SC 411.186]. It is also employed in the *Comm in Cant* pr. 2.6 [SC 375.94]. Cf. also *Hom in Num* 24.2 [SC 461.166–176], where he emphasizes that it is within this "inner man" that the reformation of the "image" takes place.

143. SC 411.202–204: *Unde et nos optare debemus non pro aetate corporis, neque pro officio presbyterii appellari et seniores, sed pro interioris hominis perfecto sensu et gravitate constantiae, sicut et Abraham appellatus est presbyter.*

ing Psalm 36.21[144] and employs it to make sense of Psalm 36.28 ("All day long he shows mercy and lends"). Once again, sound teaching and the fruit it bears in action are contrasted with heretical teaching, and the product of the "Lord's mint" (*de dominica moneta*) is presented in opposition to the "wicked and pernicious funds" garnered from the Evil One (*iniquam pecuniam et pestiferam et de malo*).[145]

Throughout these homilies, when the literal or historical sense of the Psalm text is insufficient or problematic, Origen adduces its moral, and specifically ecclesial, meaning for the believer.[146] As Origen himself had initially suggested in these homilies,[147] the Scriptures are themselves multivalent—some texts teach profound mysteries transcending speech, others adumbrate and ultimately disclose the Incarnation and its meaning, and others are given to the correction and reformation of life—and, as has been shown, the Psalms that form the basis of these homilies are to him clearly moral in tenor.

Origen's Teaching in the *Homilies on the Psalms*

Origen, within the course of his *Homilies on the Psalms,* employs three principal models of or metaphors for the soul's progress, which might be characterized as (a) agonistic/military, (b) medicinal/therapeutic, and (c) educational/pedagogical. The assumption underlying all three models is that the Christian life is one of making progress (*profectus*), and each metaphor attempts to capture or express this from a different perspective. As these are preached texts, there is no systematic presentation of these models, but rather they occur as the text of the Scriptures appears to suggest them to Origen; further, they are hardly mutually exclusive and occasionally

144. "The sinner will borrow and not return, but the just one shows mercy and lends," *Hom in Ps* 36.3.11 [SC 411.170–174].

145. SC 411.214.

146. This is quite consistent with what Edwards, *Origen against Plato,* 136, describes as the significance of the moral sense for Origen.

147. *Hom in Ps* 36.1.1 [SC 411.50].

are elided or conflated. One discovers that Origen's teaching in these homilies and the theological vision he employs are quite consistent both with the teaching found in *De principiis,* from his Alexandrian career (c. 229–230 AD), and that of his *Commentary on the Canticle,* composed at Athens in 245 AD, and so not long after these homilies were delivered at Caesarea.

The Agonistic/Military Model

The image of the Christian life as an *agon* (rendering ἀγών) or *certamen* (probably rendering ἄθλησις) figures prominently in *Hom in Ps* 36.4.[148] In explaining Psalm 36.23–24,[149] Origen employs the image of the Christian as one engaged in contest, a struggle principally with the prince of this world.[150] In this grappling, the just individual might from time to time be taken down, so to speak, but the mark of his justice is that he does not remain down; he gets up and continues the struggle. It is the devil who seeks quite literally to supplant the Christian, to trip him up, inducing a fall (*casus*).[151] Within this discussion, Origen in a passing remark distinguishes between the just person (*iustus homo*) and the pure person (*purus homo*),[152] perhaps anticipating a distinction he later makes between the person who is still making progress (*qui proficit*)—while subject to falls (*casus*), he maintains his justice through effort and repen-

148. Esp. *Hom in Ps* 36.4.2 [SC 411.188–200].

149. *A Domino gressus hominis diriguntur et viam eius cupiet. Cum ceciderit non conturbabitur* [*prosternitur*] *quia Dominus confirmat manus eius* (= "The steps of man are guided by the Lord, and he will long for his way. When he falls, he will not be thrown into confusion [remain down], for the Lord strengthens his hands").

150. *In nostro agone, qui est nobis adversum principem huius mundi: Hom in Ps* 36.4.2 [SC 411.194], alluding to Ephesians 6.12 and perhaps also to John 12.31. Discussing this *agon* in *De principiis* 3.2.5 [GK 578], Origen mixes the agonistic and athletic metaphors: *ita etiam hoc audiendum est, quod apostolus dicit, quod universis athletis vel militibus Christi conluctatio et certamen est adversum omnia ista, quae enumerata sunt.*

151. SC 411.194; in this context he also employs the verb *luctari* (= λυγίζω).

152. SC 411.194; there is a possibility (Prinzivalli and Crouzel concur on this) that *purus* in this passage simply means "without qualification" or "without specification"; however, a reasonable case can be made that *purus* here is being used synonymously with *perfectus* at *Hom in Ps* 38.1.5 [SC 411.346]. The term *homo purus/purus homo* is found in Latin literature only later (in the fifth century) and used exclusively in reference to Christ's human nature.

tance—and the one who has been made perfect (*perfectus*).[153] Repentance is understood and presented by Origen precisely in ecclesial terms: it is the one who abandons hope (*desperans*) of conversion who remains paralyzed and idled by his sin, and, like the wife of Lot, being fixed on what lay behind, is mired in failure, and renders himself incapable of returning to life in the Church (*ad ecclesiam redire*).[154] Conversion is understood not as an autonomous or private activity, but only in terms of the life of the community. One who engages in this struggle is referred to by Origen as an "athlete of piety and virtue,"[155] one whose firmness of purpose (*maneat semper immobilis*)[156] is subtly juxtaposed to Lot's wife's ultimately self-imposed intransigence: *permansit perfecta statuuncula salis.*[157] Job, who figures no fewer than five times in the *De oratione,* is called by Origen an "athlete of virtue," whose two "contests" with the Adversary Origen distinguishes from the Lord's, who, like Job, grappled—and conquered—three times.[158] In fact, in an earlier homily, in relation to Paul's teaching about all things being made subject to Christ (1 Corinthians 15.28), Origen posits that the believer's entire life is like a struggle or contest for obedience, whether to Christ or to his Adversary, with prayer and asceticism as requisite in training: *Propter ergo videntes quia omnis vita nostra agonem quendam obaudientiae gerit, sive Christi, sive huius qui contrarius Christi, conemur per orationis, per eruditionis religiosam institutionem hoc agere.*[159]

Origen, prompted by an image in 2 Timothy 2.5, furthers

153. Cf. *Hom in Ps* 38.1.5 [SC 411.346].

154. SC 411.192; 196.

155. *Athleta pietatis ac virtutis* [SC 411.196].

156. SC 411.196.

157. SC 411.192.

158. *De oratione* 30.2 [GCS 3.394]: νενικημένος δὲ ὑπὸ τοῦ τῆς ἀρετῆς ἀθλητοῦ ψευδὴς ἀποδείκνυται. Cf. *Hom in Ps* 36.4.2 [SC 411.198–200], where David, Jeremiah, Jacob, and the Innocents are brought forth as athletic exemplars.

159. *Hom in Ps* 36.2.1 [SC 411.98], with *eruditio* probably rendering ἄσκησις; here the agonistic and educational (*institutio*) metaphors are elided. On the significance of this passage from Paul and the centrality of subjection to Christ in Origen's vision of the Christian life, see also *Hom in Ps* 38.1.8 [SC 411.354] and *De principiis* 1.6.2 [GK 216–224]; 3.5.7–8 [GK 636–640]; 3.6.9 [GK 664–666].

the metaphor and speaks of the *certamen* and *agon* encountered by believers in terms of their embrace of and adherence to the Law.[160] It is important to note that for Origen, the Law, when correctly understood in terms of its spiritual meaning and in light of its genuine *telos*, Christ,[161] does not carry the pejorative connotations it frequently had in the Pelagian disputes and even later in the Reformation debates. Origen speaks of the various classes or groupings of contestants by age in the wrestling matches of an athletic competition, namely, children, adolescents, and adults,[162] implying both degrees of maturity and the progressive nature of the struggle;[163] this struggle is further defined through Ephesians 6.12 again as against the spirits opposed to Christ. The variety of "ages" is then explained by Origen in terms of the distinction between the "inner" and the "outer" man,[164] a distinction he also makes in the prologue to his *Commentary on the Canticle*;[165] these, of course, refer not to biological age, but to stages of spiritual maturity.

In *Hom in Ps* 38.1.5, the theme of the *agon* and *certamen* appear again, in this case in reference to those who might insult or speak harshly toward the believer. Origen makes use of the metaphor of a fighter who is being pummeled: the blows themselves build endurance, and the one who has been engaged

160. *Hom in Ps* 36.4.2 [SC 411.196–198].

161. *De principiis* 4.1.6 [GK 686–688]; cf. the helpful summary of Thomas Scheck, "Law," in *The Westminster Handbook to Origen*, ed. John A. McGuckin (Louisville: Westminster John Knox, 2004), 138–40.

162. Prinzivalli, *Origene, Omelie sui Salmi* (1991), here cites Origen's *Hom in Lev* 16.1 [SC 287.262], where these "classes" or ranks of athletic contestants are distinguished along the same lines: *Verbi gratia, si inter pueros quis habeat agonem, si inter iuvenes, si inter viros, quae per singulos ordines observatio haberi debeat, quid fieri liceat quidve non liceat, et quae certaminis regulae custodiri, quid etiam post haec remunerationis mereatur palma vicentis, ipsis nihilominus agonicis legibus cautum est.* Crouzel cites a parallel in Ambrose, perhaps, though not conclusively, derived from Origen: *Enarratio in Psalmum* 36.52 [PL 14.992]: *Sunt athletae qui vocentur pueri, ephebi, viri; hoc est* παῖδες, ἐφήβοι, πύκται; cf. also *De principiis* 3.2.3 [GK 570].

163. This parallels closely what Origen has to say about the stages of the soul's progress after death; see *De principiis* 2.11.5–7 [GK 446–454]; *Hom in Ps* 36.5.1 [SC 411.228–230]; *Hom in Ps* 38.1.8 [SC 411.354].

164. *Hom in Ps* 36.4.3 [SC 411.202–204].

165. *Comm in Cant* pr. 6–9 [SC 375.94–98].

in the struggle gradually becomes impervious to the blows.[166] In like manner, one who has been well trained, whose endurance has been fortified through an extended or long practice of meditation (*bene instituti sumus et animo longa meditatione roborati*) is capable of being unmoved by the blows (in this case, the insults or abusive words) of one's opponent (*antagonista*). Endurance of this sort engenders a kind of meekness in the believer that is itself imitative of God, for God has to endure the insulting language of heretics, the blasphemy of those who deny Providence,[167] and the "accusations" of those who remain unaware of the depths of God's wisdom.[168] When confronted by the sinner's provocation, the just person meditates or focuses his energies internally on what God has revealed, and so ensures his victory, even though initially such provocation might take its toll on him: *dum ipse haec apud se meditatur, irritatio ei supervenit peccatoris, quae eum conturbet quidem et fatiget, non tamen vincat.*[169] Origen then continues by distinguishing one who is making progress (*qui proficit*) from one who is already perfect (*perfectus*), suggesting how a wound sustained in combat, once reopened by another blow, is like the individual who is making progress but not yet perfect: additional blows still have some effect, but do not necessarily overcome the one who endures them.[170] For Origen, it is precisely the struggle, the contest, that produces in the believer both endurance in the face of temptation and the capacity to overcome sin in the future.

The *topos* of the Christian who must face the opposition of the sinner recurs in *Hom in Ps* 38.2.6. Here such conflicts are presented as a function of divine Providence. Commenting on

166. SC 411.344–348.

167. The denial of Providence is arguably for Origen, as for many of the Fathers, the most insidious form of atheism.

168. *Culpatur ab his qui thesauros sapientiae* [cf. Colossians 2.3] *eius ignorat,* perhaps referring to those who misconstrue the text of the Scriptures and who fail to grasp the economy articulated in them.

169. SC 411.346.

170. SC 411.346, and so conflating the agonistic metaphor with the medicinal one. Ambrose, at the outset of his *Explanatio Psalmorum,* at 1.4–8 [CSEL 64.4–7], likewise makes use of both medicinal and agonistic metaphors in describing the healing and strengthening capacities of the Psalms.

Psalm 38.10 (*Obmutui et non aperui os meum, quia tu es qui fecisti*), Origen explains that God has ordered such struggles precisely for the benefit of those who believe, as a kind of exercise or training with a view to the progress that it will both generate and facilitate: *quoniam quidem velut agonem quendam inter nos et consistentem adversum nos peccatorem describit, quia hoc ipsum indicet fecisse Deum, id est, quod exercitii nostri causa et profectus Deus fecerit ista certamina.*[171] Faced with such struggles (*agones istos*), the believer is encouraged by the Psalm to recall that these are providentially ordered exercises in endurance (*tu nobis haec exercitia patientiae praeparasti*).[172] Far from being accidental, the various *agones* or *certamina* experienced by the believer are providentially ordered occasions for growth and progress.

Closely related to agonistic metaphors are military ones, which make use of combat imagery. Origen several times draws upon the language of Ephesians 6.13–17[173] in order to emphasize the nature of the Christian battle. In *Hom in Ps* 36.2.8,[174] initiating his peroration with an explanation of Psalm 36.14,[175] Origen contrasts the armaments of the sinner and those with which the believer is fitted. The contrast is metaphorically controlled by the text of Ephesians: justice and injustice (breastplates), salvation and perdition (helmets), preaching the Gospel and the shedding of blood (shoes), faith and infidelity (shields), the Holy Spirit and evil (swords). Because the Psalm teaches that "sinners have bent their bow," Origen then speaks about different kinds of arrows (*sagittae*). Sinners and the just both possess arrows, and by these, Origen explains, one is to understand "words" (*verba*). The just person uses words to reprove the sinner, to call him to repentance.

171. SC 411.388.

172. SC 411.390.

173. διὰ τοῦτο ἀναλάβετε τὴν πανοπλίαν τοῦ θεοῦ ἵνα δυνηθῆτε ἀντιστῆναι ἐν τῇ ἡμέρᾳ τῇ πονηρᾷ καὶ ἅπαντα κατεργασάμενοι στῆναι (= *propterea accipite armaturam Dei ut possitis resistere in die malo et omnibus perfectis stare*).

174. SC 411.118–122.

175. *Gladium evaginaverunt peccatores, tetenderunt arcum suum ut deiciant inopem et pauperem, ut trucident rectos corde* (= "Sinners have drawn the sword, they have bent their bow, to cast down the needy and the poor, that they might murder the upright of heart").

Conversely, sinners use poisoned words like arrows to pierce the one who is not armed with the shield of faith, to do him in. Not only words, but sometimes the actions of sinners function as fiery darts; those who incite others to lust or anger function as *tela ignita* of the Evil One.[176]

Juxtaposed to the devil's *tela* is Christ, who, speaking through Isaiah,[177] presents himself as the chosen arrow (*sagitta electa*) for the just, and this fittingly relates Origen's explanation of *sagittae* as *verba* to the fact that Christ is *the* Word.[178] Moses and the apostles, Origen later contends, are, like Christ, *sagittae electae* insofar as they speak God's word for the salvation of the hearer, as can be any just individual or preacher who provokes his hearers to conversion.[179] And because Christ is the *sagitta electa,* the words of the Canticle ring quite literally true: *vulnerata caritate ego sum.*[180] Those who speak words that provoke to conversion are further specified later as "darts of reprimand" (*correptionis iacula*), whose words pierce the very heart of the listener.[181]

Origen again speaks about such "fiery darts" in *Hom in Ps* 37.1.1,[182] here within the context of the progressive healing that takes place for the believer within the community of the Church.[183] With keen psychological insight, Origen observes that correction of faults often is initially painful, and that frequently the wound's pain stirs in the one being treated a resis-

176. *Hom in Ps* 36.3.3 [SC 411.136]: *Non solum autem in verbis, sed in factis diriguntur in nos tela diaboli ... nonne et hic ignitum iaculum est maligni?* Cf. *Hom in Ps* 36.3.2 [SC 411.132–134].

177. Is 49.2; later, in *Hom in Ps* 37.1.2 [SC 411.272], Christ is again understood by Origen as the speaker of this verse of Isaiah: *Denique et Salvator ita dixit: Posuit me sicut sagittam electam et in pharetra sua abscondit me.*

178. SC 411.120.

179. *Hom in Ps* 36.3.3 [SC 411.134], where Antichrist is called *sagitta diaboli.*

180. Song 2.5; *Hom in Ps* 36.3.3 [SC 411.134]. Cf. *Comm in Cant* pr. 2.17 [SC 375.102], *telum quoddam et vulnus amoris.*

181. *Hom in Ps* 37.1.2 [SC 411.272].

182. *Ignita iacula,* SC 411.260–262.

183. SC 411.260: *discipuli vero eius* [*Christi*] *Petrus vel Paulus sed et prophetae medici sunt et hi omnes qui post apostolos in ecclesia positi sunt quibusque curandorum vulnerum disciplina commissa est, quos voluit Deus in ecclesia sua esse medicos animarum.* Here the military metaphor is elided into the medicinal.

tance that is against his best interest.[184] Thus, he advises, being fully fitted with the armor of God, the believer protects and fortifies his "inner man"[185] against the *tela ignita* launched by the devil.[186] One who has been wounded by such darts should first confess his sin (*confiteri peccatum*) and then keep the failure in mind (*in memoriam recordari delictum*), so as to learn from his mistake. Both elements, self-knowledge and confession, seem important to Origen. He speaks of "confession" elsewhere in the homilies, almost always in reference to self-awareness that comes from recollection.[187] In *Hom in Ps* 36.1.5, he encourages his listeners to be aware of their evil deeds and, rather than hiding them, to make them known to the Lord through confession: *per exomologesin*.[188] This "confession" is spoken of as "to the Lord" four times in as many lines (*revela ea Domino … confessus fueris et revelaveris ei delicta tua … si aliqua ei delicta revelaveris … et haec ei revelas*) and has a therapeutic effect (*sine dubio sanum te faciet*). There is no indication here of "confession" to another person or to the community. *Hom in Ps* 37.2.1

184. *Hom in Ps* 36.3.3 [SC 411.262]: *Argui vel corripi est doloris poena, cruciatus et ita gravis est ut etiam hi qui fideles et religiosi videntur, si forte ut homines aliquando in delicto aliquo incurrerint et arguantur, indignentur adversus eos qui arguunt et oderint eos. Corripiunt enim ut emendent.*

185. *Hom in Ps* 37.1.1 [SC 411.262], linking Ephesians 6.13–16 with the distinction between the "inner" and the "outer" man of which he is fond, and which reflects his interpretation of Gn 1 and 2 as mediated by Eph 3.16; cf. *Hom in Ps* 36.1.4 [SC 411.74–76] on the differences between the "outer" and the "inner," including their armature; *Hom in Ps* 36.4.1 [SC 411.186–188], on the "steps" or progress of the inner man; *Hom in Ps* 36.4.3 [SC 411.204], on "ages" of the inner man; cf. also *Comm in Cant* pr. 2.6 [SC 375.94]; *Dial Heracl* 15–24 [SC 67.86–102].

186. Cf. *Hom in Ps* 36.3.3 [SC 411.134] for *tela maligni ignita*, and *De principiis* 3.2.4 [GK 576], where they are called *ignita iacula*.

187. Cf. *Hom in Ps* 37.1.3 [SC 411.284]: *etiam haec* [sc. the words of Psalm 37.4] *debet dicere qui peccavit et post peccatum peccasse se recordatur; Hom in Ps* 38.1.7 [SC 411.352]: *quodam conscientiae suae igne succensum ex recordatione delicti, propterea dicebat "Et quis est qui me laetificet, nisi qui contristatur ex me?"*; *Hom in Ps* 38.2.7 [SC 411.392–393]: *ostendimus igitur dupliciter hominibus flagella praeparari … etiam cum ex recordatione delicti perurgentis conscientiae stimulis terebramur in corde.*

188. SC 411.84, where this self-awareness (*si malorum tibi conscius aliquorum fueris*), leading to confession, reflects pure conduct and a clear conscience (*pura est via tua et munda conscientia*) and issues forth in the "hope" spoken of in the Psalm; the term *exomologesis* is found again at *Hom in Ps* 37.2.1 [SC 411.302].

begins with a discussion of the ideal penitent, whose complete and candid confession of sin (*nolit tegere et occultare maculam suam*) emerges from self-awareness (*memor delicti sui … conscius sit sibi … ipse sui accusator exsistat*).[189] This description of "confession" is rife with both agonistic and medicinal language: the repentant sinner seeks a cure to restore health to his soul and does not remain down once fallen.[190] Unlike the earlier instance, however, which emphasized confession to the Lord, this passage seems to assume the potential embarrassment or scandal attendant upon such a candid confession and the impact this might have on the penitent. Origen feels the need to persuade his hearers that slight embarrassment in the present is far less worrisome than what they will face before the angels at the resurrection if they fail to confess, and that they should not fret about the criticisms which might be leveled against them by others.[191] One might infer that here Origen assumes some kind of public confession, one that would make an individual's failings known to others; hence his concern about embarrassment. Later in the same homily, he again draws upon a medicinal model. Here, the inability or unwillingness to be forthright is likened to indigestion, which is ultimately suffocating; confession relieves the internal pressure, so to speak.[192] Origen encourages his congregants to seek out the best doctor to whom they might confess their sin, one whom they can trust and who is skilled in mercy and compassion.[193] After such

189. SC 411.300–302; cf. Prv 18.17 (LXX): δίκαιος ἑαυτοῦ κατήγορος ἐν πρωτολογίᾳ; (Vlg): *Iustus prior est accusator sui.*

190. SC 411.300–302: *volentem tamen medelam ac salutem animae reparare … cum lapsis non iaceant … et sublevetur post casum suum.*

191. SC 411.300–302: *Si ergo huiusmodi homo memor delicti sui confiteatur quae commisit et humana confusione parvipendat eos qui exprobant eum confitentem et notant vel irrident, ille autem intellegens per hoc veniam sibi dari et in die resurrectionis pro his quibus nunc confunditur coram hominibus, tunc ante angelos Dei confusionem atque opprobria evasurum.*

192. SC 411.318: *Fortassis enim sicut hi qui habent intus inclusam escam indigestam, aut umoris vel phlegmatis stomacho graviter et moleste imminentia, si vomuerint, relevantur: ita etiam hi qui peccaverunt, si quidem occultant intra se et retinent peccatum, intrinsecus urgentur et propemodum suffocantur a phlegmate vel umore peccati.*

193. *Hom in Ps* 37.2.6 [SC 411.318]: *Tantummodo circumspice diligentius, cui debeas confiteri peccatum tuum. Proba prius medicum, cui debeas causam languoris*

a consultation, one course of action that might suggest itself to the doctor seems to be a public confession (*in conventu totius ecclesiae exponi debeat et curari*), which can, Origen suggests, provide healing for the penitent and simultaneously edify the community *(ex quo fortassis et ceteri aedificari poterunt et tu ipse facile sanari*). The perils of anachronism and the quality of other internal evidence prevent attempts to ascertain more precisely how this *confiteri* (no doubt originally ἐξομολογεῖν) is to be construed, but suffice it to say that there is reasonable evidence to infer some form of public penance to which Origen is alluding in these homilies.[194]

Agonistic and military metaphors are combined in *De principiis* 3.2.4–7, where Origen employs the language of the *agon* as a means of emphasizing the necessity of divine help in overcoming "thoughts," *cogitationes* (probably λογισμοί in the Greek), which can frequently be an instrument of demonic temptation.[195] While not ruling out the reality of demonic *incitamenta*,[196] Origen emphasizes both human freedom from fate or demonic compulsion and the reality and nature of God's Providence. He refers to believers as *athletae* and *milites* who are engaged in a *conluctatio* and *certamen* against the "principalities, powers, and the rulers of the darkness of this world" enumerated by Paul in Ephesians 6.12.[197] He makes clear that his language is metaphorical,[198] and emphasizes that the battle is spiritual: *sed spiritui adversum spiritum pugna est.* The devil will employ "fiery darts" (*ignita iacula*) to insinuate his various

exponere ... qui condolendi et conpatiendi noverit disciplinam.

194. This is the verdict found in the classic study of Bernhard Poschmann, *Penance and Anointing of the Sick,* trans. Francis Courtney (New York: Herder and Herder, 1964), esp. 66–70, who cites *Hom in Ps* 37.1.1; cf. also what is still an important study, Karl Rahner, *Theological Investigations XV: Penance in the Early Church,* trans. Lionel Swain (New York: Crossroad, 1982), esp. 246–328; and also the study of Ernest Latko, *Origen's Concept of Penance* (Quebec: Laval, 1949).

195. GK 574–584; the taxonomy of these λογισμοί will later figure heavily in the ascetic schema of Evagrius; see Robert Sinkiewicz, *Evagrius of Pontus: The Greek Ascetic Corpus* (Oxford: Oxford University Press, 2003), 66–114.

196. *De principiis* 3.2.3 [GK 572].

197. *De principiis* 3.2.5 [GK 578].

198. *De principiis* 3.2.6 [GK 582]: *Nec sane arbitrandum est qui huiuscemodi certamina corporum robore et palaestricae artis exercitiis peragantur.*

cogitationes, against which the believer is to make use of the "shield of faith" recommended by Paul in Ephesians, in language encountered repeatedly in the *Homilies on the Psalms.*[199]

One particular theme that recurs in Origen's treatment of these various *agones* or *certamina* facing the believer is the *ira* or *iracundia* incited by demons[200] or provoked by sinners. While a variety of sins and evils that afflict believers is treated in the course of these homilies, the dangers of wrath and anger seem to occupy Origen's interest and pastoral concern more than the others. In cataloguing the various ways someone may resist subjection to Christ,[201] which is constitutive of the Christian vocation, Origen counterposes a number of the ἐπίνοιαι of Christ with a corresponding vice.[202] *Iracundia* and *furor* are the opposites of the *spiritus mansuetudinis* that one sees in Christ. Later in the same homily, Origen observes that while some individuals are predisposed to particular vices, and others to different ones, all people struggle with anger; it is characterized as a *morbus* that is pandemic.[203] The kind of peace of which Psalm 36.11 speaks as the source of delight is found in one who controls his wrath both internally and externally, and the contrast with meekness is developed with obvious reference to the Beatitudes. As he begins *Hom in Ps* 36.3.1, Origen contrasts the "sword of sinners" (Psalm 36.14) with the "sword of the Spirit" (Ephesians 6.17) operative in the just.[204] The former is the instrument of contention and provocation to anger; if one were to respond not with *mansuetudo,* but in like manner with *furiosa verba,* he would reveal himself, too, as a sinner. The task that confronts

199. Cf. Eph 6.16; *De principiis* 3.2.4 [GK 577–578]; cf. above.

200. Cf. *De principiis* 3.2.6 [GK 582], where the demons are said to incite to anger, which leads through sadness ultimately to despair: *Ipsa vero certaminum species ita intellegenda est, cum damna, cum pericula, cum obprobria, cum criminationes excitantur adversum nos, non id agentibus adversariis potestatibus, ut haec tantummodo patiamur, sed ut per haec vel ad iram multam vel ad nimiam tristitiam, vel ad desperationem ultimam provocemur, vel certe, quod est gravius, conqueri adversum deum fatigati et victi taediis compellamur, tamquam humanam vitam non aeque iusteque moderantem.*

201. 1 Cor 15.28.

202. *Hom in Ps* 36.2.1 [SC 411.98].

203. *Hom in Ps* 36.2.3 [SC 411.102].

204. SC 411.126–128. Cf. *Hom in Ps* 38.1.4–5 [SC 411.338–346], where the sinner provokes to anger while the just is one who seeks to avoid wrath and rage.

the believer is slowly and over time to allow the "sword" of sin to rust and fall apart from desuetude. In the face of criticism—whether merited or not—and harsh words, the just person will enact the words of Psalm 37.15, not offering a retort out of anger. Responding with anger induces sadness, a sadness that, Origen suggests, harms, rather than reforms, the soul.[205]

In order to emphasize the ultimate insufficiency of human effort alone in the face of such an onslaught,[206] Origen adduces the account of an angel's "wrestling" with Jacob recorded in Genesis 32. He wants to avoid reading the text as implying that Jacob wrestled in opposition to an angel, and so the plain text *luctatus esse cum Iacob* [LXX 32.25 = μετ' αὐτοῦ] (Genesis 32.24) is taken by Origen to mean "wrestled alongside of Jacob" or "in support of Jacob" (against the opposing powers Paul speaks of in Ephesians 6.12).[207] After evaluating the progress Jacob had made (*cognitis profectibus eius*), the angel by his very presence offered him assistance in his struggle (*cum ipso est in agone et iuvat eum in certamine*). He also emphasizes that these *agones* encountered in the life of the believer occur neither indiscriminately nor by chance (*non utcumque neque fortuito*) but are ordered and arranged by God in his careful Providence (*diligenti examinatione*), in much the same way as one who arranges a competition seeks to match opponents by age or class.[208] Origen uses this analogy to make substantially the same point in *Hom in Ps* 36.4.2.[209]

205. *Hom in Ps* 37.2.3 [SC 411.310]: *Ex iracundia et indignatione hunc arguo, volens ei inferre tristitiam, non illam quae "secundum Deum est, quae paenitentiam in salutem stabilem operatur," sed tristitiam quae laedat animam, non emendet.*

206. The insufficiency of effort alone and the necessity of divine aid are also emphasized elsewhere; cf. *Hom in Ps* 36.4.1 [SC 411.188]: *non sufficit homini volenti istud iter incedere sola propositi sui voluntas, nisi et Dominus direxerit gressus eius.* For this emphasis on divine assistance, cf. also *De principiis* 3.1.19 [GK 536] and 3.2.2 [GK 568]. For a treatment of grace in Origen more generally, see Benjamin Drewery, *Origen and the Doctrine of Grace* (London: Epworth, 1960).

207. *De principiis* 3.2.5 [GK 580].

208. Cf. *Hom in Ps* 38.1.8 [SC 411.354], where Origen suggests a providential ordering of human life in accord with a particular *telos.* Cf. also *De principiis* 3.2.3 [GK 570] and 3.2.7 [GK 584], where Origen makes the distinction between God's direct and permissive will.

209. SC 411.196–198.

The Medicinal/Therapeutic Model

Another prominent metaphor employed by Origen in his *Homilies on the Psalms* is that of healing. The life of the believer is likened to a convalescence in the course of which sins require the correct cure. *Hom in Ps* 37.1.1 begins with the observation that God, in his Providence, has imparted the art of medicine to humanity to compensate for the fragility of the human condition;[210] further, this art makes use of the produce of the earth to craft remedies for various maladies.[211] Origen then immediately notes that medical treatment is a metaphor for the healing of the soul.[212] Sin, defined as the soul acting against its own natural good (*cum viderint animam aliquid praeter naturam gerentem*), is thus like a disease (*aegritudo*) or an injury (*vulnus*).[213] Just as from the produce of the earth cures can be wrought and applied to various physical maladies, so from the words and precepts of sacred Scripture appropriate treatments (*medicamenta*) can be found for the soul. While he does not make it explicit, on the basis of what he holds elsewhere,[214] Origen likely expects his hearers to infer that there is also a kind of craft or art to this scriptural pharmacology. Christ is called the "Chief Physician" (*archiater* = ἀρχιατρός),[215]

210. On medicine among the human arts, see *De principiis* 3.3.2 [GK 588].

211. SC 411.258.

212. *Quo nobis tendit ista praefatio? Ad animam sine dubio revocatur* [SC 411.258].

213. Cf. *Hom in Ps* 37.2.1 [SC 411.300], where a believer who is weak is spoken of as searching out a remedy for his sin: *Intellege mihi fidelem quidem hominem, sed tamen infirmum, qui etiam vinci ab aliquo peccato potuerit et propter hoc mugientem pro delictis sui et omni modo curam vulneris sui sanitatemque requirentem, licet praeventus sit et lapsus, volentem tamen medelam ac salutem animae reparare.*

214. Cf. *Hom in Ps* 36.3.6 [SC 411.148–150], where he defines what it means to be "rich in every word" (1 Cor 1.6) as a kind of resourcefulness in both knowing and applying the sacred text prudentially to the concrete situations of everyday life. Cf. also his classic statement of the problem facing believers found in *De principiis* pr. 2 [GK 84]: *Quoniam ergo multi ex his qui Christo se credere profitentur, non solum in parvis et minimis discordant, verum etiam in magnis et maximis ... propter hoc necessarium videtur prius de his singulis certam lineam manifestamque regulam ponere, tum deinde etiam de ceteris quaerere.*

215. This term is used again in reference to Christ a little later, *Hom in Ps* 37.1.4 [SC 411.288], as well as in *Hom in Luc* 13.2 [SC 87.208].

though this same work has also been entrusted to prophets, apostles, and those who have taken their place in the life of the Church (presumably bishops and perhaps presbyters) as *medici animarum.*[216] Worthy of note is that this healing process is understood and described by Origen precisely in terms of ecclesial life (*in ecclesia sua*).

The words of the sacred text are elsewhere held by Origen to heal and reform the soul,[217] and the patient is expected to "adjust his life" in accord with the medicine imparted by scriptural teaching.[218] The medicine of divine teaching is necessary for souls that are sick and weak: *Haec infirmae et fragiles animae, etiamsi non ore proferunt, in corde suo tamen loquuntur ... et ideo nobis mandati huius medela succurrit.*[219] Here, too, this *medela* is both conceived of in terms of the apt use of scriptural teaching and shaped by a common hope made possible by a shared life.[220] Origen understands his own task as preacher in terms of enabling such healing by imparting God's Word through preaching. It is the indwelling Word, imparted through sound teaching and preaching, that transforms the soul of the believer: *Ita ut possem secundum gratiam quam ipse a Domino meruissem, vobis quoque ministrare verbum Dei et serere illud in animabus vestris: tum deinde ingressus sermo Dei animas vestras et haerens in corde vestro formaret mentes vestras secundum speciem verbi ipsius.*[221] In his *Commentary on the Canticle,* within a discussion of the spiritual senses, Origen emphasizes the accommodation made by the Word in healing humankind: he makes himself accessible to the weak (*qui infirmantur*) by offering himself to them like healing herbs ([*h*]*olera*).[222] The goal of sound preaching, then,

216. SC 411.260.

217. *Hom in Ps* 36.3.1 [SC 411.128]: *Si vero in hac vita contemnimus commonentis nos divinae scripturae verba et curari vel emendari eius correptionibus nolumus, certum est quia manet nos ignis ille qui praeparatus est peccatoribus.*

218. *Hom in Ps* 36.3.6 [SC 411.150]: *vitam suam secundum verbum veritatis eius quae in scripturis continetur aptare.*

219. *Hom in Ps* 36.2.2 [SC 411.100].

220. SC 411.100: *sed recogitare debemus quia praesens saeculum eorum qui est futurae beatitudinis non habent spem.*

221. *Hom in Ps* 36.4.3 [SC 411.210–212].

222. *Comm in Cant* 1.4.13 [SC 375.228]: *Denique his qui ex corruptibili semine*

is a personal encounter and engagement with the *Logos*, which transforms the soul of the hearer.[223]

In *Hom in Ps* 37.2.6, Origen likens the effect of unconfessed sin to indigestion, which causes both pressure and discomfort.[224] A flesh wound (*vulnus*) and injury to the eye are also brought forward as metaphors to describe the effects of sin: in each case, the correct remedy is to be sought so as to avoid further problems.[225] Relief is sought—and found—in the community of the Church and with the right doctor, one who is versed in mercy and compassion and who knows precisely what course of action should be taken.[226] The very discomfort of the indigestion, for example, serves to prompt the individual to action in seeking the right cure, and the "pain" caused by sin should do the same. Additionally, in the same way that one suffering from indigestion has neither the appetite nor the capacity for the food enjoyed by the healthy, so too those who are unfit to approach but attempt to share in the Eucharist bring only ruin upon themselves.[227]

Origen twice uses the image of indigestion in his *De principiis* with a similar import and emphases. The degree of discomfort to the stomach depends largely on the nature of what is consumed, and so too the conscience (*mens ipsa vel conscientia*) is provoked to a greater or lesser degree depending upon

regenerantur, rationabile et sine dolo efficitur lac; his vero qui infirmantur in aliquo, [h]olera se praebet ad hospitalitatis amicitiam et gratiam.

223. Cf. the instructive discussion of the relationship between biblical interpretation and personal transformation in John David Dawson, *Christian Figural Reading and the Fashioning of Identity* (Berkeley: University of California Press, 2002), 194–206.

224. SC 411.318.

225. SC 411.320.

226. SC 411.318: *Tantummodo circumspice diligentius, cui debeas confiteri peccatum tuum. Proba prius medicum, cui debeas causam languoris exponere ... qui condolendi et compatiendi noverit disciplinam: ut ita demum si quid ille dixerit, qui se prius et eruditum medicum ostenderit et misericordem, si quid consilii dederit, facias et sequaris, si intellexerit et praeviderit talem esse languorem tuum qui in conventu totius ecclesiae exponi debeat et curari, ex quo fortassis et ceteri aedificari poterunt et tu ipse facile sanari, multa hoc deliberatione et satis perito medici illius consilio procurandum est.*

227. SC 411.320–322: *Patiuntur hoc quod febricitantes pati solent, cum sanorum cibos praesumunt, sibimetipsos inferentes exitium.*

the severity of its sins.[228] Honest acknowledgment of one's sins obtains relief in the same way as one who suffers from indigestion relieves himself by vomiting forth what is causing the pressure and his discomfort. In the lengthy discussion of free will that forms the centerpiece of his *De principiis*,[229] Origen again uses the metaphor of indigestion (here implied rather than explicit) to explain sin and its healing. An expert physician will sometimes delay or extend treatment until the right moment, rather than settle for a quicker but less certain treatment. God, whom Origen identifies as ἰατρός, in his Providence (γινώσκων καὶ ... προγινώσκων τὰ μέλλοντα) allows the evils hidden within the individual (τὰ κρύφια τῆς καρδίας) ultimately to be vomited out (ἐμέσας), though for a time God may allow them to accumulate. Similarly, in dealing with an open wound, a shrewd physician must in some circumstances not seek to cover it, but allow it to breathe, so that the infection may drain and not become gangrenous.[230] Sometimes the medicine needed for health is bitter, especially if it follows on the heels of gluttony: *si enim ad corporis sanitatem pro his vitiis quae per escam potumque collegimus, necessarium habemus interdum austerioris ac mordacioris medicamenti curam.*[231] Some ills can be cured only through excision with the knife, and, failing that, the last resort for the physician is sometimes the use of flame, to heal and cauterize. Elsewhere Origen contends that fire, as Paul knew (1 Corinthians 3.13), could test and prove one's mettle, burning off what is sinful:

> *Est ergo hoc peccatum etiam unum ex illis quod aedificium deferet ligna, fenum, stipulam et necesse est huiusmodi materias, sicut scriptum est, per ignem probari, ita ut permaneamus tamdiu in igne, donec de nobis ligna iracundiae consumantur et fenum indignationis et stipula verborum, eorum videlicet quae huiuscemodi vitiis exagitati protulimus.*[232]

228. *De principiis* 2.10.4 [GK 428–430].

229. *De principiis* 3.1.13 [GK 506–508]. This longest chapter in the *De principiis,* with its extended discussion of free will and divine Providence, is arguably the cardinal or pivotal chapter of the work—both structurally and in terms of the argument.

230. GK 506.

231. GK 432.

232. *Hom in Ps* 36.2.3 [SC 411.104].

The allusive account given by Paul in 1 Corinthians 5.1–5 of the individual who was cut off from community life because of πορνεία serves Origen's purpose in demonstrating the medicinal or therapeutic purpose of such a course of action; in fact, he refers to Paul's treatment as *medicinalis disciplina*.[233] The sinner's willingness both to accept correction and to endure the requisite punishment demonstrates the genuineness of his repentance and the presence of charity within him. Later in the same homily, in an effort to explain Psalm 37.4 ("there is no health in my flesh"), Origen offers a gloss on Paul's advice to the Corinthians: "Hand over one such as this to Satan for the destruction of the flesh" (1 Corinthians 5.5).[234] "Flesh" for Origen is not a reference to physical life or to the body itself, but rather the lower element or activity of the soul, a term for all that drags or attracts the soul away from the spirit and toward the material and transient. Origen insists that it is for the well-being of the individual (*pro salute eius*) that this "handing over for the destruction of the flesh" take place. He contends that in the sinner the "flesh" is "alive," but in the just person the flesh is "dead." Because *caro* (σάρξ) is here understood in terms of Romans 8.6 (τὸ φρόνημα τῆς σαρκός), the "dying off" of the flesh means being "dead" to sin.[235] So the "destruction" of the unnamed Corinthian's "flesh" is expressive of the healing process entailed in conversion, culminating in his eventual readmission to community life. Paradoxically, the weakening of the flesh enhances the life of the spirit: *Si vero infirmatur quidem caro sed redit ad sanitatem suam, id est ut sapiat quae sunt carnis ac desideret malum, tunc sanitas est in carne, quod utique spiritui non est bonum.*[236] To elucidate this further, Origen draws on Christ's words in Matthew 26.41, *spiritus quidem promptus est, caro autem infirma*, and offers a rather striking interpretation. To the degree that the flesh is weak, to that degree the spirit is ready; elsewhere, in discussing the soul of Christ, Origen

233. *Hom in Ps* 37.1.1 [SC 411.264].

234. *Hom in Ps* 37.1.2 [SC 411.278].

235. SC 411.280: *Delictum autem semper ex sensu carnis* [= ἐκ φρονήματος τῆς σαρκός] *venit.*

236. SC 411.280.

asserts that the soul is the medium between the "ready spirit" and the "weak flesh."[237] The "weakening" of Christ's flesh on the cross completes the "readying" of his spirit, which is at that moment "handed over" to the Father.[238] Thus by an intriguing juxtaposition of images, the physical "weakness" of Christ on the cross becomes instructive of the kind of metaphorical "weakening" of the flesh that must occur in the life of the believer: *Haec autem ille in se describens nostris eruditionibus praebebat exemplum. Propter nos enim et nobis infirmus est.*[239] For the believer, this "weakening" is effected through self-denial (*abstinentiam*) and self-restraint (*continentiam*).

The Educational/Pedagogical Model

The third metaphor or model used by Origen in the *Homilies on the Psalms* for the life of the believer is educational or pedagogical. In his treatment of Psalm 37.2 (*Domine ne in furore tuo arguas me neque in ira tua corripias me*), Origen tells his hearers that it is necessary to offer some words on correction, which often takes the form of a "reprimand" (*correptio*).[240] The context of this discussion is life in the Church, for references to the role of the bishop as one who rebukes (*episcopi arguentis*)[241]

237. *De principiis* 2.8.4 [GK 396]: *Nam cum passionem aliquam vel conturbationem sui vult indicare, sub nomine animae indicat, cum dicit: "Nunc anima mea turbata est" et "Tristis est anima mea usque ad mortem" et "Nemo tollit a me animam meam, sed ego pono eam abs me." "In manus," autem "patris commendat" non animam sed "spiritum," et cum "carnem" dicat "infirmam," non dicit animam "promptam" esse sed "spiritum"; unde videtur quasi medium quiddam esse anima inter carnem infirmam et spiritum promptum.*

238. *Hom in Ps* 37.1.2 [SC 411.282]: *Antequam Salvator noster veniret ad crucem et crucifigeret carnem atque emori eam faceret, antequam perfecte mortificaretur, prius dixit infirmari carnem suam; et donec infirmabatur quidem caro, spiritum promptum esse dicebat, cum vero cruci eam tradit et perfecta morte consummat, tunc non iam promptum spiritum, sed in manibus Patris positum esse testatur.*

239. SC 411.282; cf. *Dial Heracl* 1.7–8 [SC 67.70–74], where Origen is at pains to emphasize the reality of Christ's body, soul, and spirit, and his "handing over" of the spirit to the Father on the cross: the spirit, incapable by nature of descending at death *ad infera,* was "deposited" with the Father (ταύτην τὴν παραθήκην παραθέμενος τῷ πατρί), to be reclaimed at the Resurrection.

240. *Hom in Ps* 37.1.1 [SC 411.266]: *Oportet ergo nos aliqua et de correptione dicere.*

241. SC 411.266.

and to bishops, presbyters, and deacons as educating through verbal reprimand (*omnes episcopi atque omnes presbyteri vel diacones erudiunt nos et erudientes adhibent correptiones et verbis austerioribus increpant*)[242] form an *inclusio* that frames his discussion of the divine pedagogy that shapes the life of the believer. Quoting Hebrews 12.11, Origen remarks that the benefits of correction and instruction are not immediate, nor are they usually received with pleasure; however, the long-term benefits outweigh the immediate discomfort and pain that are inflicted. Correction and rebuke are exercises intended to engender justice. He then turns to the example of children, who experience correction at the hands of pedagogues (*paedagogi*) and teachers (*doctores*). Even if cognizant of the fact that such correction is ultimately helpful and that genuine progress (*profectus*) depends upon such measures, students still bristle at such correction.[243] This is no less true of adults, Origen contends. He then employs language found in Galatians 3.24 and 4.2 to discuss the various types and degrees of correction experienced by the mature: he speaks of the "steward" (*dispensator/ actor/* οἰκόνομος), the "tutor" (*procurator/* ἐπίτροπος), and the "pedagogue" (*paedagogus/* παιδαγωγός).[244] This triplet is introduced by Origen immediately after mentioning the instructional and corrective roles exercised by the threefold order of bishops, priests, and deacons;[245] however tempting it may be to infer a more precise correlation between these two sets of three, the text offers nothing further, and, given what follows, it is unlikely that he intended such a strict parallelism. What is important, however, is that he sees the work of instruction and correction as taking place on two levels or in two modes, as it were: within ecclesial life and under the tutelage of the angels (with no suggestion that these are exclusive of each other); this is the real state of affairs (*res*), which his comparison (*similitudo/ exemplum*) with the education of the young is intended to illustrate. Life in the community of

242. SC 411.268.

243. *Hom in Ps* 37.1.1 [SC 411.266].

244. *Hom in Ps* 37.1.1 [SC 411.268].

245. *Hom in Ps* 37.1.1 [SC 411.268]: *Si intellexisti similitudinem, transi mihi ab exemplo ad rem, et intellege de nobis hominibus quae dicuntur. Omnes episcopi atque omnes presbyteri vel diacones erudiunt nos.*

the Church is understood as educative, and Origen wants his hearers to understand that this *eruditio* is carried out both by the ordained who shepherd the community and by angels who act as instructors and guides. The roles of steward and tutor, he suggests, belong to the angels, to whom care for the believer is entrusted: *Est autem quando erudimur etiam a procuratoribus et actoribus, id est ab his angelis quibus creditae sunt dispensandae et regendae animae nostrae.*[246] To support this he offers the example of the Angel of Repentance (ὁ ἄγγελος τῆς μετανοίας), who guides, not infrequently chastises, and ultimately tutors Hermas in the *Shepherd.*[247] In fact, the *De principiis* indicates that Origen had elaborated a rather developed angelology. Within his discussion of the origin and end of created things, he teaches that, in this age, humans who have not become totally depraved are entrusted to a kind of angelic management, described explicitly as an education: *Sciendum tamen est quosdam eorum, qui ex illo uno principio quod supra diximus, dilapsi sunt, in tantam indignitatem, ac malitiam se dedisse, ut indigni habiti sint institutione hac vel eruditione, qua per carnem humanum genus adiutorio caelestium virtutum instituitur atque eruditur.*[248] His understanding in this text is very much tied to his theorizing about the soul's origin, a topic he never addresses nor even approaches in the *Homilies on the Psalms.* These angels, Origen suggests, are sometimes referred to in the Scriptures as "princes" or "rulers," and they are responsible for the management and instruction of those in this world: *Sed et principes et rectores intellegendi sunt hi qui inferiores et regunt et erudiunt et edocent atque instituunt ad divina.*[249]

In this tripartite scheme, the Law, understood spiritually, serves as the pedagogue, and this is based on Origen's understanding of Galatians 3.24: *Itaque lex paedagogus noster fuit in Christo.* One can infer from his presentation that there is a kind of hierarchy of guardians, disciplinarians, and educa-

246. SC 411.268.

247. *Shepherd of Hermas;* see, e.g., Vision 5 (25) [SC 53bis.140–144].

248. *De principiis* 1.6.3 [GK 224]; cf. 2.9.3 [GK 406]: *Sunt etiam quaedam invisibiles virtutes, quibus quae super terram sunt dispensanda commissa sunt.*

249. *De principiis* 2.11.3 [GK 444].

tors, beginning with the angelic tutors and stewards, and from time to time (*quoque interdum*) progressing for more serious correction to the pedagogue; throughout his discussion, education (*eruditio*) is understood as primarily about correction by verbal reprimand (*correptio*). In *De principiis* 3.6.8, he speaks of the Law as a pedagogue, but here more as a propaedeutic for the fullness of the revelation of God in Christ. In this context, he draws on the language of Hebrews 10.1 and compares the Law to the "shadow" of that which was to be revealed in Christ. Instruction and training in the Law (*eruditi ab ea et instituti*) increased one's capacity for the more perfect teaching of Christ (*ut facilius possent post institutionem legis perfectiora quaeque Christi instituta suscipere*);[250] and all this in anticipation of the "eternal gospel" (εὐαγγέλιον αἰώνιον), which will not be superseded.[251] Given what Origen teaches in *De principiis*, the "*lex paedagogus … in Christo*" of Galatians, evoked in *Hom in Ps* 37.1.1, is thus perhaps best understood as intimating the Law's role in forming and directing the believer toward Christ, who is himself the Law's *telos*, as is made clear at the end of *De principiis* 3.6.9, where the ultimate end of this educational and corrective enterprise is to make believers fit to receive God himself: *id est ut cum capaces Dei fuerint effecti, sit eis Deus omnia in omnibus.*[252]

Origen emphasizes the distinction, however, between these preliminary educators (the steward, tutor, and pedagogue) and the "Head of the Household" (*paterfamilias*/οἰκοδεσπότης), to whom ultimate correction belongs. He discusses the increasing severity of punishment, noting that the pedagogue is more demanding than the steward or tutor, but then equating the Head of the Household with the very "hand of God" (*divina manus*).[253] Origen then invites his hearers to consider the deeper meaning (*altior intellectus*) of these metaphors, which is that the believer should respond to correction so as not to provoke divine wrath (*ira Dei*).[254]

250. GK 664.

251. On the "eternal gospel," see *De principiis* 4.3.3 [GK 770–772] and *Comm in Jn* 1.40 [SC 120bis.78–80] and 1.84 [SC 120bis.100].

252. GK 666; cf. 1 Cor 15.28.

253. *Hom in Ps* 37.1.1 [SC 411.270–272].

254. SC 411.272.

This divine pedagogy, however, extends beyond the grave.[255] In *Hom in Ps* 36.5.1, Origen refers explicitly to an education or instruction that will occur in the Kingdom. There is an intentional ambiguity, however, in the language he chooses:

> *Ultra enim non erit aliquis imperitus in regno Dei, non indocilis permanebit, nullus erit a rerum scientia peregrinus ... ibi iam illuminabitur perfectioribus disciplinis et ea quae hic studio ac labore quaesita sunt, ad compendium futurae inibi institutionis accedent.*[256]

The juxtaposition of *ibi* and *hic,* as well as the reference to a *disciplina* and *institutio* yet to come, suggests that while there is a kind of completion or fruition achieved in the Kingdom, there is simultaneously a continuation of education as well. The mouth of the just person, it is said, will meditate upon or "rehearse" (*meditabitur*—μελετήσει) wisdom (Psalm 36.30); Origen makes much of the future tense of the verb, finding in it a reference to the age to come, and he implies that this Wisdom will become the source of nourishment, a kind of food. He makes a very similar point in *De principiis* 2.11.3,[257] in discussing the fate of those who die "insufficiently instructed" (*minus eruditus*), but whose lives are marked by worthy behavior (*probabilia tamen opera detulerit*). Origen suggests that they can continue their education in the heavenly Jerusalem. Further, he likens Wisdom to a food (*cibus/ esca*) on which they will be nourished.[258] The passage has strongly eucharistic overtones

255. Cf. *De principiis* 3.1.13 [GK 508], where this post-mortem healing is explicit: θεὸς γὰρ οἰκονομεῖ τὰς ψυχὰς οὐχ ὡς πρὸς τὴν φέρ' εἰπεῖν πεντεκονταετίαν τῆς ἐνθάδε ζωῆς, ἀλλ' ὡς πρὸς τὸν ἀπέραντον αἰῶνα. ἄφθαρτον γὰρ φύσιν πεποίηκε τὴν νοερὰν καὶ αὐτῷ συγγενῆ καὶ οὐκ ἀποκλείεται ὥσπερ ἐπὶ τῆς ἐνταῦθα ζωῆς ἡ λογικὴ ψυχὴ τῆς θεραπείας; cf. also the essay of John Anthony McGuckin, "Origen's Use of the Psalms in the Treatise *On First Principles,*" in *Meditations of the Heart: The Psalms in Early Christian Thought and Practice,* ed. A. Andreopoulos, A. Casiday, and C. Harrison (Turnhout: Brepols, 2011), 97–118; McGuckin demonstrates how, in *De principiis,* the Psalms are mined by Origen as witnesses to and in service of a soteriological *paideia* of the *Logos,* both pre- and post-mortem; this seems remarkably consistent with what Origen is seeking to accomplish in the *Homilies on the Psalms.*

256. SC 411.228.

257. GK 444.

258. See *De oratione* 27.10 [GCS 3.369–370], where, in explaining the "daily bread" of the Lord's Prayer in light of Psalm 77.25 ([LXX], ἄρτον ἀγγέλων

(though without explicit reference to the sacrament), as Wisdom is spoken of as "preparing her table" (Proverbs 9.2–5) and the activity that marks this continuing post-mortem instruction is "eating the bread of life," glossed by Origen as the soul's nourishment and enlightenment by Truth and Wisdom.[259]

In *Hom in Ps* 38.1.8, in explaining the Psalmist's entreaty, "Make known to me, Lord, my end and what is the number of my days, so that I might know what is lacking in me,"[260] Origen suggests that, like the human τέχναι, each of which possesses a particular τέλος, the entire creation is ordered to a particular end,[261] as is each believer within this larger scheme. As a child does while learning to speak, one begins by stammering (*balbutiens*) and finally achieves the capacity to speak clearly with age and progress; so one's life in this age is marked by a stammering, but will reach its perfection with God in heaven (*consummatur vero et ad summum pervenit in caelestibus apud Deum*).[262] Progress is viewed, then, in terms of the *telos* articulated in 1 Corinthians 15.24–28—an end achieved only in the age to come—and begins with a recognition of what is lacking (*quid desit*) or imperfect in light of that end. It is this awareness of what is lacking in the self that is the condition of possibility for the genuine healing and growth envisioned in his lengthy account of human freedom that forms the centerpiece of his *De principiis*.[263]

ἔφαγεν ἄνθρωπος = [Vlg] *panem angelorum manducavit homo*), he notes that both angels and humans share the "bread" of Wisdom. See also *Comm in Cant* 1.4.13 [SC 375.228], where this "bread of angels" is called a "small, delicate food" (cf. Exodus 16.14) offered to those who follow the "pillar and cloud" into "the wilderness," presumably a metaphor for those "making progress."

259. GK 442–444: *Hi vero, qui secundum apostolorum sensum theoriam scripturarum recipiunt, sperant "manducaturos" quidem esse sanctos, sed "panem vitae," qui veritatis et sapientiae cibis nutriat animam et inluminet mentem et potet eam divinae sapientiae poculis.*

260. SC 411.354: *Notum fac mihi, Domine, finem meum et numerum dierum meorum qui est ut sciam quid desit mihi,* quoting Ps 38.5.

261. That end is here once again supplied by 1 Cor 15.24–28, the subjection of all things to God in Christ.

262. SC 411.354.

263. *De principiis* 3.1.12 [GK 504]: *Ita et si qui non prius animae suae vitia et peccatorum suorum cognoverit mala ac proprii oris confessione prodiderit, purgare is*

Quoting Psalm 119.6 (*multum enim incola fuit anima mea*) and explaining Psalm 38.5 in terms of the exodus from Egypt (characterizing the plea as their desire to know where they were going), Origen then goes on to explain what the text means by *numerum dierum meorum*. He offers two ways of understanding this. The first is rooted in the distinction between the temporal "day" marked by the sun's movement across the sky and (drawing on the dual meaning of *caelum*) the "second" and "third" heavens spoken of by Paul in 2 Corinthians 12.2–4, as representative of different "days," and a progressive revelation of the truth in each. This is quite similar to his teaching in *De principiis* 1.6.3, where he speaks of three "times" (*in primis alii, alii in secundis, nonnulli etiam in ultimis temporibus*)[264] in which beings are arranged in accord with their proportionate perfection, and in 3.6.6, where he discusses the *telos* of creation. While not specifying a tripartite progression, here he emphasizes that the restoration of all things (*tunc cum omnia restituentur*) will happen gradually and in varying degrees (*paulatim et per partes*) over a period of endless and immeasurable ages (*infinitis et immensis labentibus saeculis*).[265] The second possible interpretation he offers of these "days" is related to Christ as the *Sol iustitiae* (cf. Malachi 3.20 LXX), who illumines with knowledge and truth: the individual who allows this Sun to shine on his heart experiences this "day," and the frequency and regularity of such illumination increase the "number" of

---

absolvique non poterit, ne ignoret sibi per gratiam concessum esse quod possidet et divinam liberalitatem proprium bonum putet. Here, this awareness of sin necessarily requires verbal acknowledgment or "confession."

264. GK 226. Origen is fond of this threefold division among believers, the differences among them, however, being not a matter of nature (as in the various gnostic systems), but reflecting degrees of progress and healing. He posits three classes of athletic competitors in *Hom in Ps* 36.4.2 [SC 411.196–198], and in *Comm in Cant* 2.4.4–6 [SC 375.332], the three types of companions mentioned in the Canticle, the *reginae,* the *concubinae,* and the *adulescentulae,* are understood mystically (*requiramus intelligentiam mysticam*) as referring to believers at different stages of progress: *istae autem omnes differentiae eorum sunt, qui in Christo credentes diversis ei affectibus sociantur.* Cf. also *Hom in Num* 27 [SC 461.270–346], the lengthy treatment of Israel's progress in the desert through various stops or stations (*mansiones*).

265. GK 658.

those days.[266] Similarly, in *De principiis* 2.11.6, Origen describes the continuing pedagogy in the life to come as a "school for souls" (*in quodam eruditionis loco et, ut ita dixerim, auditorio vel schola animarum*).[267] This pedagogy both involves a greater understanding of what has already transpired in the life of the believer (in the light of God's Providence) and includes a making known of what is to come.[268]

Future Judgment

Origen also addresses the judgment to come (*iudicium futurum*) in the *Homilies on the Psalms.* As a matter of faith, awareness of the coming judgment should prompt the believer to undertake a more careful examination of conscience and recollection of his sins: *Ut mens credens de iudicio futuro, recordationem delictorum suorum non absque lacrimis et lamentatione recenseat, cum quis resolutus in lacrimis dicit ad Dominum, "Effundo in conspectu tuo orationem meam."*[269] Drawing on a distinction he had made earlier in his *De oratione,*[270] he notes that the "Kingdom of Heaven" refers to those who are still making progress, while the "Kingdom of God" refers to those who have reached the end: *Et ut memini me iam saepe dixisse, regnum caelorum est eorum qui adhuc in profectionibus sunt; regnum vero Dei, eorum qui iam ad perfectum venerunt finem.*[271] This distinction is made possible by his conviction that progress (*profectus*) can continue after death. In *Hom in Ps* 36.5.7, in explaining how the Lord is the "protector in time of trouble" (Psalm 36.39), Origen describes what happens at

266. *Hom in Ps* 38.1.8 [SC 411.358]. Cf. *Comm in Cant* 2.4.29 [SC 375.346], where it is purity of heart that constitutes midday (*meridies*) in the believer, allowing him to see God; *Hom in Ps* 36.3.9 [SC 411.156–158], where each believer is spoken of as "making a day proper to himself."

267. GK 452.

268. GK 452: *De omnibus his, quae in terris viderant, doceantur, indicia quoque quaedam accipiant etiam de consequentibus et futuris, sicut in hac quoque vita positi indicia quaedam futurorum.*

269. *Hom in Ps* 38.2.10 [SC 411.400].

270. *De oratione* 25.1 [GCS 3.357], composed at the request of his patron Ambrose early in his Caesarean career, c. 233–234 AD, and so likely a decade or so prior to the delivery of these homilies.

271. *Hom in Ps* 36.5.7 [SC 411.250]; from the *saepe dixisse,* one can infer that this teaching was a regular feature of Origen's catechetical enterprise.

death. Many are troubled when they ponder the coming judgment and probe themselves to discover anything that might be grounds for accusation.[272] He speaks of how, at the separation of the soul from the body (*cum anima separatur a corpore*), opposing powers, whom he qualifies as "sinful demons" (*peccatores daemones*), the "spirits of the air" mentioned in Ephesians 2.2, led by the "prince of this world," go out to meet it (*occurrunt*).[273] Should they recognize in the soul anything of their own—Origen offers the examples of greed, wrath, and wanton behavior generally—they claim their right over that soul, detaining it and calling it to themselves, ultimately diverting it (presumably from its progress toward God) to the lot assigned to the sinful. Even the just, however, Origen contends, can expect to be so assailed; but the Lord, who is their "protector in time of trouble," will not allow the demons to overtake or misdirect them. This, he suggests, is the meaning of the dominical injunction that the believer pray, "deliver us from evil." Moreover, beyond the moment of individual death, the just also must hope for the Lord to deliver them later on the day of Judgment.[274]

Origen offers a similar account in *Hom in Ps* 38.2.2. Explaining the meaning of Psalm 38.7 (*Quamquam in imagine ambulet homo*) in light of the Pauline teaching found in 1 Corinthians 15.49 (*Sicut portavimus imaginem terreni, ita portemus et imaginem caelestis*), Origen discusses what it means to "bear the image of the earthly" and to "bear the image of the heavenly."[275] Both hostile powers and divine virtue[276] produce images in the soul;

272. SC 411.252: *Tribulantur enim considerantes tempus iudicii et semetipsos discutientes ne forte aliquid inveniatur in eis quod vocetur ad culpam.*

273. Cf. *De principiis* 2.11.6 [GK 450–452], where this "air" (cf. Eph 2.2 and 1 Thes 4.17) between earth and heaven is the realm of angelic and demonic activity as well as the "place" of the continued instruction (it is within this discussion of this "air" that he speaks of the *schola animarum*) that Origen envisions as necessary for the soul.

274. SC 411.252–254.

275. This "bearing the image" is also treated, but in relation to the *interior* and *exterior homo,* in *Comm in Cant* pr. 2.16 [SC 375.102]. Cf. *De principiis* 3.4.2 [GK 604–606], where "earthly" and "heavenly" are spoken of as aspects or tendencies within the soul.

276. It is not entirely clear whether by *virtus divina* he means "divine power," "moral virtue," or perhaps rather angelic assistance.

he even goes so far as to use the language of an image "being painted" (*depingitur*) on the soul.[277] Yet even among those who bear the "heavenly" and among those who bear the "earthly" there is a considerable diversity, a diversity that reflects the individual's inclinations (*singulae harum imagines quasdam exprimunt in anima eorum qui se ad receptaculum earum diversis studiis exhibent*). Paul and Timothy, Origen argues, each possessed the "image of the heavenly," but in different ways. So too, among the sinful, the "image of the earthly" impressed upon the soul varies depending upon the specific inclinations of the individual, and so the nature and extent of that "image" is particular to each, and Origen implies a willed cooperation on the part of the individual, that is, cooperation with the power impressing the image. Those who depart this life bearing the "image of the earthly" will be reduced to nothing in God's city (*in civitate illa Dei ad nihilum redigetur*).[278] The "image of the heavenly," however, and the various virtues that instantiate it, are in this life experienced only partially. Origen reminds his hearers that, as Paul taught, knowledge (*scientia*) can be only partial in this life: there is not yet "face to face" (*facie ad faciem*) knowing. The "real" and complete experience of the various virtues (those he enumerates are all also *epinoiai* of Christ) is to be had in the life to come: *huius quidem mundi vita et conversatio imaginaria quaedam sit et imago, futura autem non sit imaginaria sed vera.*[279] In reference to *iustitia* (its cognate *iustus* is the most common appellation for the believer in these homilies), Origen notes that believers might walk "in the image of Justice," but that they do not yet make progress in Justice *facie ad faciem.* It is clear that, in this age, the experience of virtue is *in imagine,* while in the age to come, *facie ad faciem;* moreover, from Origen's language, the inference can be drawn that, even "face to face," there is progress to be made.[280] The limitations of knowledge, which Origen associates with the human condi-

277. SC 411.382.

278. *Hom in Ps* 38.2.1 [SC 411.374].

279. *Hom in Ps* 38.2.2 [SC 411.374].

280. *Hom in Ps* 38.2.2 [SC 411.374]: *Eadem audeo de iustitia Dei dicere, quod in imagine iustitiae ambulamus et nondum in illa iustitia quae est facie ad faciem incedimus.*

tion in this age, necessitated the economy of the Incarnation: incapable by its own power to grasp the full, naked, and pure splendor of Justice, humanity required the divine *kenosis* elucidated in Philippians 2 in order to grasp Christ as the fullness, as it were, of all the virtues experienced only partially by the believer in this age.[281]

The *Epinoiai* of Christ

While Christ, the Incarnate *Logos,* in his work as mediator between God and the created order, constitutes the "fullness" of the virtues, the believer nonetheless experiences this fullness in a partial or fragmentary way. That is, Christ is customarily encountered or grasped under one or more of the facets or dimensions of this mediating activity, which Origen calls ἐπίνοιαι, usually translated as "concepts," "titles," or "aspects."[282] Origen provides the foundation for this in *De principiis* 1.2. He begins by immediately emphasizing that Christ possessed both a divine and a human nature, and that the Incarnation is the pivotal moment in the divine economy (*dispensatio,* rendering οἰκονομία).[283] The method he then employs to plumb this

281. *Hom in Ps* 38.2.2 [SC 411.374–376]: *Neque enim capere poterat humana natura pellibus et carne vestita, ossibus et nervis inserta, nudam ipsam iustitiae sinceramque veritatem ferre et tolerare secundum naturae suae potentiam ac virtutem, si quidem ipse Christus est natura virtutum: ipse enim iustitia, quae humano generi non in plenitudinem splendoris advenit, quia Iesus Christus seipsum exinanivit forma Dei, ut formam servi acciperet.* Here, Christ is spoken of as the *natura virtutum;* in the *Comm in Cant* 1.6.13 [SC 375.256], he is referred to as *ipsarum virtutum substantia.* It is possible that *natura* and *substantia* are both attempts to render οὐσία or perhaps even ὑπόστασις; on the relative synonymity of these two terms in Origen's thinking, see Rowan Williams, *Arius: Heresy and Tradition* (Grand Rapids: Eerdmans, 2002), 132–33.

282. For a very convenient summary, see Ronald Heine, "*Epinoiai,*" in *The Westminster Handbook to Origen,* ed. John Anthony McGuckin (Louisville: Westminster John Knox, 2004), 93–95. The most celebrated discussion of the ἐπίνοιαι is found in the first book of his massive *Commentary on John,* though, as will become clear, the foundations for it are laid in *De principiis,* contemporaneous with, if not composed prior to, the *Commentary;* both were begun sometime c. 220–230 AD.

283. *De principiis* 1.2.1 [GK 122]: *Primo illud nos scire oportet, quod alia est in Christo deitatis eius natura, quod est unigenitus filius patris, et alia humana natura, quam in novissimis temporibus pro dispensatione suscepit.*

mystery is an extended reflection on the various titles (*diversis nominibus*) found in the different scriptural texts. Principal among these, and the first to receive Origen's attention, is Wisdom, which he contends must be understood as possessing individuated existence.[284] It is this Wisdom that is the condition of possibility for human wisdom, as it makes humans wise by "attaching itself" to the human mind: *quae sapientes efficiat, intellegamus, praebentem se et mentibus inserentem eorum, qui capaces virtutum eius atque intelligentiae fiunt.*[285] Further titles include Word, Truth, Life, Way, Splendor, and Resurrection, though this preliminary accounting is hardly exhaustive.[286] While Origen's central concern in elucidating these various titles is to demonstrate the special relationship between the Father and the Son, what is important for present purposes is that these *epinoiai* also serve a pedagogical function in the economy of salvation, slowly and gradually revealing to the soul the fullness of the mystery of Christ and simultaneously enabling its progress in that mystery. For example, as Way he leads to the Father, as Word he makes accessible and meaningful the hidden mysteries of God, and as Splendor he exercises and trains the internal vision of the rational creature gradually to receive the fullness of Light.[287]

Not surprisingly, these *epinoiai* figure heavily in the *Homilies on the Psalms*. There are at least eighteen instances in these homilies where one or more of these *epinoiai* appear.[288] Christ

284. *De principiis* 1.2.2 [GK 122–124]: *Nemo putet aliquid nos insubstantivum dicere, cum eum "Dei sapientiam" nominamus … unigenitum filium Dei sapientiam eius esse substantialiter subsistentem.* Origen is further concerned to demonstrate that individuated existence does not necessarily imply corporeality or materiality.

285. GK 122.

286. *De principiis* 1.2.4 [GK 126–128]; others include Light, Door, Justice, Sanctification, and Redemption, at 1.2.13 [GK 154–156].

287. *De principiis* 1.2.7 [GK 136–138]: *Secundum haec namque, quae superius exposuimus, quomodo via sit et ducat ad patrem, et quomodo verbum sit arcana sapientiae ac scientiae mysteria interpretans ac proferens rationabili creaturae … consequenter intellegere debemus etiam splendoris opus: per splendorem namque quid sit lux ipsa agnoscitur et sentitur. Qui splendor fragilibus se et infirmis mortalium oculis placidius ac lenius offerens et paulatim velut edocens et adsuescens claritatem luminis pati.*

288. Cf. *Hom in Ps* 36.1.1 [SC 411.58], Law; 36.1.4 [SC 411.80], Truth, Wisdom, Justice, Sanctification; 36.1.6 [SC 411.88], Light; 36.2.1 [SC 411.92],

is presented as Justice repeatedly throughout these homilies, though this is not surprising given the fact that much of Origen's pastoral energy is expended on describing the life, characteristics, and progress of the just or righteous (*iustus*/δίκαιος) person, one who is imbued with Justice by participating in it. Christ is also the Way, and it is precisely in or on him that the believer must walk as he progresses.[289] By walking on the Way who is Christ, the believer thus avoids errant steps either to the left or to the right. Origen suggests that this might include philosophical inquiry that is without reference to God.[290] He further elaborates what "left" and "right" might mean in this case: those wandering off to the left include those heretics who do not read the Scriptures with sensitivity to their spiritual sense; this may be a less than veiled criticism of the Marcionites, whose rejection of the Old Testament was the product of a deficient manner of reading that hindered them from grasping the deeper meaning of its seeming contradictions or less savory episodes.[291] Those who wander off to the right include those who possess the capacity for spiritual reading, but who fail to hold on to the rule of faith (here *regula veritatis*) and thus misunderstand the text; this no doubt refers to gnostic readings of Scripture.[292] It is adherence to Christ as Way that assists the believer in avoiding these errors.

Justice, Truth, Sanctification, Peace; 36.2.4 [SC 411.108], Hope, Patience, Wisdom, Peace, Justice; 36.3.8 [SC 411.154], Word, Wisdom; 36.3.9 [SC 411.158], Light, Sun of Justice; 36.4.1, three times [SC 411.182; 186; 188], Knowledge, Wisdom, Word; Power; Way; 36.4.3 [SC 411.210], Wisdom, Knowledge; 36.4.8 [SC 411.218–220], Word, Wisdom, Light; 36.5.1 [SC 411.224], Word, Wisdom; 36.5.4 [SC 411.234], Justice; 36.5.6 [SC 411.246], Equity, Truth, Justice, Life; 38.1.8 [SC 411.358], Sun of Justice; 38.2.3 [SC 411.382–384], Wisdom, Justice, Sanctification, Hope, Patience, Redemption; 38.2.7 [SC 411.390–392], Wisdom, Prophet.

289. *Hom in Ps* 36.4.1 [SC 411.186–188].

290. SC 411.188: *Ut illi qui in philosophiae eruditione versantur, videntur quidem iter virtutis incedere, sed quia a Domino non diriguntur gressus eorum, non tenent iter rectum.*

291. *Hom in Ps* 36.4.1 [SC 411.188]: *Sed et haeretici nihilominus ingrediuntur etiam ipsi iter, sed cum scripturas carnaliter, non spiritaliter intellegunt, declinant in sinistram.*

292. *Hom in Ps* 36.4.1 [SC 411.188]: *Si vero spiritaliter intellegant, in ipso autem spiritali intellectu apostolicae non teneant regulam veritatis, decidunt nihilominus et ipsi*

Word and Wisdom often appear together as *epinoiai* of Christ, and this is not surprising, given his predilection for these two titles in his discussion in *De principiis*.[293] In explaining Psalm 36.30, "the mouth of the just will meditate on wisdom," Origen describes the believer as one who is "always speaking Christ" (*Christum semper loquamini*).[294] This is not merely a matter of verbalization. Drawing on Deuteronomy 6.7, the injunction to "speak these things" (*loqueris haec*)[295] in the circumstances of daily living, including "on the way" (*pergens in via*), Origen can then associate this "speaking" with life "in Christ."[296] He plays on the various nuances of *meditari* (μελετᾶν), and it is clear that he understands the Psalm text not merely as an activity of mental reflection (which it necessarily involves), but more deeply an engagement with Christ that is simultaneously an exercise, a rehearsal, and a practice.

Word and Wisdom are also spoken of by Origen as offering support and assistance to the believer.[297] In explaining Psalm 36.17 (*Suffulcit autem iustos Dominus*), Origen first notes that the propensity to fail is common to weak human nature (*omnis autem homo, quantum ad humanam fragilitatem spectat, et infirmus est et promptus ad lapsum*).[298] Assistance, however, is available for those who are alert enough to ask for help: *Tantum est ut nos exspergiscamur aliquando et evigilemus, ut si quando per infirmitatem casus aliquis imminet, deprecemur Dominum ut mittat nobis verbum suum et sapientiam suam, quae suffulciat casuros et erigat.*[299] Here

---

ad dexteram, diabolo, ut ita dixerim, gressus eorum non dirigente, sed detorquente a via recta. There are three instances in the *Hom in Ps* when particular heretics or their followers are explicitly mentioned: 36.2.6 [SC 411.114], Valentinians; 36.3.11 [SC 411.170], Valentinus, Marcion, Basilides; 37.2.8 [SC 411.322], Marcionites, Valentinians, followers of Basilides. In addition, though not explicit, their positions are implied here, at 36.4.1, and at 36.5.5 [SC 411.244–246], in both instances in reference to inadequate readings of Scripture. Cf. now A. Le Boulluec, "La polémique contre les hérésies dans les *Homélies sur les Psaumes* d'Origène," in *Adamantius* 20 (2014): 256–74.

293. *De principiis* 1.2.2–3 [GK 122–126].

294. *Hom in Ps* 36.5.1 [SC 411.224].

295. The LXX here employs its customary imperatival future, λαλήσεις.

296. SC 411.224.

297. *Hom in Ps* 36.3.8 [SC 411.154].

298. SC 411.154.

299. *Hom in Ps* 36.3.8 [SC 411.154].

self-awareness is linked to divine assistance, in this case God's Word and Wisdom, which are sent to support and lift up the one about to fall. While the antecedent of *quae* might arguably be simply *sapientia,* context and sense demand that it refer to both *verbum* and *sapientia* acting jointly; for Origen, in light of 1 Corinthians 1.24, they are univocal terms and *epinoiai* for Christ. Further, this kind of correlativity had already been exploited in the late second century by Theophilus of Antioch. For Theophilus, God as Physician employs both his Word and his Wisdom in the art of healing; they are also related to God's creative activity and are the source of life.[300] Similarly, Irenaeus spoke of the Son and the Spirit as the two "hands" of God used in the formation of the human person.[301] Here, of course, Origen is not so much making a distinction within God (as Irenaeus does between Son and Spirit), but rather employing his two favored *epinoiai* to describe God's action of "reaching out" (almost as if with "hands") in Christ to those on the verge of falling.

Prompted by the text of Psalm 36.37 (*Custodi innocentiam et vide aequitatem*), Origen speaks of this *aequitas* (probably rendering the Greek εὐθύτης, as will become clear below) as being among the *epinoiai* of Christ.[302] If the believer maintains innocence, which Origen understands to mean offering offense to no one, and if the believer is attentive and vigilant (*semper intento animo et vigilanti*), then he is capable of seeing *aequitas.* He makes it clear that "seeing equity" in conjunction with the other aspects or *epinoiai* of Christ—he explicitly enumerates Truth, Justice, and Life—is what it means to see God: *Aequitatem ergo in hoc loco sic accipio, sicut veritatem, sicut iustitiam, sicut vitam quod Christus est. Haec enim videndo simul etiam Deum videbimus.*[303] Origen is convinced that to know God is to know

300. *Ad Autolycum* 1.7 (ed. Robert M. Grant [Oxford: Clarendon, 1970], 10): τίς ἐστιν ὁ ἰατρός· ὁ θεός, ὁ θεραπεύων καὶ ζωοποίων διὰ τοῦ λόγου καὶ τῆς σοφίας. ὁ θεὸς διὰ τοῦ λόγου αὐτοῦ καὶ τῆς σοφίας ἐποίησε τὰ πάντα. Word and Wisdom are later spoken of as part of the triad who is God, at 2.15 (ed. Grant, 52): αἱ τρεῖς ἡμέραι πρὸ τῶν φωστήρων γεγονυῖαι τύποι εἰσὶν τῆς τριάδος, τοῦ θεοῦ καὶ τοῦ λόγου καὶ τῆς σοφίας.

301. *Adversus haereses* 4.20.1 and 5.1.13 [SC 100.626 and 153.26].

302. *Hom in Ps* 36.5.6 [SC 411.246].

303. SC 411.246.

the Son, as he elsewhere makes explicit: it is in understanding Christ that the Father is made known and revealed.[304]

In addition to being adduced by Origen in conjunction with various other *epinoiai* for grasping the mystery of God, Christ under the aspect of *aequitas* is also important for the moral life. In *Comm in Cant* 1.6.6–14, he treats Song of Songs 1.4, *aequitas dilexit te.* Playing on the semantic relation *aequitas–iniquitas,* he notes that perfection is constituted by charity, and he defines *aequitas* negatively in terms of the absence of iniquity: *caritas autem nihil iniquitatis admittit; ubi autem nihil iniquitatis est, ibi sine dubio est aequitas.*[305] Iniquity is understood as disregard for Christ's commandments, and thus *aequitas* is essential in keeping the commandments and so maintaining charity (love for Christ). For the believer, then, *aequitas* (εὐθύτης) functions quite literally as a norm or standard (*regula directa/ directoria*), making or keeping straight what is crooked or distorted:

> *Et ideo regulam quandam directam ponamus esse aequitatem, ut, si quid in nobis iniquitatis est, hanc adhibentes et superducentes directoriam mandatorum Dei, si quid in nobis curvum, si quid tortuosum est, ad huius regulae lineam resecetur, ut possit de nobis dici, "Aequitas dilexit te."*[306]

One who lives in accord with *aequitas* fulfills the words of the Song of Songs and, by keeping the commandments, indeed loves Christ.

The *epinoiai,* then, have at least two distinct yet related functions. Not only do they make Christ known through the various aspects of his mediation to the created order and thus ultimately reveal God, but participation in them also furthers the progress of the believer in living "in Christ," the *telos* of the moral life.[307]

304. *De principiis* 1.2.6 [GK 136]: *Revelat autem per hoc quod ipse intellegitur. A quo enim ipse fuerit intellectus, consequenter intellegitur et pater, secundum hoc quod ipse dixit, "Qui vidit me, vidit et patrem."* Cf. Irenaeus, *Adversus haereses* 4.6.3 [SC 100.442], extant in Latin: *Agnitio patris est filii manifestatio.*

305. *Comm in Cant* 1.6.8 [SC 375.254].

306. *Comm in Cant* 1.6.11 [SC 375.254–256].

307. Cf. *Comm in Cant* 1.6.14 [SC 375.256], where these *epinoiai* are said both to mediate who Christ is and collectively to embrace his fullness: *quae utique omnia et ipse esse et rursum ipsum dicuntur amplecti.*

Conclusion

While several metaphors are employed to describe the life of the believer, Origen's teaching in the *Homilies on the Psalms* presupposes degrees of progress (*gradus profectuum*)[308] in the life of the Christian. The agonistic, therapeutic, and pedagogical images employed throughout the *Homilies on the Psalms* serve to underline the ongoing struggle, gradual healing, and progressive education of the soul that mark the believer's life in this age; indeed, they may even continue after death. His teaching in these homilies, as has been demonstrated, is largely consistent with his more speculative teaching in *De principiis* and the more elaborate nuptial theology found in the *Commentary on the Canticle.*

Origen's interpretation of these Psalms is essentially moral, and this is consistent with his understanding of the "soul" of the Scriptures. Further, this moral interpretation both assumes and at times makes explicit that progress takes place and is worked out within the context of the community of believers, the Church.

Self-awareness (*sui agnitio*)[309] is an essential prerequisite for

308. Cf. *De principiis* 1.3.8 [GK 182]: *Ita ergo indesinenti erga nos opere patris et filii et spiritus sancti per singulos quosque profectuum gradus instaurato, vix si forte aliquando intueri possumus sanctam et beatam vitam; in qua cum post agones multos in eam perveniri potuerit, ita perdurare debemus, ut nulla umquam nos boni illius satietas* [probably = κόρος] *capiat, sed quanto magis de illa beatitudine percipimus, tanto magis in nobis vel dilatetur eius desiderium vel augeatur, dum semper ardentius et capacius patrem et filium ac spiritum sanctum vel capimus vel tenemus.*

309. This is the expression found in *Comm in Cant* 2.5.21 [SC 375.366]. Such emphasis on self-awareness permeates these homilies; cf., e.g., *Hom in Ps* 36.1.3 [SC 411.72]: *iubemur ... considerare eam* [*animam*] *diligentius;* 36.2.1 [SC 411.98]: *si teipsum perscrutari vis et videre si iam subiectus es Deo;* 37.2.1 [SC 411.302]: *non ergo cogitet de talibus sed cogitet de anima sua;* 38.2.2 [SC 411.380]: *scrutari debemus actus nostros et nosmetipsos probare;* and expressed negatively, 37.1.1 [SC 411.262]: *quod si per negligentiam sui atque animi desidiam incurrerit in peccatum;* 37.2.6 [SC 411.320]: *quoniam non seipsos diiudicant neque seipsos examinant nec intellegunt quid est communicare ecclesiae.* Cf. also, e.g., *Comm in Cant* 2.5.7 [SC 375.358]: *Videtur ergo mihi duplici modo agnitionem sui capere animam debere, quidve sit ipsa et qualiter moveatur, id est quid in substantia et quid in affectibus habeat;* and 2.5.28 [SC 375.370]: *Et quid opus est plura memorare, quibus ex causis semetipsam*

this progress, and Origen draws continually upon the idiom provided by the text of Scripture to elucidate the nature of the Christian vocation. Whether in terms of being "subject to God in Christ" (1 Corinthians 15.28), "always speaking Christ" (cf. Psalm 36.30), "the putting to death of the flesh" (1 Corinthians 5.5), or "walking in the image of the heavenly" (1 Corinthians 15.49), the person of Christ is central in Origen's teaching as the one who, in and through his various *epinoiai,* mediates the believer's progress and who heals, trains, and educates the soul in reference to its *telos.* Assimilation to the *Logos,* incarnate in Christ, encountered in and through the words of Scripture and the sacraments of the Church, is the proximate *telos* of Christian living, while the ultimate end is spoken of by Origen as nothing less than "seeing God."[310] By this Origen understands a deepening awareness of and a share in God's life as triune mystery. Moreover, this growing awareness (*agnoscere*) of God as triune is itself progressive:[311] it begins with recognition of Christ as the Word and Wisdom of God and continues with the recognition of and faith in the Holy Spirit. Ultimate vision is the knowledge (*scientia*) of the Trinity, expressed metaphorically by Origen as the soul's "food," necessary both for growth and for the maintenance of life. The soul is nourished eternally on the contemplation (*theoria*) and understanding (*intellectus*) of God, a *telos* very much in accord with the soul's nature.[312]

---

cognoscat anima, ne forte si neglexerit perfecte semetipsam cognoscere, exire iubeatur in vestigiis gregum et pascere haedos.

310. Cf. *Hom in Ps* 36.4.1 [SC 411.182]: *magna ergo est visio, cum puro corde Deus videtur.*

311. Cf. a similar accounting in *De principiis* 1.2.8 [GK 138–140] and 3.6.9 [GK 664–666], where those who are capable of grasping the Word and Wisdom of God ultimately are made capable of receiving God, and thus the end becomes like the beginning, and God will be "all in all."

312. *Hom in Ps* 36.4.1 [SC 411.182–184]: *Magna est visio cum puro corde verbum Dei et sapientia Dei qui est Christus eius agnoscitur. Magna visio est agnoscere et credere in Spiritum Sanctum. Magna ergo haec visio scientia Trinitatis est.* The choice of verbs is intriguing: *agnoscere* (implying perception) in reference to Christ, Incarnate Word and Wisdom, and the addition of *credere* (perhaps implying faith in what is not seen) to acceptance of the Spirit. Cf. *Comm in Cant* 2.5.20 [SC 375.366], where the highest function of knowledge is the recognition of the

A Note on the Translation

This translation of these nine homilies from the Latin of Rufinus was undertaken before the discovery of the Munich Codex, which includes the Greek text of the first four homilies on Psalm 36. While it would be tempting to seek to revise these four homilies in accord with the newly discovered Greek text, this was not done for two reasons. First, Joseph Trigg has now prepared a translation of the entire corpus of homilies found in the Munich Codex.[313] Second, allowing the Greek text to affect the translation made from Rufinus's Latin, while perhaps bringing the text closer to Origen's Greek—an obviously worthy aim—would at the same time risk losing the voice or tonality of Rufinus. Rufinus, for reasons of his own, selected these nine homilies to translate and, as his Preface indicates, understood them as an ensemble. While it is no doubt important to discover what Origen said and how he said it, it

---

Trinity, and its secondary function is the understanding of his creation: *Igitur principale munus scientiae est agnoscere Trinitatem, secundo vero in loco cognoscere creaturam eius;* and his account of the human *telos* in *De principiis* 2.11.7 [GK 456]: *Et ita crescens per singula rationabilis natura, non sicut in carne vel corpore et anima in hac vita crescebat, sed mente ac sensu aucta ad perfectam scientiam mens iam perfecta perducitur, nequaquam iam ultra istis carnalibus sensibus impedita, sed intellectualibus incrementis aucta, semper ad purum et, ut ita dixerim, "facie ad faciem" rerum causas inspiciens, potiturque perfectione, primo illa, qua in id ascendit, secundo qua permanet, cibos quibus vescatur habens theoremata et intellectus rerum rationesque causarum. Sicut enim in hac vita nostra corporea primo in hoc ipsum, quod sumus, corporaliter crescimus, in prima aetate ciborum sufficientia nobis incrementa praestante, postea vero quam crescendi ad mensuram sui fuerit expleta proceritas, utimur cibis iam non ut crescamus, sed ut vivamus et conservemur in vita per escas: ita arbitror et mentem etiam cum iam venerit ad perfectum, vesci tamen et uti propriis et conpetentibus cibis cum ea mensura, cui neque deesse aliquid debeat neque abundare. In omnibus autem cibus hic intellegendus est theoria et intellectus Dei, habens mensuras proprias et conpetentes huic naturae, quae facta est et creata; quas mensuras singulos quosque incipientium "videre Deum," id est intellegere per puritatem cordis, conpetit observare;* earlier at 2.11.5 [GK 448], Origen suggests that this knowledge of *rationes et causae rerum* will include an understanding of the significance of all that has transpired in this age: *omnium quae geruntur in terris manifestius agnosceret rationes.*

313. Origen, *Homilies on the Psalms: Codex Monacensis Graecus 314,* trans. Joseph W. Trigg, Fathers of the Church 141 (Washington, DC: The Catholic University of America Press, 2020).

is also important to understand how Rufinus understood what Origen said and how he chose to communicate it. Thus, because the temptation has been resisted regularly to consult the Greek and because the Latin text instead has been the source of this translation, it is hoped that this translation will help the reader better to understand these homilies on Rufinus's terms, so to speak. Further, a Greek text for the remaining five homilies in Rufinus's collection is not extant; for now, Rufinus is our only source of access to them. Therefore, other than on a couple of technical points indicated in the notes, the Greek text was consulted only minimally.

HOMILIES ON PSALMS 36–38

THE *PREFACE* OF RUFINUS

Since[1] the interpretation of Psalms 36, 37, and 38 is entirely moral and presents certain principles conducive to a reformed way of life, it teaches at one moment the path of conversion and penance, and at another that of purification and progress. So I have produced a translation into Latin for you, dearest son Apronianus, of nine short addresses, which the Greeks call *homilies,*[2] arranging them virtually as a single unit, so that you might possess in one volume their teaching,[3] which is devoted entirely to improvement and moral progress. Indeed, reading this volume will be beneficial insofar as an understanding of its plain teaching may be grasped without much effort on the part of the reader, and simplicity of life may be taught in clear and straightforward language, and less sophisticated minds may be able to be nurtured—thus making progress accessible not only to men, but also to devout women. May your sister in Christ,[4] my devout daughter, not be without gratitude for my efforts, should she experience these as an ongoing challenge to her understanding due to the difficulty of the subject matter. For the human body would not have been able to exist composed solely of sinews and bones, had divine Providence not woven them together with the softness of flesh and a fullness that is attractive.

1. Text, SC 411.46 [= CCL 20.251]; for the literary background, see Tore Janson, *Latin Prose Prefaces: Studies in Literary Conventions* (Stockholm: Almqvist and Wiksell, 1964); also, Marti, *Übersetzer der Augustin-Zeit,* 204–6.

2. *In novem oratiunculis, quas Graeci* ὁμιλίας *vocant;* for a classic discussion of the developing terminology of preaching in Christian antiquity, see Christine Mohrmann, "*Praedicare–Tractare–Sermo:* Essai sur la terminologie de la prédication chrétienne," in *La Maison-Dieu* 39 (1954): 97–107.

3. *Dictionem;* cf. *OLD* s.v. § 4. In the same sentence, he uses the terms *oratiuncula, homilia,* and *dictio* seemingly synonymously, at least in reference to these texts.

4. Presumably Avita, Apronianus's wife.

FIRST HOMILY ON PSALM 36 [37]

"IN MANY AND various ways God has spoken to our ancestors through the prophets."[1] Sometimes he teaches us ineffable mysteries through the things that he speaks, and at other times it is about the Savior and his coming that he instructs us, but from time to time he corrects and reforms our behavior. For this reason, we will attempt to point out differences of this kind in each passage of divine Scripture and to distinguish when there are prophecies and it is speaking of things to come, or when mystical realities are being announced, or when the passage is moral.

As we begin, then, an explanation of Psalm 36, we discover that the entire Psalm is moral and that it has been given as a kind of cure and medicine for the human soul, since it rebukes our sins and instructs us how to live according to the Law.

But let us now see what kind of starting point the first verse gives us: *Do not,* it says, *provoke jealousy among the wicked nor envy those who do evil: for they wither quickly like grass and like green herbs soon die.*[2] Through these words it teaches us that there are two

1. Heb 1.1.

2. Ps 36.1. There is a difficulty here in that the LXX employs two cognate verbs, [μὴ] παραζήλου and [μηδὲ] ζήλου (both active, it should be noted, despite the claim of J. Lust et al., that the former is middle voice; however, if that were the case, the ultima should have been printed with a circumflex. Cf. *Greek-English Lexicon of the Septuagint,* ed. J. Lust, K. Hauspie, E. Eynikel [Stuttgart: Deutsche Bibelgesellschaft, 2003], 462) respectively, where Rufinus simply uses the construction *noli aemulari ... neque aemulatus fueris* (in both cases, a deponent). Crouzel and Bresard note the ambivalence and render them as follows: "ne provoque pas la jalousie ... ne sois pas jaloux" (SC 411.51). As will become clear below, however, 1 Corinthians 10.22, where παραζηλοῦμεν is employed (*aemulamur* in the Vulgate), offers to Origen the basis for his interpretation of παραζήλου as "provoke jealousy" in Psalm 36.1. Erasmus was suspicious of Rufinus's style and

particular things which we ought not to do. First, we should not provoke jealousy among the wicked; second, we should not envy those who do evil: for the consequence for one who provokes jealousy among the wicked is that he withers like the grass, and that this happens to him quickly, not slowly. The consequence for one who envies those who do evil is that he soon dies, like green herbs.

According to the simple, literal understanding, the meaning of "not to provoke jealousy among the wicked" seems to be: one should not live as a provocateur[3]—that is, a leader and instigator—of evil among the wicked and worst of humanity, offering to others, as it were, a model of shameful behavior. But "to envy those who do evil," means to be an imitator and learn to act wickedly. This is what is said in each of these: that you should neither offer a bad example to others nor yourself follow the bad examples of others.

But in order to discover more fully the inner meaning of this word, I think it fitting to adduce from the divine Scriptures this word wherever we happen to find it and to compare spiritual things with what is spiritual.[4] In this way, the meaning of these passages might be made clearer.

It is written in Deuteronomy: "They have excited in me jealousy for what is no god, they have aroused me to ire through their idols, and I will lead them to jealousy for what is no peo-

---

translation, particularly regarding his rendering of παραζήλου; see his *Censurae, Desiderii Erasmi Roterdami Opera Omnia,* ed. Jean Leclercq (Lugduni Batavorum, 1703–1704), 8.434.

3. *Aemulator;* from Rufinus's use of *aemulari;* in this context, "provocateur" or "one who provokes" is preferable to "emulator."

4. See 1 Cor 2.13; Rufinus makes use of this principle, which is central to his approach to the sacred text, in his *Comm in Cant* 3.13.8 [SC 376.62]; see as well Claude Jenkins, "Origen on 1 Corinthians," *Journal of Theological Studies* 9 (1908): 231–47, esp. 240, and the discussion of Daniel Sheerin, "Rhetorical and Hermeneutic *Synkrisis* in Patristic Typology," in *Nova et Vetera: Patristic Studies in Honor of Thomas Patrick Halton,* ed. John Petruccione (Washington, DC: The Catholic University of America Press, 1998), 22–39, esp. 31–33; see also Alberto Viciano, "*Homeron ex Homerou Saphenizein:* Principios Hermenéuticos de Teodoreto de Ciro en su Comentario a las Epístolas Paulinas," in *Scripta Theologica* 21 (1989): 13–61.

ple."[5] Where this is said in Latin, "They have led me to jealousy (*in zelum adduxerunt*)" and "I will lead them to jealousy (*ego in zelum adducam*)," in the Greek text it is the same word that is said at the beginning of the Psalm, that is, "they have provoked me, and I will provoke them." Although the Greek word itself, παραζήλωσαν, seems to be expressed more clearly in Latin if we were to say, "they incited me," nevertheless it is the same word. Yet in the Apostle it is also written, "Do we provoke the Lord to jealousy? Are we stronger than he?"[6] In some manuscripts, "Do we incite the Lord?" is written in place of "Do we provoke the Lord to jealousy?"

From all this evidence, *aemulari in aliquem* means to incite or to provoke another. Let us, for instance, use this example: there are certain immodest and good-for-nothing women who, if they happen to beguile men and entice them into a clandestine love-affair, over time are no longer satisfied with their hidden wantonness and wish to make known also to the men's chaste wives the fact that they are being loved by their husbands so as to incite their jealousy and disturb them and wreck others' families. If you understand the power of this example, how a concubine arouses a wife's jealousy, you should also grasp what *aemulari inter aliquos* means: when incitements to some evil are presented to them.

Finally, since this is the meaning of the passage from Deuteronomy in which it says, "They have led me to jealousy"—that is, παραζήλωσαν—"for what is no god," from this it becomes clearer what is written elsewhere, where it is said that our God is a jealous God.[7] For a husband is customarily spoken of as jealous of his wife because out of deep concern he watches carefully over her modesty and does not permit his wife's chastity to be defiled. This is why it follows that a person who sins against God (who is called "jealous") incites and arouses his jealousy. But all these things are to be understood imprecisely[8] when referring to God, just like the things

5. Dt 32.21.
6. 1 Cor 10.22.
7. Cf. Ex 20.5.
8. *Abusive* [= καταχρηστικώτερον ἀκουστέον], "unidiomatically" or "in a

said regarding the wrath of God or sleep or sadness; what is to be understood through them is what each one of us deserves from God on account of our actions. This is why he spoke thus in Deuteronomy: "They have led me to jealousy for what is no God and have stirred me through their idols";[9] that is, they have stirred up jealousy in me because they worship idols. But what follows? "And I," it says, "will lead them to jealousy for what is no people, and I will provoke them to jealousy through a foolish people."[10]

This is why even now the Jews are not moved against the pagans, against those who worship idols and blaspheme God. They do not hate them, nor is their ire raised against them; yet they bear an insatiable hatred toward Christians who have abandoned idols and turned to God,[11] and in this respect at least—if in no other—the Jews have become like the pagans.

So when you observe the Jews holding the Christian in contempt and plotting against him, understand this as the fulfillment of the prophecy that says, "And I will stir up in them jealousy against a non-people."[12] For we are the "non-people," we few from this city who have come to believe and others from different cities, and an entire people has been enlisted from no particular place from the very beginning of the faith.[13] For unlike the nation of the Jews or the nation of the Egyptians,

---

misapplied way"; Origen makes the same distinction between language used properly or appropriately (*proprie*) and inexactly or loosely (*abusive*) regarding the term *caritas* in the Scriptures in his *Comm in Cant,* pr. 2.33: *sciendum est in his* [*locis*] *non proprie sed abusive caritatem nominari* [SC 375.114]; also, *De principiis* 1.2.13 [GK 156], on the "accidental" rather than substantial goodness of created things: *haec omnia abusive dicuntur.* Cf. also Bernhard Neuschäfer, *Origenes als Philologe* (Basel: Friedrich Reinhardt, 1987), 222.

9. Dt 32.21.

10. Dt 32.21; Origen also addresses divine "jealousy" in *Ex ad Mart* 9 [GCS 2.9–10] and *De principiis* 4.1.4 [GK 680–682].

11. Cf. 1 Thes 1.9.

12. Dt 32.21: Rufinus's rendering of this passage from Deuteronomy poses a challenge for the translator, as Rufinus translates it differently each time; the Greek text as found in the Munich manuscript is consistent throughout [ἐγὼ παραζηλώσω αὐτοὺς ἐπ' οὐκ ἔθνει].

13. *Qui pauci ex ista civitate credidimus et alii ex alia et nusquam gens integra ab initio credulitatis videtur assumpta;* cf. *OLD,* s.v. *assumo* § 8.

the race of Christians is a people that is united and complete, but gathered from various places and from different nations.[14] He therefore says, "I will lead them to be jealous for what is no people, I will provoke them to jealousy of a foolish people."[15] This is why they are provoked against us and hold us in contempt as a foolish people, calling themselves wise, since, granted, it was to them that God's revelation was first entrusted. Yet meditating on the Law of God from youth to old age, they have not entered into the Law of God.[16] But "God has chosen the foolish things of this world to confound the wise,"[17] and thus what was written is fulfilled: "I will provoke them to jealousy of a foolish people."[18]

But what else does the Apostle say: "Do we provoke the Lord to jealousy? Are we stronger than he?"[19] Let us see what this means. In this passage, he spoke these things while discussing sacrifices and offerings made to idols. "Do we"—he says—"provoke the Lord to jealousy?" That is, do we incite jealousy in the Lord when we eat what was offered to idols, just as the Jews had stirred up his jealousy through their idols? Do we really wish to do the same? Therefore, he says, "Do we provoke the Lord to jealousy? Are we stronger than he?" This is what he is saying: if indeed we, by our strength, stir up jealousy in one who is weaker, we are easily able to disregard him; but if we stir up the jealousy of one who is strong, are we not working toward self-destruction? If, then, we eat what has been offered to idols and stir up the Lord's jealousy, we provoke against ourselves the wrath of One who is stronger, and this results in our own ruin. So when you see a thoroughly wicked person, watch out and beware lest you stir up his jealousy against you, lest you carelessly do something to provoke his wickedness.

14. *Gens* is used throughout this passage, but for the sake of the English it is rendered variably as "people" or "nation." The noun "race" here renders the Latin noun *genus*.

15. Dt 32.21.

16. Cf. Rom 9.31; as Crouzel notes, one of the ἐπίνοιαι of Christ, SC 411.58, n. 2.

17. 1 Cor 1.27.

18. Dt 32.21.

19. 1 Cor 10.22.

Let an example clarify what is being said. Blessed David stirred up resentful Saul to jealousy when he led the army and slew Goliath and when choruses of young girls and women walked in procession, singing, "Saul has killed thousands, and David tens of thousands."[20] Now if David had done this by design, he would, in fact, have provoked jealousy in bitter Saul.[21] But as it is, this was not done with the intention that choruses of young girls would go out and sing a song such as this: "David has killed tens of thousands, and Saul thousands."

This is what the Psalm is teaching us. Since the human race is prone to jealousy[22] and is quite easily inclined toward this vice, take heed lest your actions provoke the wicked to jealousy of you, either stirring them to plot against you or arousing hatred for you. This is the full meaning of these words, namely, that you yourself should neither provoke the wicked to jealousy against you nor emulate the wickedness of another.

How then does a person emulate the wickedness of another? Doubtless it is when he engages in the very same behavior. What I am saying is this: if someone who was once poor becomes rich through evil-doing, and if his neighbor is in need, and sees him who rose from the ground up and reached the pinnacle of wealth, and begins so to rival him so as to grow rich in the same way through evil-doing, this is what it means to emulate those who do evil. Moreover, if someone wishes to rival the person who, through sly sexual affairs or illicit schemes, forces access to marriages, households, and wealth that are beyond his position and means, this person has envied those who do evil. Even more, in the case of those who have, through various criminal acts or unworthy and illegal campaigning, reached undeserved heights of public office or who have, through unjust political activity or even bloodied hands, seized offices of importance that are not their due, if someone, observing these people, should be inflamed toward a similar madness, he has envied those who do evil.

20. 1 Sm 18.7.

21. *Aemulatus fuisset in malignante Saul:* clearly an attempt to link this biblical passage to the Psalm.

22. *Zelotypiam.*

2. For this reason, then, we are enlightened by the Lord's command[23] that, when the flame of wrongful emulation singes[24] our mind and heart, we should use the words we have learned and say, "If I ever wish to provoke jealousy among the wicked or envy those who do evil, see what happens next: *for,* it says, *they wither quickly like grass and like green herbs soon die.*"[25]

Do you want to be supported further by the authority of another prophet concerning such warnings? Listen to what Isaiah, too, declares about all fleshly glory. "All flesh is grass," he says, and "all its glory is like the flower of the field."[26] Do you now want to see a series of examples of how the glory of the flesh is but the flower of the field? Look who assumed power some thirty years ago; see how his empire flourished. But it immediately began to wither like the flower of the field; then there was another after him; and then, one after another, leaders and princes and all their honor and glory not only withered like a flower but also like dry dust were blown about by the wind, and have left not even a trace of themselves behind.[27]

Others, too, borne up by riches and swollen with honors, are anxious to be considered either worthy of praise through their feigned goodness or worthy of hatred through their unrelenting cruelty. If one among them thinks that such empty pursuits are enviable, let him go now to the remains of their corpses (if even these can be found—for there are a considerable number to whom not even this has been granted), and

23. Cf. Ps 18.9.

24. *Pulsaverit,* rendered here as "singes" for the sake of the metaphor introduced by *flamma.*

25. Ps 36.2.

26. Is 40.6; "flower of the field" is the Douay-Rheims rendering.

27. Crouzel posits that this is a reference to Septimius Severus (193–211 AD), placing the homily c. 241; Harnack had suggested Caracalla (Aurelius Antoninus), who reigned 211–217 AD, thus making for a slightly later date of delivery, c. 247; SC 411.64, n. 1. See Marie-Josèphe Rondeau, *Les commentaires patristiques du Psautier (IIIe–Ve siècle),* 2 vols. (Rome: Institutum Studiorum Orientalium, 1982–1985), 1.53, n. 90. In the light of the Munich Codex and subsequent research, Lorenzo Perrone has suggested Macrinus (217–218), thus placing the homily even later, 247–248; see "The Dating of the New *Homilies on the Psalms* in the Munich Codex: The Ultimate Origen?" in *Proche-Orient Chrétien* 67 (2017): 243–51, at 244.

then he will discover how "all flesh is grass, and all its glory is like the flower of the field. The grass has withered, and its flower has fallen."[28] But the one who neither loves the flowering of the flesh nor lives in a fleshly fashion, but loves the Word of God and makes progress in it, hear what he has to hope for: "The Word of the Lord," it says, "abides forever."[29]

But further I do not think that this very saying—*they*—that is, the wicked—*wither quickly like grass*—comparing them to grass, is without purpose, since certainly there could be some other substance to which those who act with malice might be compared. Grass is the food of dumb and irrational animals. Quite possibly it is because all who are foolish and ignorant and who live in contradiction to reason and the wisdom of God follow those who are in the forefront[30] of wickedness and are said to feed on the life and actions of those men whom they also obey, and for this reason they are compared to grass. For no one who is wise follows their example. For, as the wise person is the one "who hears the words of the Lord and acts on them,"[31] it is he who eats "the bread that comes down from heaven,"[32] and his food is Jesus, because he is nourished on his words and lives by his commands.[33] In the same way, too, those who are conspicuous in wickedness become grass for those who follow their example or who emulate them in evil-doing.

Moreover, similarities are to be perceived also in green herbs, to which evildoers are compared because they pass away swiftly. Nevertheless, we also discover on occasion in the divine Scriptures vegetables that are the object of praise, the ones that, at the Apostle's instruction, the weak are commanded to

28. Is 40.6–7.

29. Is 40.8.

30. *Principes;* earlier, *auctor et dux,* at 36.1.1 [SC 411.2].

31. Mt 7.24.

32. Jn 6.33.

33. Cf. *Contra Celsum* 8.22, where the one making progress is described as "feeding on the flesh of the Word": ἐσθίοντα τῆς σαρκὸς τοῦ λόγου [SC 150.224]; in the context of sacrifice in which it is used, the language is arguably eucharistic. In his *Hom in Gen* 10.3 [SC 7bis.264], the same phrase is used in reference to *hearing* the Word in the liturgy: *carnes Verbi cotidie sumunt.*

eat.[34] But there are others that are opposed to these, in reference to which it is said that water, coming down from above, feeds the rivers of Egypt like a vegetable garden.[35] Evidently, the Egyptian is not spoken of as a "tree," nor is he even called "vine," but green herbs that die quickly. Do you want to see how quickly the Egyptian dies? See what is said about them in Exodus: "But the Egyptians hastened," it says; "they shattered their axles and quickly disappeared under the water."[36] Therefore, *like green herbs they soon die.*[37]

Finally, there is also that wicked man, Ahab, who was prepared to plant vegetables like these in the vineyard of Naboth the Jezreelite,[38] for which reason Naboth chose death rather than allow vegetables to be planted in an expropriated vineyard of Israel. He acted as a just man, so as not to allow the expropriation of the vineyard of justice, whose produce, when mixed in the bowl of wisdom, gladdens the human heart,[39] nor to allow the planting of vegetables of iniquity, which green quickly but soon dry up.

I therefore think that, in the hearts of us who believe in the Savior, there is also a kind of vineyard planted, just as it says, "A vineyard was planted for my beloved in a fertile place on a crest."[40] But this was said also to those to whom the saying, "I planted you as a complete, true vineyard,"[41] was first given. There is then within us a kind of vineyard out of which we press the fruit of knowledge (knowledge that gladdens the human heart)[42] by means of the gift of wisdom in the winepresses of the Scriptures when we more perfectly and more joyfully contemplate the mysteries of the divine law. But to us who are making progress in these pursuits and who are striving toward spiritual understanding with the vision of an Isra-

34. Cf. Rom 14.2.
35. Cf. Dt 11.10b.
36. Cf. Ex 14.25.
37. Ps 36.2.
38. Cf. 1 Kgs 21.
39. A conflation of images from Prv 9.5 and Ps 103.15.
40. Is 5.1.
41. Jer 2.21.
42. Cf. Ps 103.15.

elite, comes wicked and impious Ahab, the enemy of our vineyard, who, against these pursuits of wisdom, stirs up envy,[43] initiates discord, contrives deceptions and factions through Jezebel—that is, through the wisdom of the flesh[44]—and means to expropriate this vineyard of spiritual understanding and to plant it with vegetables, that is, so that we understand what we are reading in a fleshly manner. For indeed, as all glory of the flesh is vegetables, so the condemnation of the Apostle is fulfilled in us when he said to the Galatians, "Are you so senseless, that while you began with the Spirit you now are finishing with the flesh?"[45]

Moreover, as to the fact that there exist in the holy soul vineyards and fields blessed by the Lord, listen also to Isaac speaking to his son Jacob: "Behold, the smell of my son is like the smell of a full field that the Lord has blessed."[46] For it is to our great advantage that we cultivate the vineyard in our soul and dig out the winepress of the Scriptures and harvest the clusters of grapes and press the wine from the vineyard of Sorek,[47] so that we too might say to the Lord, "How splendid your cup, which intoxicates me!"[48]

3. After it said that those who do evil die like green herbs and it proscribed provoking jealousy among the wicked and

43. *Invidia.*

44. *Hoc est per carnalem sapientiam;* cf. τὸ φρόνημα τῆς σαρκὸς of Rom 8.6–7.

45. Gal 3.3.

46. Gn 27.27.

47. Cf. Is 5.2; the fertile valley of Sorek, between Ashkelon and Gaza, is mentioned as the home of Delilah in Jgs 16.4. Unfortunately, the nine extant homilies of Origen on Judges [SC 389] treat passages in the first seven chapters of the book and do not mention Sorek. Eusebius identifies Sorek both as a χειμάρρους, a wadi that is dry in the summer but swells in the winter (cf. the Kidron Valley of Jn 18.1), as well as a city near Zorah, the birthplace of Samson; see R. Steven Notley and Zev Safrai, *Eusebius, Onomasticon: The Place Names of Divine Scripture, including the Latin edition of Jerome* (Boston: Brill, 2005), 150.

48. Ps 22.5; While Origen's extant works do not witness his use of the precise term, on *sobria ebrietas* (θεία μέθη) see R. P. Lawson, trans., *Origen: The Song of Songs: Commentary and Homilies* (Westminster, MD: Newman Press, 1957), 346–47, n. 51; also, Hans Lewy, *Sobria Ebrietas: Untersuchungen zur Geschichte der antiken Mystik* (Giessen: Verlag von Alfred Töpelmann, 1929), 119–28, who demonstrates similar ideas in Origen's works. Ambrose's later use of the concept is likely directly from Philo.

imitating evildoers,[49] it then tells us what we ought to do. *Hope in the Lord*, it says, *and do good.*[50] Holding in contempt all those things condemned earlier—public office, wealth, all glory of the flesh, and all the goods of this world—*Hope,* it says, *in the Lord.* But while you hope in the Lord you are not to be idle; rather, hope in him as you do good.

Let us see what this goodness is. It is one of those fruits that the Apostle reckons as fruits of the Holy Spirit. "But the fruits of the Spirit are love, joy, peace, patience, goodness, and justice."[51] *Do good,* therefore, as if one were saying to the field, "Produce this or that fruit."[52] So now it is to you as a hearer of the divine Scriptures that the divine Word speaks as to a field. *Do good and dwell in the land, and you will be fed with its riches.*[53] Do not be like grass, which withers; do not become like green herbs, which soon die; but *hope in the Lord and do good and dwell in the land.*

What is the land in which it commands us to dwell if we do good? Certainly, if it is referring to this land where we are now dwelling, then both those who do good and those who do not do good dwell in this land. The command, then, seems unnecessary if it is this land that is understood. But let us see if it is not rather referring to that land about which it is written, "Another seed fell upon good ground,"[54] which bore fruit; now this "ground" seems to signify the heart and soul of the one who hears. We are therefore commanded to dwell in this land, that is, not to wander too far afield, nor to dash haphazardly near and far, but rather to dwell and abide steadily within the boundaries of our soul and to examine it quite carefully and to become its farmer, as Noah was,[55] and to plant a vineyard in it and to cultivate the ground that is within us, "to break

49. See Ps 36.1–2.

50. Ps 36.3.

51. Gal 5.22.

52. It is not possible to reproduce in English with the same verb all that one can infer from *facere,* used throughout this section.

53. Ps 36.3.

54. Lk 8.8; *terra,* of course, can be rendered both "land" and "ground."

55. Cf. Gn 9.20.

up anew[56] the fallow ground of our soul and not to sow seed among thorns";[57] that is, when we cleanse our soul from vices and cultivate our untilled and rough character toward gentleness in imitation of Christ, only in this way are we at last fed from the riches of the virtues. For it must never be thought that we are instructed to seek earthly riches: these we are commanded to disregard and to scorn.

It then says, *Dwell in the land.* That is, always tend to the field of your soul; remain there permanently and cultivate your ground, so that when you have begun to abound with the fruits of justice, then *you will be fed with its riches.* But what does "fed with its riches" mean? It means, "whatever a person has sown, this he will also reap."[58] And "the one who sows in the flesh will reap corruption from the flesh. But the one who sows in the spirit reaps eternal life from the spirit."[59] So then, if you dwell in your land and sow seed in it not with the flesh but with the spirit, *you will be fed with its riches,* like those sheep who are described as being fed in a verdant place, of whom the divine Word says: "He has placed me there in a verdant place."[60] From this it is clear that every one of us prepares a verdant place within himself in which he is fed by the Lord, when he cultivates the fields of his soul and, sowing always in the spirit, progresses toward the joy of spiritual husbandry.

4. *Find delight in the Lord, and he will grant you the requests of your heart.*[61] It is customary for the divine Scriptures to offer for consideration two men, and to speak in the same terms [ὁμώνυμα] about one, drawn from the other, that is, to apply characteristics of the "outer" man also to the "inner."[62] What I am saying is this: the outer, bodily man feeds on corruptible foods and things proper to him. But there is a kind of food of the inner man of which it is said, "Man lives on every word

56. *Innovare.*

57. Jer 4.3.

58. Gal 6.7.

59. Gal 6.8.

60. Ps 22.2.

61. Ps 36.4.

62. Cf. 2 Cor 4.16; this is treated as well in the prologue to his *Comm in Cant,* pr. 2.6 [SC 375.94].

of God."[63] There is a drink proper to the outer man, and there is another proper to the inner man. For we drink from the spiritual rock that follows us,[64] and we drink its water, just as Jesus says, "The one who drinks will never thirst."[65] There is a clothing for the outer man, and there is one for the inner man. Indeed, if someone is a sinner, "he clothes himself with a curse like a garment."[66] But if someone is just, he hears, "Put on the Lord Jesus Christ,"[67] and, "Clothe yourself with heartfelt mercy, kindness, humility, gentleness, and patience."[68] But why is it necessary to describe in detail how the inner man is spoken of in the same terms as the outer man? Both the outer man and the inner man possess armor.[69] The one who engages in battle according to the inner man is clothed in the armor of God so as to be able to stand against the cunning ploys of the devil.

But after many examples, let us come to the subject at hand. Let us see what is meant by the passage, *Find delight in the Lord, and he will grant you the request of your heart.* First it must be kept in mind that what in Latin is "Find delight in the Lord" (*delectare in Domino*) is, in Greek, "Delight in the Lord" (*deliciare in Domino*). For this is what the Greek term κατατρύφησον means.[70] For just as, in the case of the outer man, it is possible not only to make use of foods, but also to enjoy them with delight (and it is the wealthy especially who make use of delicacies),[71] so too the inner man is capable not only of making use of foods but also of enjoying them with delight.

I think this happens in this way: if someone hears only the

63. Dt 8.3.
64. Cf. 1 Cor 10.4.
65. Jn 4.14.
66. Ps 108.18.
67. Rom 13.14.
68. Col 3.12.
69. Cf. Eph 6.13.
70. Rufinus is fond of distinguishing in meaning *delectare* and *deliciare* (here both used in the imperative; later, *Hom in Ps* 36.2.6 [SC 411.114–116], in the future tense, *delectabuntur* and *deliciabuntur*); I have attempted to capture a slight difference by using "find delight" and "delight," respectively.
71. *Deliciis perfrui* (contrasted with *cibis uti*); the various senses in which this construct is used in the following paragraph require a paraphrastic translation.

words that summon him to the fear of God, this man receives only food from this kind of word. But the one who makes an effort to understand the Law, to examine carefully the prophets, to make sense of the parables in the Gospel, to clarify the meaning of the words of the apostles, he who directs his efforts toward knowledge and understanding of all these, he is one who enjoys them with delight. For he is making use of the food of the commandments not solely for the purpose of sustaining his life, but he finds delight in the full attainment of knowledge.

This is what I think is meant in that passage where God is said to have planted in the beginning a paradise of delight,[72] in which we were doubtless to enjoy spiritual delights. But also in another place it says: "You will give to them"—that is, to the saints—"a cup brimming with delights."[73] Yet I am also aware that "brimming with your pleasure (*voluptatis tuae*)" is usually found here in the Latin manuscripts, but the Greek has τρυφῆς, that is, "with delights (*deliciarum*)."

But further, to the saints and those for whom contempt for bodily foods is prescribed, the hope of spiritual delights is promised in return. Do you also want to receive the authoritative witness of the divine Scriptures? There was a certain rich man and Lazarus, who was poor. The rich man abounded in delights of the body; Lazarus was worn out by starvation. Both departed this life, and Lazarus was carried up by the angels to the bosom of Abraham that he might rest in the delights there; but the former, who had enjoyed the delights of the body, went off, as it is written in the Gospel, to fiery Gehenna, and he heard from Abraham: "You obtained good things in your life"—that is, you misused delights—"and Lazarus, bad. Now, however, he rests here, but you are in torment."[74] No one is capable of possessing delights both in the flesh and in the spirit. But if one delights in the flesh, as that rich man did, he will be deprived of Abraham's lap and its delights. But the one who

72. Cf. Gn 2.8.
73. Ps 35.9.
74. Lk 16.25.

eats the bread of affliction[75] in this present life, as that poor man did, when he departs from here, will experience delight.

Therefore, *Delight in the Lord, and he will grant you the request of your heart.*[76] But if you wish to contemplate still more fully how one will delight in the Lord, observe that the Lord is Truth,[77] and that he is Wisdom,[78] and that he is Justice, and that he is Holiness.[79] So if you abound in the wealth of Truth, if you abound in the understanding of Wisdom, if you are overflowing with works of Justice, then you will delight fully and completely in the Lord. And when you fulfill this, then you will also attain what follows: for *the Lord will grant you the requests of your heart.*[80]

Nevertheless, it was necessary to add *requests of your heart,* although it could have said simply "your requests." But what is said can be understood quite easily if one imagines a kind of personality proper to each of the parts of the body. For example, if the eye had a voice, would it not say, "I seek light, so that I might look upon things the sight of which brings me delight; for I avoid looking at anything awful and everything which distresses or saddens my vision"? Similarly, if the sense of hearing had a voice, would it not say, "I desire a sound composed with musical artistry, a sound that brings delight, but I avoid listening to anything caustic or dreadful"? So, too, if speech were granted to the sense of taste or of touch, all these senses of ours would without doubt also seek the things agreeable to their own sense.

Let us pass from these senses to the heart, in which exists the mind and the governing intellect,[81] and let us see what

75. Cf. Dt 16.3.

76. Ps 36.4; here Rufinus employs *deliciare* in place of *delectare* used initially in quoting the Psalm.

77. Cf. Jn 14.6.

78. Cf. 1 Cor 24.30.

79. Cf. 1 Cor 1.30.

80. Ps 36.4.

81. *Principalis intellectus,* the probable equivalent of the Greek τὸ ἡγεμονικόν, the higher of the two activities of the soul; cf. the summary discussion of Crouzel, *Origen,* trans. A. S. Worrall (San Francisco: Harper and Row, 1989), 88–89. Elsewhere the term will be rendered *principale cordis,* e.g., in Rufinus's translation

the heart desires and requests, just as we have shown above concerning the eye, the ears, and the other senses. Without a doubt, the heart, in accord with its own nature, seeks understanding. As the eye seeks vision, so the heart searches for understanding. As the ear desires a pleasing sound, so the heart finds delight in wise conceptions. As the sense of taste finds joy in sweet flavor, so the heart finds joy in prudent thoughts. As the sense of smell is gladdened by a pleasant fragrance, so the heart is gladdened by rational endeavors. As the sense of touch finds delight in what is smooth and soft, so the heart finds delight in the best and most beneficial counsels. If, then, you delight in the Lord and thoroughly enjoy the abundance of wisdom and truth and justice and their delights, the Lord *will grant you the requests of your heart,* requests oriented to the delights just described.

5. After this, it says, *Reveal your way to the Lord; hope in him, and he will act.*[82] "Everyone who does evil hates the light and does not come to the light lest his works be criticized. The one who does the truth, he comes to the light."[83] Since, then, the one who does evil hates the light, he also, to the degree he can, covers up and conceals his path, hiding his wicked deeds and, fearful of being accused, cloaking them in order to mask them. For example, if one of you—though I would hope that there is no one of this sort in this congregation—nevertheless, if one among you (whether a catechumen or even someone from among the many faithful) is aware that he has fornicated and hides the sin, does it not seem to you that this person is hiding and covering up the path that he is taking?

The one, however, who lives chastely and who has confidence concerning the purity of his own life does not wish to cover up his way, but desires that it be manifest; when I say "manifest," I mean to God, not to human beings (lest perhaps he receive his reward from humans).[84] This is the reason, there-

of the *Comm in Cant* 1.2.3; 6; 7 [SC 375.192; 194] and in Jerome's translation of Origen's *Hom in Ez 3* [PL 25.714C].

82. Ps 36.5.

83. Jn 3.20–21.

84. Cf. Mt 6.2–6.

fore, why it is said: *Reveal your way to the Lord.* But even if you are aware of some evils, do not hide them, but through confession[85] *reveal* them *to the Lord* and *hope in him, and he will act.* That is, when you confess your sins and reveal your faults to him, hope in him because you can win forgiveness from him and *he will act.* What will he do? Without doubt he will make you whole.[86] He will say to you, "Behold, you have been made whole; sin no more, lest something worse befall you."[87] He will do this, if you reveal some of your faults to him.[88] Indeed, if your path is pure and your conscience is clean and you reveal these things to him, *hope in him.*

6. Learn what he does from what then follows: *he will bring forth your justice like a light and your judgment like the midday.*[89] God brings forth your justice, which you have carried out in secret[90] and have revealed only to God, like a light, and presents you to heaven and earth as a just person enlightened by the Sun of Justice;[91] he shows the light of your justice to all who are in heaven, and he takes pride in you, so to speak, as a son,[92] as one who has received the spirit of adoption.[93] Thus, *he brings forth your justice like a light,* for the one who is just in accord with the Lord's command carries out his deeds of justice exactly as the Lord himself commanded: "But you, when you carry out your deeds of justice, do not let your left hand know what your right is doing."[94] Therefore, justice such as this, which is carried out not to be shown to human beings nor to pursue human glory, but which is done instead in secret—and which the Father, who sees in secret,[95] will reward openly in his own

85. *Sed per exomologesin* [=ἀλλὰ δι' ἐξομολογήσεως].

86. *Sanus.*

87. Jn 5.14.

88. *Haec faciet, si aliqua ei delicta revelaveris;* as above, SC 411.84: *si malorum tibi conscius aliquorum fueris;* alternately, taking *aliqua* adverbially, "if you reveal your faults to him in some way."

89. Ps 36.6.

90. Cf. Mt 6.4.

91. Cf. Mal 3.20.

92. *Iactabit se de te tamquam de filio;* cf *OLD* s.v. *iacto,* § 13.

93. Cf. Rom 8.15.

94. Cf. Mt 6.3.

95. Cf. Mt 6.4.

time—is brought forth by God like a light and *your judgment like the midday.*

All judgments whatsoever, then, which the just person makes will be not only like light but like the midday light, which is certainly clearest and brightest. For indeed the fullness of light is indicated by midday. If, then, you are just and good, God *will bring forth your justice like a light and your judgment like the midday.* And assuredly at the judgment, when your case is considered, God will make the justice of your case manifest like the light, and the judgment that he renders he will also make as clear as at midday.

Aware, then, of what is thus to come, let us entreat the mercy of God, that he may grant us to be among those who are found worthy, and that God himself may bring forth the light of our justice and our judgment, clear and bright like the midday, for he possesses in himself the True Light,[96] our Lord himself, "to whom are glory and power forever and ever. Amen."[97]

96. Cf. Jn 1.9.

97. 1 Pt 4.11. On the doxologies with which Origen concludes his homilies, see Henri Crouzel, "Les doxologies finales des homélies d'Origène selon le texte grec et les versions latines," *Augustinianum* 20 (1980): 95–107.

SECOND HOMILY ON PSALM 36 [37]

SEEING THAT the command admonishes us and says, *Be subject to the Lord,*[1] it seems necessary to investigate what it means to be *subject to the Lord* and what it means not to be *subject to the Lord.* For just as "Not everyone who says, 'Lord, Lord,' will enter the kingdom of heaven, but the one who does the will of my Father who is in heaven,"[2] so too not everyone who claims to be subject to the Lord is subject to him, but the one who has made himself subject[3] in fact and deed. For the act of subjecting oneself, not the claim that one has done so, reveals that one is truly subject to the Lord.

What we are saying is better understood in this way: Our Lord Jesus Christ is Justice.[4] Therefore, no one who acts unjustly is subject to Christ, who is Justice. Christ is Truth.[5] No liar, whether he lies in deed or in teaching, is subject to Christ, who is Truth. Our Lord Jesus Christ is Holiness.[6] No one, when defiled and impure, is subject to Holiness. Our Lord Jesus Christ is Peace.[7] No one who is quarrelsome and factious is subject to Christ, who is Peace; but rather, the one who says, "I was at peace with those who have hated peace," is subject to him.[8] This is why in another Psalm also, the prophet says to

1. Ps 36.7. The text of the Psalm quoted here employs *subditus* (also found in the Vulgate *iuxta* LXX), but Rufinus prefers *subiectus* and its cognate *subiectio* in explaining the text.
2. Mt 7.21.
3. Taking *subiectus est* as a medial passive.
4. Cf. 1 Cor 1.30.
5. Cf. Jn 14.6.
6. Cf. 1 Cor 1.30.
7. Cf. Eph 2.14.
8. Ps 119.7.

his soul, "Nevertheless be subject to God, my soul, for from him comes my patience."[9]

But the Apostle also indicates great, indeed, and spiritual realities concerning this "being made subject" when he says, "When all things have been made subject to him, then the Son himself will be made subject to him who has made all things subject to himself."[10] Listen to what he is saying: it is necessary that all things be made subject to Christ and that then he himself be made subject by a subjection that is, of course, appropriately understood as having been effected by the Spirit.[11] In the meantime, it is necessary that all things be made subject to Christ so that, when at last all things have been fulfilled and brought to completion through subjection, he too (as though bringing back this [subjection] as the palm of his victory) may eventually be described as made subject to the Father. But unless this is understood spiritually, it is held to mean surely something impious to those who are not attentive. For it should not be thought that the Son of God is not at all now subject to the Father, but that in the end times, when all things have been made subject to him [the Son], he will then himself also be made subject. On the contrary, because he makes his own everything belonging to us[12] and says that it is he who hungers in us, and that it is he who thirsts in us, and that it is he who is naked and sick, that he is the stranger and the imprisoned, and asserts that whatever is done to one of his disciples has been done to him,[13] logically and appropriately, then, does he attest that he has been made subject when each of us is fully and perfectly subject to God, such that he shows himself to be in no way whatsoever disobedient.[14]

What we are saying can also be more clearly understood in

9. Ps 61.6.

10. 1 Cor 15.28. On the centrality of this text to Origen's thought, see Henri Crouzel, "Quand le Fils transmet le Royaume à son Père: L'interprétation d'Origène," in *Studia Missionalia* 33 (1984): 359–84.

11. *Subiectione videlicet illa quam de Spiritu intellegi dignum est.*

12. *Omnia nostra in se recipit.*

13. Cf. Mt 25.35–40.

14. Cf. *De principiis* 1.6.1 [GK 216]: *subiectionis enim nomen, qua Christo subicimur, salutem quae a Christo est indicat subiectorum.*

another way. If some part of our body aches, though our soul remains unharmed and all the other parts of our body are healthy, nevertheless because the whole person suffers from the pain of one part, we do not say that we are healthy, but that we are ill. For example, we say, "He is not well." Why? Because his feet or kidneys or stomach aches. And no one says that he is healthy but that his stomach aches, but rather that he is not healthy because his stomach aches.

If you have grasped this example, let us now return to the subject at hand. The Apostle says that we are "the Body of Christ and individually are members."[15] Therefore, Christ, whose Body is the entire human race—or perhaps rather the whole of the entire creation[16]—and each one of us is a member of it; if someone from among us who are called his members is sick and is afflicted with some disease of sin, that is, if the stain of some sin is branded upon him and he is not subject to God, he [Christ] is correctly said not yet to be made subject, for his members include those who are not subject to God. But when he possesses all those who are called his Body, and its members are in a healthy state, so that they suffer from no disease of disobedience, when all the members are healthy and subject to God, he rightly describes himself as subject, when we his members are in every respect obedient to God.

But if you wish to examine yourself thoroughly and see whether you are now subject to God, or if you are as yet still disobedient, this is the way to scrutinize yourself: if there is nothing contrary to God in you, then you are subject to him.[17] But we mean "contrary" in this way: "God is love";[18] if there is

15. 1 Cor 12.27: ὑμεῖς δὲ ἐστε σῶμα Χριστοῦ καὶ μέλη ἐκ μέρους; the text of Rufinus reads *et unusquisque nostrum membra ex parte;* the Vulgate has simply *et membra de membro.*

16. Cf. *Fragm in Jn* 45 [GCS 4.520]: καὶ ἑτέρᾳ δὲ ἐκκλησίᾳ γράφων ὁ αὐτὸς ἀπόστολος μνημονεύσας τοῦ Ἀδὰμ καὶ τῆς γυναικὸς ἐπιφέρει. Τὸ μυστήριον τοῦτο μέγα ἐστιν, ἐγὼ δὲ λέγω εἰς Χριστὸν καὶ τὴν ἐκκλησίαν, ἵνα ὡς ἐκεῖνοι γονεῖς ἐγένοντο πάντων ἀνθρώπων, οὕτως ὁ Χριστὸς καὶ ἡ ἐκκλησία πάντων τῶν ἀγαθῶν ἔργων, νοημάτων τε καὶ λόγων, γεννήτορες ὦσιν. Cf. also Origen's account of Christ's Body in an explicitly apologetic context, *Contra Celsum* 6.48 [SC 147.298–300].

17. Jas 4.7–10 seems to be the "lens" through which the following is understood.

18. 1 Jn 4.16.

no hatred in you, you do not have what is contrary to God. God is Truth;[19] see that there is no deceit in you, for it is opposed to the Truth. For if there is deceit in you, you are not subject to God, but to him who is the father of lies.[20] If there is injustice in you, you are subject to the father of injustice rather than to God, who is Justice.[21] If you detect the remaining vices[22] in yourself, know that as long as they remain, you are subject not to God, but to the devil. For example, it is clear that, at the moment of fornication, we are subject to the spirit of fornication and opposed to the spirit of chastity. At the moment of rage or wrath, we are subservient to the spirit of anger and resistant to the spirit of gentleness. For this reason then, seeing that our entire life is lived as a kind of struggle for obedience,[23] whether to Christ or to the one who is opposed to Christ, let us make every effort through the devout practice of prayer and training[24] to accomplish this: that we may never find ourselves obedient to the devil or to his wickedness, but that our every action, word, and thought may be found to be subject to Christ.

But what if perhaps you say, "What benefit is there if I am now subject when I have sinned previously and already been hindered by my failures?" There is no doubt that when we have done wrong we have not been subject to God, but when we stop our wrongdoing, then we have taken the first step toward subjection. When, therefore, we have been made subject to the fear of God and we stop sinning, then, too, do we receive the confidence to ask forgiveness for our earlier failures. But as long as we persist in our failures, we seek forgiveness of our sins in vain. This is also why I remember telling you often that we ask for the forgiveness of our failures worthily when, situated far from sin, we are able to say, "Do not recall our sins of old."[25] It does not say "those things that we are doing," but

19. Jn 14.6.

20. *Mendacii pater;* cf. Jn 8.44.

21. Cf. Ps 16.1.

22. *reliqua in te ... vitia.*

23. *Agonem quendam obaudientiae.*

24. *Per orationis, per eruditionis religiosam institutionem,* taking *eruditio* as a Latin equivalent for ἄσκησις.

25. Ps 78.8.

rather, "those things that we once did." Therefore, *be subject to the Lord* and—being made subject—sin no more, *and* then *pray to him*[26] for your failings, both more recent and from of old.[27]

2. *Do not be jealous of him who is successful in his way, of the man who does evil.*[28] This describes human experience. For not infrequently if we see a wicked person prospering and living what people call the "happy life," we are scandalized and our faith is endangered; in our hearts we grumble against divine Providence and say, "What profit is there in good behavior? See, just persons experience hardships, but this unjust person lives happily. He is unjust, yet he has obtained the greatest wealth, he has climbed to the highest pinnacle of public office and power; perhaps being unjust is preferable to being just!" Unhealthy and fragile souls such as these, even if they do not utter a word, nevertheless say this in their heart when they see the wicked enjoying prosperity in their way of life.[29] And so this command comes to our aid as a medicine so that we do not become jealous when we see these things, that is, so that we do not provoke the Lord to anger against us by saying such things in our hearts. Instead, we ought to recall that this present age belongs to those who do not possess hope of the happiness to come.

So let us therefore endure patiently those who live prosperously here, who receive good things in their life,[30] until our own age arrives, the age to which we have been invited and whose goods have been promised to us, the age to which we look forward, in which we place our hope, whose goods do not pass away as a shadow does[31] in this age, but which last forever. Moreover, it is impossible to obtain good things both in this

26. Ps 36.7.

27. *Pro delictis praeteritis et antiquis;* while perhaps seemingly synonymous, the use of both *praeteritis* and *antiquis* may signal a distinction between recently past and long past; it is also possible that *praeteritis* implies not only "former," but also "previously omitted [withheld]" or "neglected [and only now recognized]."

28. Ps 36.7.

29. *Cum viderint iniquos prosperis successibus agere in via sua;* on this use of *via,* cf. *OLD* s.v. § 7.

30. Cf. Lk 16.25.

31. Cf. Wis 5.9.

present age and in the age to come. For it is inevitable that it be said to one individual: "You received your goods during your life"; and to another, "You received bad things," so that one receives good things in place of bad ones and the other bad things in place of good ones, just like, for example, that rich man and Lazarus.[32] For this reason, then, *Do not be jealous of him who is successful in his way, of the man who does evil.*

3. After this, it calls to our attention the vice by which nearly all of us are troubled, and I do not know if anywhere that rare individual is to be found who is so perfect as to be free from this affliction. It says, *Cease from anger and let go of indignation.*[33] There are many vices that are easily avoided by many people. For example, if someone has made a greater effort at chastity, he has cast off the evil of impurity. A considerable number of people have also mastered greed, so that, even though they are not perfect in other respects, they nevertheless seem to avoid this evil, and even a few others. But the vice of anger is harsh and sharp, and it inflames and disquiets even those who appear to be wise. This is why Solomon says in Proverbs, "Anger destroys even the wise";[34] that is, he is saying, "Do not be astonished if anger inflames the fool, the wicked, the unbeliever: it frequently disquiets even good and wise men."

This sin, then, is one of those that will add wood, straw, stubble to the building, and it is necessary that materials of this kind be tested, as it is written,[35] through fire, so that we remain in the fire as long as it takes for us to be purged of the wood of anger, the straw of indignation, and the stubble of words—words, that is, that we have uttered at the prompting of such vices. For this reason, then, *cease from anger and let go of indignation,* which is to say, when you are moved to anger, do not give in to your wrath,[36] but stop, let go, and disregard it.

But when we receive these commands, and are moved in precisely the opposite direction, we cease not from anger but

32. Cf. Lk 16.25.
33. Ps 36.8.
34. Cf. Prv 29.8.
35. Cf 1 Cor 3.11–13.
36. *Animis; animus* here is likely the equivalent of θυμός.

from gentleness, and we abandon not indignation, but meekness. But let us at least begin now to reform ourselves, and, little by little, soothing anger through self-control and continuous reflection,[37] let us also reach the point where we are angry no longer; and, continually beating back the onset of indignation, which is aroused through wrath, let us arrive even at the point at which we are no longer troubled by the impulse toward indignation. *Do not be zealous to do evil.*[38] Do not, it says, become evil yourself by provoking others to emulate your wickedness, because zeal for what is evil is always eager to outdo another in wickedness.

4. *For those who act wickedly will be driven away; but those who wait for the Lord will possess the land as an inheritance.*[39] It appears that wickedness is some other kind of evil, in addition to the rest of the sins.[40] This is why this sacred passage portrays one man as a sinner and another as wicked, just as it also employs a similar distinction when it says, "Break the arm of the sinner and of the evil-doer (*maligni*),"[41] meaning the wicked (*nequam*). But in the Gospel, the Lord also called the devil not only a sinner, but wicked or evil (*malignum vel malum*),[42] and when he teaches on prayer, he even says, "Deliver us from the Evil One,"[43] and elsewhere says that "an evil man (*malus*) has done this,"[44] meaning an evil-doer (*malignus*). Some define πονηρία, that is, wickedness (*nequitiam*), as intentional or voluntary wrongdoing (*malitiam*). For it is one thing to do evil through ignorance as if overcome by evil, but it is another to do what is

37. *Assiduam meditationem;* this could be rendered "constant practice" or "continuous exercise."

38. Ps 36.8; *aemulari* is explained in *Hom in Ps* 36.1.1 [SC 411.50–58]; cf. also SC 411.105, n. 2.

39. Ps 36.9.

40. This distinction occurs below at 7.

41. Ps 9.36 LXX (10.15).

42. Cf. Mt 13.19.

43. Mt 6.13; this is Origen's interpretation of this petition, rather than understanding it as a neuter substantive; cf. his *De oratione* 29.1–30.3 [GCS 3.381–395].

44. Mt 13.28; cf. Mt 13.38: τὰ δὲ ζιζάνιά εἰσιν οἱ υἱοὶ τοῦ πονηροῦ (Vlg = *zizania autem filii sunt nequam*).

evil willfully and with intent,[45] and this is wickedness [*nequitia*]. This is why the devil is rightly called by the name πονηρός, that is, Evil or Wicked One. But the Savior also chastises us when he said, "If then you, though wicked, know to give good things to your children."[46]

Therefore, now it says, *For those who act wickedly will be driven away; but those who wait for the Lord will possess the land as an inheritance.* There is, in addition, another kind of land, which Scripture says is "flowing with milk and honey,"[47] a land that the Savior also in the Gospels promised in return to those who are gentle (*mansuetis*) when he said, "Blessed are the meek (*mansueti*), for they will inherit the land."[48] This land of ours, in which we dwell, is appropriately called "dry land,"[49] just as this heaven, the one we gaze upon, is appropriately termed the "firmament."[50] But this firmament also takes the name "heaven" from the title of the other heaven, as the text of Genesis clearly teaches. What does this mean then? In this present life we use the terms "heaven" and "earth" for those visible entities in which we find nothing of the true heaven and true earth except the names. But I think they are called such here so that, when these are so named, those that are true and great will come to mind and engender a longing in those who use these names.

Who are the ones who will possess the land as an inheritance? *Those,* it says, *who wait for the Lord.* We wait for the Lord, for he is our Hope[51] and our Patience, as it is written: "And what now is my hope? Is it not the Lord?"[52] For just as our Savior is Wisdom[53] and Peace[54] and Justice,[55] so too he is also

45. *Voluntate et studio.*
46. Mt 7.11.
47. Cf. Ex 3.8.
48. Mt 5.5.
49. Cf. Gn 1.10.
50. Cf. Gn 1.8; cf. *De principiis* 2.11.6 [GK 450–454].
51. *Exspectatio;* the pun on the verb *exspectamus* ("we wait for") is lost in English.
52. Ps 38.8.
53. Cf. 1 Cor 24.30.
54. Cf. Eph 2.14.
55. Cf. 1 Cor 1.30.

our Hope and Patience. And just as we are made just through participation in his justice, and we become wise through participation in his wisdom, so also we are made patient by participation in his patience. Therefore, he is like an everlasting spring,[56] from which we can draw patience and justice and wisdom and everything whatsoever that is good from the virtues, but only if the vessels we bring to the spring are worthy and clean. Thus it says, *But those who wait for the Lord will possess the land as an inheritance.*

5. But after these words a certain mystical saying is added, one that is above my hearing and beyond my speech, and which transcends my understanding. For it speaks, whether in reference to all sinners or to some individual sinner, in the singular: *A little while longer, and the sinner will be no more.*[57] It speaks of this "little while" as being really from the present time until the end of the age, or, perhaps, even beyond the end of the age and until that avenging fire consumes those who are enemies.[58] But if it happens in some other way that "the sinner will be no more," then let one who is able investigate and determine how it can come about that "the sinner will be no more."

Nevertheless, *a little while longer, and the sinner will be no more; you will seek his place and you will not find him.*[59] Moreover, not only will the sinner no longer exist, but not even the sinner's place will exist. What does the "place of the sinner" mean except those things that pass away? For it says, "Heaven and earth will pass away."[60] Without a doubt, then, along with the sin that has passed away, the place of the sinner will also pass away.[61] "Heaven," it says, "and earth will pass away, but my words will not pass away."[62] Let us be eager, then, to do the words of God, which do not pass away, lest perchance we perish along with those things that pass away. For if we commit sin, which passes

56. Cf. Jn 4.14.
57. Ps 36.10.
58. Cf. Dt 9.3; Heb 12.29.
59. Ps 36.10.
60. Mt 24.35.
61. *Praeteriet* = *praeteribit;* cf. the Vulgate text of Wis 1.8 and Sir 39.37.
62. Mt 24.35; *terra,* of course, being rendered both "earth" and "land."

away, we will doubtless also be counted among those things that pass away. But if we act with justice,[63] which does not pass away, neither will we pass away, but we will abide in the company of the Justice that abides, according to what is written: "Is my hand not able to save you? Have I dulled my ear so that I do not hear you? Rather, it is your sins that cause separation between you and God."[64]

But further, it is not without some spiritual basis that from the beginning of creation a firmament is said to have been made which was to cause a separation between the waters and to divide the dwelling place of mortals from the abodes and dwelling places of the angels. It follows, then,[65] that this dry ground,[66] which the Lord also called "land,"[67] has been appointed as the place for us sinners. But there are also certain other places called "waters," over which the Spirit of the Lord is said to have hovered. There are certain other places called "the abyss," over which darkness is reported to have been placed.[68] Indeed, it is said in reference to the waters in another passage of Scripture that "the waters saw you, God; the waters saw you and were afraid."[69] But in reference to the abyss it says that "the abyss was thrown into confusion";[70] without doubt, this is because the abyss does not have peace, but darkness, placed over it. Moreover, the demons too are said in the Gospel to have asked not to be commanded to go off into the abyss,[71] as though into a kind of place of punishment suited to them and their activities. Not only, then, will the sinner be no more, but even his place, whatever it is, will be sought for and will not exist.

63. *Si autem facimus iustitiam,* correlated to *studeamus ergo nos facere verba Dei* and *si enim peccatum facimus,* hard to duplicate in English.

64. Is 59.1–2. The text here is substantially the same as found in the Vulgate; the LXX text is in the third person: ἢ ἐβάρυνεν τὸ οὖς αὐτοῦ τοῦ μὴ εἰσακοῦσαι.

65. *Ex eo ergo:* offering the *mystica ratio* referred to in the previous sentence. The link among all these texts is, of course, *terra.*

66. *Haec arida.*

67. Cf. Gn 1.10.

68. Cf. Gn 1.2: καὶ σκότος ἐπάνω τῆς ἀβύσσου.

69. Ps 76.17.

70. Ibid.

71. Cf. Lk 8.31.

6. *But the meek will possess the land.*[72] This verse is to be brought forward against the Valentinians and other heretics, who think that my Savior says in the Gospel things that are not found in the Old Testament,[73] just as we have learned from a certain elder[74] to bring forth such texts in order to confute them. But as to what is said in the Gospel: "Blessed are the meek, for they will possess the land,"[75] see how what was already said before by the Holy Spirit through David, Christ himself now speaks in the Gospel: "Blessed are the meek, for they will possess the land as an inheritance."

The prophet also rightly adds something more than we read in the Gospel when he says: *And they will find delight in an abundance of peace.*[76] Here the Greek also uses the same word, about which we have spoken earlier:[77] κατατρυφήσουσιν, meaning "they will delight," (*deliciabuntur*) rather than "they will find delight" (*delectabuntur*). In either case,[78] the meek *will find delight in an abundance of peace.* If men are fleshly, they find delight in the foods that will be destroyed along with their belly, just as the Apostle says: "Food is for the belly and the belly is for food, but God will destroy them both."[79] The saints, however, think little of these delights and spit them back;[80] for they possess their delight[81] *in an abundance of peace.* Yet "the abundance of peace" is said to exist in the days of the Christ, for so it is written: "And there will be an abundance of peace in his days, until the moon be taken away."[82]

Whoever, then, *ceases from anger and lets go of indignation,*[83] whose mind is not aroused to wrath, and who does not use

72. Ps 36.11.

73. *In antiquis litteris;* cf. Prinzivalli, ed., *Origene, Omelie sui Salmi* (1991), 424.

74. *Sicut et nos didicimus a quodam presbytero.*

75. Mt 5.5.

76. Ps 36.11.

77. Here again Rufinus distinguishes between *delectari* and *deliciari;* cf. *Hom in Ps* 36.1.4 [SC 411.76–80].

78. The best possible way, I think, to render: *Igitur deliciabuntur sive delectabuntur mansueti in multitudine pacis.*

79. 1 Cor 6.13.

80. *Respuunt;* fitting, given the metaphor.

81. Here Rufinus opts for the present idiom *habent delicias* for *delectabuntur.*

82. Ps 71.7.

83. Ps 36.8.

angry words, and who is totally at peace, not only externally but also internally, who does not succumb to one who provokes him to anger and does not himself provoke another to anger, but who keeps peace with himself and with others in the face of possible disagreement, who encourages the love of meekness, which is the guardian of peace, and who lives up to all his responsibilities faithfully,[84] this person delights or finds delight *in an abundance of peace.*

7. *The sinner will watch the just one and will grind his teeth against him.*[85] Just as, in nature, light is opposed to darkness, so too the sinner and the just person are opposed one to the other. If, at some point, you see a just person being hated,[86] do not hesitate to say about the one who hates the just person, "he is a sinner." If you see someone who lives a good life suffering persecution, do not hesitate to say concerning the one who is doing the persecuting, "Not only is he a sinner, he is wicked."[87] *The sinner,* then, *will watch the just one*—and, watching him—*will grind his teeth against him.* As to its saying: *he will grind his teeth,* I do not know if this should be understood in reference to bodily teeth, though it is possible that this too be done by a sinner against a just person. When he threatens him, when he rages against him, when his voice is silent but his rage is roaring,[88] when he lays traps for the just person and plots every kind of evil against him, then what is said is fulfilled in a bodily way also: *he will grind his teeth against him.* But when the sinner does these things against the just man, *The Lord,* it says, *will laugh at him, for he foresees that his day will come.*[89] What day belonging to the sinner does the Lord foresee? That day, no doubt, when the sinner will be sought for, but will be no more.

8. *Sinners have drawn the sword; they have bent their bow to cast*

84. *Fidelissimaque cuncta moderatur;* more literally, "and who governs all things in a most dependable fashion"; or, perhaps alternately and even more loosely, "and is completely reliable."

85. Ps 36.12.

86. *Odio haberi;* cf. *Hom in Ps* 37.2.8 [SC 411.322].

87. This distinction between *peccatum* and *nequitia* is found earlier at 4. See above, pp. 100–101.

88. *Cum silet voce clamat furore.*

89. Ps 36.13.

down the needy and the poor.[90] Not that every kind of sinner[91] possesses a bodily (*corporalem*) sword; rather, let us see if perhaps, just as there are certain armaments of God (among which are said to be the breastplate of justice and the sword of the Spirit and the shield of faith),[92] there are not also certain armaments of the devil with which a sinful person is clad. Therefore, let us understand this opposition on the basis of contraries:[93] let us imagine two armed soldiers, one a soldier of God, the other a soldier of the devil. If indeed the soldier of God possesses a breastplate of justice, without a doubt the soldier of the devil wears a breastplate of injustice opposed to it. And if the soldier of God shines in a helmet of salvation,[94] in opposition the sinner, who is a soldier of the devil, wears a helmet of perdition. And if the feet of the soldier of Christ are readied for the race of preaching of the Gospel,[95] on the contrary the feet of the sinner are swift to spill blood,[96] and his shoes (that is, what he is prepared for) are readied for sin. The soldier of God, then, possesses a kind of shield of faith while the soldier of the devil has a shield of infidelity.

So, too, there is what one might call a sword of the Holy Spirit in the possession of those who are soldiers for God;[97] but there is also a sword of evil in the possession of those who are soldiers for sin; this is the sword sinners are here said to draw.[98] But in what way are we to think of sinners as drawing a sword? When without shame or any pretense of embarrassment, they carry out their wicked designs and neither blush nor show fear, and do not put away their malice as in a scabbard and conceal it, but with a proud and exalted spirit flash it like some kind of sword. Similarly, they also act out what follows: namely, *they have bent their bow.*[99] But the just, too, have a bow, and they also

90. Ps 36.14.
91. *Non quo omni genere peccatores.*
92. Cf. Eph 6.13–17.
93. *A contrariis igitur intellegamus contraria.*
94. Cf. Is 59.17; Eph 6.14–16.
95. Cf. Eph 6.14–16; 2 Tm 4.7.
96. Cf. Is 59.7; Rom 3.15.
97. Cf. 2 Tm 2.4.
98. In reference to Ps 36.14.
99. Ps 36.14.

have arrows. In fact, one of their arrows is the Lord Jesus, for he himself professes: "And he placed me as a chosen arrow."[100] And so the just possess arrows, as do sinners.

A word is an arrow. Indeed, a word from a just person, when it reproves and corrects the sinner, punctures and pierces the heart of the sinner like an arrow so that he might be converted to penance and be saved. A word from a sinner, however, is poisoned and shoots and wounds the one who is not protected by the armaments of God. For the words of the wicked prevail against us when we are less than carefully protected by the shield of faith.[101] *They have bent their bow,* then, *to cast down the needy and the poor.* Sinners know that they are unable to cast down the rich person, and so they do not lay snares for him, but all their snares are designed against the poor man, as it is also said elsewhere that "he lurks like a lion in his den; he lurks that he might seize the poor man."[102]

And so "the ransom of a man"—a rich man—"is his wealth, but the poor cannot sustain threats."[103] And so let us become rich in spiritual goods,[104] rich, that is, "in every word and in all knowledge,"[105] in good works,[106] casting aside the riches of sin, looking ahead "not to the things that are seen, but those that are not seen. For those riches that are seen are temporary; but those that are not are eternal."[107] And if we grow wealthy in such riches, we cannot be wounded by the arrows of sinners. For they will be deflected[108] by the shield of faith,[109] through Christ our Lord and Savior, "to whom are glory and power for ever and ever. Amen."[110]

100. Is 49.2. For Origen, it is Christ who is speaking through Isaiah; cf. *Hom in Ps* 37.1.2 [SC 411.272].

101. Cf. Eph 6.1.6 and above.

102. Ps 9.30.

103. Prv 13.8; "ransom" (here *redemptio*) renders the LXX λύτρον.

104. Cf. 1 Tm 6.18.

105. 1 Cor 1.5.

106. Cf. 2 Cor 9.8.

107. 2 Cor 4.18.

108. *Restinguentur;* or "neutralized"; cf. *OLD* s.v. § 2.b.

109. Cf. Eph 6.16.

110. 1 Pt 4.11; 5.11.

THIRD HOMILY ON PSALM 36 [37]

IN AN EARLIER homily, we were speaking about the sword and the bow of sinners and about the armor of God, and that all people have been fitted with armaments. And since I said "all people," I will now add what was left unsaid earlier, namely, that these are people who are capable of sinning or refraining from sin. For infants are incapable of handling either the armaments of God or those of the devil. But those who have become capable of knowing what is right and of avoiding what is contrary to it—in word, thought, or action—these are the ones who are all said to possess armaments. And so, if they sin, they possess the armaments of the devil and of iniquity; but if they act rightly, they will be said to be clothed in the armor of God.

We were explaining what was said, *Sinners have drawn the sword, they have bent their bow,*[1] with reference to the Apostle, who spoke concerning their opposite: "And the sword of the Spirit which is the Word of God";[2] for the sword of sinners is the wicked spirit that is in them, who inspires them to blasphemous, wicked, and disgraceful words. For example, if you see pagans bickering and disputing among themselves, throwing various impieties against each other with the tricks of dialectic, then you can correctly say, *Sinners have drawn the sword.* But even I, who am called a believer, if I am perhaps engaged in a struggle with someone, and if, having been provoked to wrath and having abandoned meekness, I should spout ravings from a lying spirit[3] and reveal that I am swollen with poisonous

1. Ps 36.14.
2. Eph 6.17.
3. Crouzel suggests this *spiritus mendacis* refers to a line above: *spiritus … nequam, qui eos inspirat ad verba blasphemiae* [SC 411.128].

words, I, too, am rightly said to be a "sinner who has drawn his sword."

Therefore, the best thing[4] is not even to possess a sword of sin, or at least[5] not to draw it, but to keep it in its scabbard. For if the sword is not pulled from its scabbard, nor made use of, its edge becomes dull and it rusts, and if it never sees action, it will be thoroughly destroyed. The Lord also makes this promise: that he will destroy the sword[6] (that is, sin), so that the sinner will be no more.[7] But certainly if, because of the admonitions of God's Word, we anticipate this task, and if, while in this life, we make the sin in us perish, so that the sword of sin is never at all drawn by us—whether in thought, deed, or word—we will have no need[8] for the punishment of eternal fire,[9] nor will we be condemned to the outer darkness,[10] nor will we find ourselves under those penalties that threaten sinners.[11] But if, in this life, we disregard the words of divine Scripture that admonish us and we do not wish to be healed or reformed by its words of correction, it is certain that that fire which has been prepared for sinners awaits us, and we will encounter that fire which "will test the quality of each one's work."[12]

Further, in my opinion, it is necessary for all of us to encounter that fire. Even if one be a Paul or a Peter, he will nevertheless come to that fire. But individuals like these hear: "Even though you pass through fire, the flame will not burn you."[13] But if someone is a sinner like me, he will indeed come to that fire like Peter and Paul, but he will not pass through it in the same way as Peter and Paul.

4. *Bonum igitur primum.*

5. *Secundum vero est saltim.*

6. Cf. Ps 9.7 [LXX]; *romphaeam* [= ῥομφαίαν]; cf. also below, at 5, p. 116 n. 58.

7. Cf. Ps 36.10.

8. Here, typical of Origen, penalties and punishments are understood as remedial.

9. Cf. Jude 7.

10. Cf. Mt 8.12.

11. Cf. Mt 25.46.

12. 1 Cor 3.13.

13. Is 43.2.

Just as the Hebrews came to the Red Sea, so too the Egyptians came, but the Hebrews passed through the Red Sea, while the Egyptians were drowned in it.[14] In this way, too, if we are indeed Egyptians and we follow Pharaoh, the devil, and are obedient to his commands,[15] we sink into that river[16] or lake[17] of fire, since sins have been discovered in us that surely we have chosen under the commands of Pharaoh. If, however, we are Hebrews, and have been redeemed by the blood of the spotless lamb,[18] if we do not carry with us the leaven[19] of wickedness,[20] we also enter the river of fire. Yet just as the water was a wall for the Hebrews on the right and on the left,[21] so also there will be a wall of fire, if we, too, do what was said of the Hebrews, that "they had faith in God and in his servant, Moses,"[22] that is, in his law and his commandments, and if we follow the pillar of fire and the pillar of cloud.[23] We have brought these things to mind as an admonition as we review the explanation of how *sinners have drawn the sword.*

2. But we should not carelessly pass over the fact that they are said to have *bent their bow.*[24] This we manage not by a juxtaposition of contraries as in the other passages, but from a comparison.[25] In the tenth Psalm it is written: "Sinners have bent the bow, they have readied arrows in the quiver that they might shoot the upright of heart in the dark."[26] Hence it is clear that the heart of the impious, like a quiver, is filled with poisoned arrows. The arrows of the impious are therefore their utterly wicked plans and designs; in fact, their mouth and lips are like

14. Cf. Ex 14.22–29.
15. Cf. Jos 24.24.
16. Cf. Dn 7.10–11.
17. Cf. Rv 19.20.
18. Cf. 1 Pt 1.19.
19. Cf. Ex 12.34.
20. Cf. 1 Cor 5.8.
21. Cf. Ex 14.29.
22. Ex 14.31.
23. Cf. Ex 13.21.
24. Ps 36.14.
25. Cf. above, contrasting the *arma diaboli* to the *arma Dei;* cf. also *Hom in Ps* 36.2.8 [SC 411.118].
26. Ps 10.2.

a kind of bow, by which, once expanded and stretched, they hurl darts from a poisoned heart. Moreover, the words "in the dark" are said fittingly. For individuals such as these do not move about in the day,[27] that is, in the light of God, but walk rather in the darkness and lurk in the shadows of wickedness and ignorance. Now as to their shooting the upright of heart, that means the simple and those who are unaware of their malicious designs. I think, however, that this phrase is uttered not so much about sinful humans as about the opposing powers;[28] for they are the ones who "shoot the upright of heart in the dark."

For this reason, then, those who are upright of heart should be alert day and night because "they have readied arrows." It did not say "they have hurled" but rather "they have readied arrows"; they have not shot them yet, nor have they caused wounds, but they are readying themselves to shoot. You see that we are warned before we are wounded, so that we can defend ourselves against their blows[29] and take every precaution to safeguard our heart.

3. I also want to uncover something further while we find ourselves among these passages, so that we might not always be speaking to you concerning lower things, but that we might also from time to time take a stab at some of the higher things. I think, then, that just as the Savior is the arrow of God, as is written, "And he placed me as a chosen arrow,"[30] without doubt in a similar way, Moses, in whom he has spoken, is also an arrow of God. And it is certain that the other prophets and apostles of Christ, in whom Christ himself was speaking,[31] wounded and pierced with the arrow of God the heart of those to whom they were speaking the word of God, so that those who heard them speak would say, "I am wounded with charity."[32] Then again, on the other hand, in the same way that Christ is the

27. Cf. Rom 13.13.

28. *Contrariis potestatibus;* cf. Eph 6.12. Eph 6.10–17 appears to provide an interpretive "lens" for understanding these verses.

29. *Ab illorum vulneribus;* here meaning "blows" more than "wounds."

30. Is 49.2.

31. Cf. 2 Cor 13.3.

32. Song 2.5.

chosen arrow of God,[33] so also Antichrist is the arrow of the devil. And, following this comparison, just as all the prophets and apostles in whom Christ has spoken or is speaking were themselves also the arrows of God, and every just person and preacher who speaks the word of God for the salvation of others can be called an arrow of God, so too, all sinners in whom the devil speaks can be called arrows of the devil. So, then, when you see yourself wounded by arrows of the devil through the mouth of a sinner, have compassion for the one who reveals himself to be a servant of the devil for this task.[34] You, however, take thought for yourself[35] and take hold of the shield of faith, so that you might be able "to extinguish all the fiery darts of the Evil One"[36] with it.

Yet the darts of the devil are directed at us not only verbally, but also in deeds. If you see a woman lying in wait to beguile you, is she not also a fiery dart of the devil, since she speaks to you in such a way as to kindle in you the fire of lust? In like manner, if someone should arouse you to anger through bitter and harsh words, is he too not a fiery dart of the Evil One, by which you are inflamed and are kindled toward rage?[37] Or further, if someone provokes you and goads you in some other way, which you are unable to bear patiently, and you fall into sin, understand carefully and observe that all these individuals are fiery darts of the Evil One, by means of which he can wound the upright of heart and inflame[38] them toward sin.

But even more unhappily, I see few arrows of God, few in-

33. Cf. Is 49.2.

34. Origen here presumes a distinction between the devil, who is the source of the verbal barbs, and the sinner, who is merely the instrument.

35. Nice parallelism with genitive objects: *illius quidem miserere ... tu autem memor esto tui.*

36. Eph 6.16; Origen elsewhere treats the issue of the "fiery darts" of the Evil One: cf. *De principiis* 3.2.4 [GK 574–576], in relation to the *cogitationes* (= λογισμοί, later developed taxonomically by Evagrius), which are insinuated by the demons, as well as to particular memories, *memoriae quaedam*, aroused by demonic influence; and 4.3.12 [GK 766–770], where the military language of Eph is explicitly evoked; and *Hom in Gen* 10.4 [SC 7bis.268], where he speaks of the *concupiscentiae iacula* directed by the devil at the soul.

37. There is a less than subtle play on the various words for heat–flame–fire.

38. Cf. Ps 10.2.

dividuals who speak in such a way as to inflame the heart of their hearer and draw him away from sin that he might be converted[39] to penance. There are few who speak in such a way that elicits a tear of repentance from the eye of the hearer whose heart has been struck. There are few who, revealing the light of future hope and bearing witness to the greatness of the world to come and the glory of the Kingdom of God, are capable of persuading men to think little of the things that are seen and to seek out what is unseen, to reject what is temporal and to pursue what is eternal.[40] Such as these are quite few, and in the case of these few (if there are any), because of envy and resentment they are unable even to be of benefit to any.

But the arrows of the devil abound everywhere; the entire earth is rife with them. The peoples, the cities, the military are, for the most part, arrows of the Evil One—would that they were found only there!—and the Enemy held sway among them so as to possess them solely as arrows of his own. But as it is, I am fearful also for those who are within,[41] and I fear for myself, lest the devil lead me into some scandal and make use of me as an arrow against another's soul![42] For the one who would scandalize anyone, whether in word or in deed, becomes an arrow and a dart of the devil for that soul which he has scandalized.

See what greater misfortune befalls us. When from time to time we consider speaking against someone and blurt out words recklessly, when we act quite contentiously and are eager to prevail by means of any words whatsoever, it is then that the devil makes use of our mouth like a bow, through which he points his arrows and shoots the upright of heart,[43] that is, those who hear us saying things that cause them to suffer scandal.

39. *Sed quod est infelicius, paucas video sagittas Dei, pauci sunt qui ita loquuntur ut inflamment cor auditoris et abstrahant eum a peccato et convertatur ad paenitentiam* [SC 411.136]; *convertatur,* taken here as passive; one is tempted to emend the text to *convertantur,* understanding it as deponent and whose subject is *pauci* rather than *auditor,* and thus paralleled with *abstrahant,* whose shared direct object is *eum.*

40. Cf. 2 Cor 4.18.

41. *Eos qui intus sunt* = members of the Church.

42. *Adversus animam hominis,* lit., "against a man's soul."

43. Cf. Ps 10.2.

In the same way that God placed a bow in the clouds,[44] that a flood should not occur and that the storm should dissipate, so too—in an opposite fashion—the devil places a bow, not to cause them to dissipate, but to stir up storms, to disturb the soul's calm, to dispel peace, to incite conflicts, and to arouse winds and tempests. For when you see someone going around driven by vices and passions and setting everything on edge, do not doubt that this individual is an arrow of the devil and that the devil has placed his mouth as his bow and that he has aimed his words as arrows, to shoot the upright of heart.[45] But those who are protected by the armor of God are incapable of being wounded by such arrows.[46]

4. Moreover, as to its having added, *that they might murder the upright of heart,*[47] since, just before, it had said *that they might kill the needy and the poor,*[48] it has connected the upright of heart with the poor. I think the Lord also, in the Gospels, links them in a similar way, for where he says the poor are blessed,[49] there he also declares blessed the clean of heart,[50] and I do not think there is any difference between the clean of heart and the upright of heart. Now this is how they are murdered. If someone who is simple in mind and in intention enters the Church that he might make progress, so that he might become better than he is, if this person sees us, who have been established in the faith for some time, either not acting rightly or speaking scandalously, we become for him the cause of his fall into sin. Moreover, when he sins, he has been murdered, the blood of his soul spills out, and his very life departs from him.

And if you hear it said in Genesis that "I will require the blood of your souls from every brother and every beast,"[51] you should not think that its admonition is so much about bodily blood as it is about the blood of the inner man, that is, the life

44. Cf. Gn 9.13–16.
45. Cf. Ps 10.2.
46. Cf. Eph 6.16.
47. Ps 36.14b.
48. Ps 36.14a.
49. Cf. Mt 5.3; Lk 6.20.
50. Cf. Mt 5.8.
51. Gn 9.5a.

of the soul and the blood of the spirit. For the blood of the soul of one who has been scandalized is poured out when he has fallen into sin, and this is why it says that blood is required from his brother.

But why also from a beast? If it is a believer who scandalizes you, he is a brother from whom your blood must be required. For it is your brother who has spilled your blood, and for this reason it was said, "From the hand of the brother I will require blood."[52] But when the opposing power, wild and wicked, stirs a person into action, and when it is an unbeliever through whom he secretly works, if he has been able to spill the blood of your soul (that is, to throw you into sin), he is a beast from whom the Lord requires your blood. Further, the prophet Ezekiel, when he calls himself a watchman appointed for the house of Israel,[53] if he announced the coming sword, would not be made guilty of blood, but if he did not announce it, he would be guilty of blood;[54] and when it says in the Law, if one does these things, he will be innocent of blood,[55] this too without a doubt is a reference to the blood of the soul, which is poured out through sin. For this reason we all ought to fear lest perhaps the blood of another who is scandalized be required of us, as the prophet indicates.

It was necessary for us to go over these matters again in order to show more fully how *Sinners have drawn the sword,* and *have bent their bow,*[56] and who the poor one is whom they kill and how the upright of heart are murdered and in particular what it means to say that their blood is poured out.

5. But now let us see what is to become of these very sinners who do these things, that is, who use the sword of the devil and the darts of the Evil One; [let us see] what the Divine Word again says about them: *Let their two-edged sword* (*framea*), it says, *enter into their own heart, and let their bow be broken.*[57] A two-edged sword is a type of weapon called by this name

52. Gn 9.5b.
53. Cf. Ezek 3.17.
54. Cf. Ezek 3.18–19.
55. Cf. Dt 21.8–9.
56. Ps 36.14.
57. Ps 36.15.

(*framea*).[58] It says that these words, then, which the wicked and the sinful, under the devil's inspiration, direct against the just in order to *murder the upright of heart,*[59] are to be turned against those very ones who shoot them and are to return to the place from which they had come. Just as it is said by the Lord to the just and to the holy apostles, "Into whatever house you enter, say, 'Peace to this house'; and if a son of peace is there, your peace will come upon him. If not, your peace will be returned to you,"[60] so also here conversely the sword of the impious that is drawn to murder the upright of heart is said to be turned back against them and plunged into their heart, and their bow is said to be broken while the Lord frees the just one from their snares.

6. *A small amount is better to the just than the abundant riches of sinners.*[61] This admonition is, on the literal level, immediately useful to those who are more simple, and this must be spoken of first, though there is also here something more profound, which, "if someone is able to receive, let him receive it."[62] So let us see what the letter teaches us.

In this world, both the just and the unjust share a concern for life, to have the things necessary for survival. Yet the just are less inclined to be concerned about their survival than they are earnestly concerned about justice, so that, although they must seek things that are necessary for their survival,

58. Prinzivalli, *Origene, Omelie sui Salmi* (1991), 428–29, citing TLL, VI.1.1239, notes that *framea* translates ῥομφαία and renders *genus teli est* as "un tipo di lancia"; it is used earlier, at 1. Throughout the Vulgate Psalter *gladius* is generally used to render ῥομφαία, including Ps 36.15, and, e.g., 43.4 and 7; 88.44; and 149.6 (cf. also Rv 1.16), where it is modified as *gladii ancipites* (=ῥομφαία δίστομοι). An exception is the Vulgate Ps 16.13 (*iuxta* LXX, though not the *iuxta* Hebraicum, which uses *gladius*), where *framea* renders ῥομφαία of the LXX. It is unclear why Rufinus would here employ *framea* for ῥομφαία (and feel the need to explain it) when earlier (above at 1, p. 109 n. 6) he was content to use the transliterated *romphaea.* The earlier classical use of *framea* is for a spear or javelin, i.e., some kind of missile (which is why it is explained as *genus teli est*).

59. Ps 36.14.

60. Lk 10.5–6.

61. Ps 36.16.

62. Mt 19.12.

they are sought without injustice,[63] so that their very income, necessary for their daily use, is acquired with complete justice. But the unjust care nothing for justice, but devote their entire concern to this: how to acquire. All their striving is devoted to seizing whatever profits they can in whatever manner they can. They do not ask if they are acquiring honestly, if they are acquiring with justice; they do not care whether in the judgment of Christ their possessions are determined to have been sought justly. How can they do such things, those who annex one field to another and appropriate property after property[64] so as to snatch something from their neighbor?

Since, then, one of two things necessarily happens—either many things are acquired with injustice or a small amount is acquired with justice—it says, *A small amount is better to the just than the abundant riches of sinners.*[65] In fact, "abundant riches" in wickedness are designated by a particular name.[66] This is also why I think that our Lord and Savior proclaimed the Mammon of wickedness to be very much a kind of god and lord[67] when he says, "Make for yourselves friends from wicked Mammon."[68] This is the literal meaning.

Let us now see if these words also contain something hidden. There are, in this world, many different literary studies, and you may see a great number of individuals starting out by

63. *Absque iniustitia quaerantur;* a nice example of litotes.

64. Cf. Is 5.8; 1 Kgs 21; cf. *Hom in Ps* 36.1.2 [SC 411.68–70].

65. Ps 36.16.

66. Which he explains as "Mammon."

67. A clever juxtaposition of "Lord and Savior" (*Dominum et Salvatorem*) with "god and lord" (*deum et dominum*).

68. Lk 16.9: *Facite vobis amicos de iniquo mammona.* This is an uncommon reading. The Vulgate reads *mammona iniquitatis.* The bilingual Codex Bezae and the earlier 4th-century Latin Vercellensis read ἀδίκου μαμμωνᾶ and *iniquo mammona,* respectively. Cf. Adolf Jülicher, *Itala: Das Neue Testament in altlateinischer Überlieferung* (Berlin: De Gruyter, 1954), 4.186. This is the reading known to and used by Ambrose, *De Abraham* 1.5 [CSEL 32.528] and *Expositio evangelii secundum Lucam* [SC 52.99], as well as his biographer Paulinus [PL 14.41]. Unfortunately, Origen's extant *Homilies on Luke* do not cite this verse. On the value of the Vercelli manuscript and the Latin of Codex Bezae, see Philip Burton, *The Old Latin Gospels: A Study of their Texts and Language* (Oxford: Oxford University Press, 2000), esp. 21–23.

learning from grammarians the songs of the poets and comedic stories, the fictitious and harrowing accounts found in the tragedies, the lengthy and diverse volumes of histories, and then next moving on to rhetoric, there to pursue every conceit of eloquence. After these things, they come to philosophy, to a thorough examination of dialectic, to investigate the relations among syllogisms, to probe the powers of geometry, to examine astronomy[69] and the courses of the stars, not to mention music, as well.[70] Thus educated in all such varied and different disciplines, through which they have learned nothing about the will of God, they have indeed gathered abundant riches, yet these are the riches of sinners.

You may see, however, a member of the Church, unskilled indeed in word and lacking in education, but full of faith and the fear of God, who, because of that fear of God, does not dare to sin in any way, but is quite afraid to open his mouth, lest by chance a bad word come forth from it, and, further, keeps his guard up against failing in the slightest way. The one who is rich in the wisdom of this world is incapable of being on guard against such things. It is in comparing these two that the divine word says, *A small amount is better to the just than the abundant riches of sinners.*[71] Even though the "riches of sinners"[72] do exist—the wisdom of this world, in which they are rich and abounding in eloquence—nevertheless they do not succeed, by means of these things, in keeping themselves from sin, while the "small amount" of the just person, who has faith as small as a mustard seed,[73] nonetheless a fully alive and ardent faith, by means of which he protects himself and keeps himself from

69. *Astrorum leges:* a calque for ἀστρονομία.

70. For the view that this ancient *paideia* was ultimately concerned with moral formation, see Ilsetraut Hadot, *Arts libéraux et philosophie dans la pensée antique* (Paris: Études Augustiniennes, 1984).

71. Ps 36.16; it is worth noting that the contrast between the sinners and the just is heightened by the contrast between the plural (*peccatores*) and the singular (*iusto*), which is not easily replicated in English; this is carried over in Origen's interpretive scheme.

72. *Ut sint divitiae peccatorum,* a concessive clause correlated with the following *nec tamen.*

73. Cf. Mt 17.20.

sin, this *small amount* of faith *is better to the just than the abundant riches of sinners,* which they possess in eloquence and in the wisdom of this world, which is brought to nothing.[74]

Nevertheless, if someone is able to possess riches, but not the riches of sinners, and to gather some things from the treasuries of Moses the Lawgiver, and also to acquire some other things from the wealth of the prophets, from Isaiah, from Jeremiah, and from Ezekiel, to examine as well the mysteries of Daniel, and to penetrate the hidden and concealed treasuries of the other prophets, this person is no longer compared to the wise of this world, so as to be called better than they, but is instead regarded as equal to those to whom it is said, "For you have become rich in every word and in all knowledge."[75] These, who are destroying the wisdom of this world and who have become as it were its conquerors, say that they are ready to take captive "all understanding that exalts itself and sets itself up against the knowledge of Christ."[76] And although the one whom we have mentioned before is uneducated and unlettered, yet he is a believer and is God-fearing, that *small amount* of faith *is better to* this *just* person *than the abundant riches of sinners,* which they acquire from the wisdom of this world.[77] But superior to both of these[78] is one who is rich in the word of God and in the knowledge of truth, namely one who (as Paul says) is rich both "in every word and in all knowledge"[79] and who is no less rich in good works.

But if you want to know what it means to be rich in every word, I will teach you briefly. Begin your inquiry first with the word[80] of Genesis, then on to the word of Exodus, after these

74. *Destruitur,* possibly rendering καταργεῖτε; cf. 1 Cor 2.6 and 1.19 (quoting Is 29.14).

75. Emending the text, which has *qui dicebant,* to *quibus dicebatur,* as Paul is the one speaking in 1 Cor 1.5.

76. 2 Cor 10.5.

77. Cf. 1 Cor 2.6.

78. "Both of these" refers to (a) the just and (b) sinners to whom the Psalmist refers.

79. 1 Cor 1.5.

80. A synecdoche, as the use of *verbum* here seems a reference to the text of the Scriptures taken as a whole unit; the "word of Exodus" seems to mean, for example, the text or teaching of Exodus as a whole; but one should not overlook

in the word of Leviticus, in Numbers, and in Deuteronomy; enrich yourself from Joshua son of Nun, and likewise from all the Judges; then from there in order from each and every one of the books of divine Scripture, until you reach the riches of the evangelists and apostles.

For example, someone who directs his attention to a word of the Psalms and who chants the entire Psalter[81] at will is certainly rich, but not "in every word and in all knowledge," but rich in the word of the Psalter alone. Or if someone should direct his efforts to the Gospels and to a reading of the apostles and exercises himself in the teachings of the New Testament, this one is rich too, but not in every word, but only in the word of the evangelists and apostles. But if he is capable of thoroughly learning the Old and the New Testament with equal devotion and is informed by means of all his learning, so that he is ready to offer an account concerning each word that has been written and to adjust his life in accord with the word of the truth that is contained in the Scriptures, then this is a person who is truly rich in every word[82] and in every good work.[83] In my view, these are the riches about which it is said: "The redemption of a person's life is his riches."[84] *A small amount,* then, *is better to the just than the abundant riches of sinners.*[85]

7. *For the arms of sinners will be broken.*[86] How can this stand in a literal sense, even if someone might try unwittingly to do violence? There are many things in the Scriptures expressed in this way, which are capable of arousing even one who is profoundly dense and sleepy, indeed of forcing him to see that it

the fact that for Origen all the *words* of Scripture convey and ultimately reveal *the* Word.

81. For the use of the Psalter in the early Christian communities, see James McKinnon, *Music in Early Christian Literature* (Cambridge: Cambridge University Press, 1986), esp. 10–11 on the difficulty of reconstructing much of what went on with psalmody in the first Christian centuries; for other texts of Origen regarding psalmody and hymnody, see 36–41.

82. Cf. 1 Cor 1.6, which has formed the "lens" for interpreting this passage for the last two paragraphs.

83. Cf. 2 Cor 9.8.

84. Prv 13.8.

85. Ps 36.16.

86. Ps 36.17.

is necessary for him to make every effort, once he has abandoned the letter, to rise up to a spiritual understanding; it is in just this way that these "arms of the sinner" are now functioning, whose "breaking," it warns, is near at hand. But in another place it says, "Break the arm of the sinner and evildoer."[87] What then? Are we to think that the bodily arm of the sinner is to be broken? We see that this does not easily happen.

But if we look at how sinners, when puffed up with pride, have both their bows and those arrows of theirs (about which we have already spoken) ready and have drawn them against the just, and when we see this entire scheme of theirs shattered by the might of the Lord, it is in this way that the arm of the sinner is rightly said to have been broken. Or in another sense, the hand and the arm signify work. If, then, you should see a sinner not reaching out his hand to a good work, a work of mercy,[88] it will not be unreasonable to say that his arm has been broken. But it must not be believed that this kind of breaking comes from God, but from the devil. For he is the one who breaks and binds[89] the arms of sinners so that they do not extend them in mercy.

Therefore, a certain kind of breaking of sinners comes from God, when he destroys and frightens off those who plot against the just one. But there is also what one might call a breaking that comes from the devil, when he hinders the exercise of a good deed as if by binding and breaking the arms of unbelievers. There is also another breaking, which is indeed permitted by God but which is carried out by the devil, that breaking about which the devil spoke to the Lord: "But stretch forth your hand and touch all that he [Job] possesses, if he should not bless you to your face";[90] and then he received him into his power. This is why Job himself said, "For it is the hand of the Lord that has touched me."[91]

87. Ps 10.15.

88. *Ad opus bonum, ad opus misericordiae;* a clear reference to the various works of mercy that follow in the homily.

89. *Conterit et constringit.*

90. Jb 1.11.

91. Jb 19.21.

8. *But the Lord supports the just.*[92] Those who are weak and frail need another for support.[93] Where collapse and fall threaten, there support is sought. Moreover, taking into account human frailty, every human is both weak and liable to fall. Indeed, in this Psalm it is written that *the Lord supports the just,* yet in another it says, "The Lord supports all who fall and raises those who are crushed."[94] It only remains for us to stir ourselves[95] at last and wake up, so that if, when some fall[96] threatens through weakness, we might beg the Lord to send us his Word and his Wisdom,[97] which supports and raises up those who are about to fall.

9. *The Lord knows the days of those without blemish, and their inheritance will be forever.*[98] According to the Scriptures, as we have seen in many other passages, the Lord does not know all things, but only those things that are good; he is said not to know the bad, not because there is actually something that is hidden from his knowledge, but he is said not to know those things that are not worthy of his knowing. We have also demonstrated this on the basis of the Scriptures, when the Apostle says, "If there is a prophet or spiritual one among you, he should know what I am writing to you, for it is of the Lord. But if someone does not know, he will not be known";[99] and in the Gospel, when the Lord speaks to sinners: "I do not know

92. Ps 36.17.

93. *Suffultore;* taking the *-or* ending as indicative of an agent.

94. Ps 144.14.

95. Understanding *expergiscamur* as a medial passive.

96. *Casus aliquis* [= *aliqui*]; the indefinite pronoun used for the indefinite adjective.

97. Cf. *Hom in Ps* 36.4.2 [SC 411.200]: *Vides ergo quia semper Dei auxilio indigemus. Primo ne cademus, tum deinde etiam si ceciderimus, ut resurgamus.* For Irenaeus, the Son and the Spirit are the two "hands" of God employed in the creation of humankind; cf. *Adversus haereses* 4.20.1 [SC 100.626] and 5.1.3 [SC 153.26]. Cf. also Theophilus, *Ad Autolycum,* 1.7 and 2.15 [*Ad Autolycum,* ed. Robert M. Grant (Oxford: Clarendon, 1970), 10, 50–52]; at 1.7 God is called the Physician who employs his Word and Wisdom in the art of healing. Origen understands Christ as both the Word and Wisdom of God (in light of 1 Cor 1.24), and hence here *suffulciat* and *erigat* are singular; cf. *Hom in Ps* 36.4.1 [SC 411.182].

98. Ps 36.18; the verb used throughout this paragraph is *cognoscere,* taken in a pregnant sense.

99. 1 Cor 14.37–38.

you: depart from me, you evildoers";[100] just as it is said elsewhere, "The Lord knows those who belong to him,"[101] so here the Lord is said to know the days not of the impious, but of those without blemish. For the days of those without blemish are worthy of the Lord's knowledge.

Yet I do not know if this passage can be explained coherently according to its literal sense. For what possible days are there that belong to those without blemish which do not also belong to sinners? Since a "day" in this age is one and the same for all, and, whether just or sinners, all pass their days in the same light, just as the Lord himself says concerning the Father: "He commands his sun to rise on the good and the bad,"[102] how, then, is the *Lord* here said to know the *days of the those without blemish* as though something distinct and separate? But let us see whether each individual does not perhaps make a "day" proper to himself. If, when we put aside duplicity, we speak the truth with our neighbor,[103] we are living in the day of truth and by the light of the truth; similarly, when we withdraw ourselves from those who hate the brothers[104] and who walk in darkness,[105] and we abide in fraternal love, we make for ourselves days[106] of charity. But further, when we safeguard justice and when, "visiting widows and orphans in their distress, we preserve ourselves without blemish from this world,"[107] we make for ourselves *days of those without blemish,* these are the "days" that the Lord is said to know when he *knows the days of those without blemish.*

But if we wish to examine a yet more sacred meaning[108] in this passage, we can say that the evil days belong to this age, in accord with what is written: "for the days are evil."[109] But there

100. Lk 13.27.
101. 2 Tm 2.19.
102. Mt 5.45.
103. Cf. Eph 4.25.
104. A reference to the community of the baptized.
105. Cf. 1 Jn 2.11.
106. Origen has moved from the singular "day" to the plural "days."
107. Jas 1.27.
108. *Sacratiorem adhuc sensum.*
109. Eph 5.16.

are other, good days, which belong to those who are without blemish, [days] which the Lord knows, [days] in which their inheritance will abide forever. It is then, without doubt, that the just will receive the inheritance of life eternal and obtain "what eye has not seen, ear has not heard, nor has it entered the human heart what God has prepared for those who love him."[110] For those are the days of those without blemish, in which not this sun, which its setting removes and whose light the ensuing night extinguishes, but the Sun of Justice, will shine,[111] who knows not the night,[112] who is the eternal Light, as it is written: "The Lord himself will be for them an eternal light."[113]

10. *They will not be ashamed in the time of evil.*[114] Only the just will be unashamed in the time of evil. But here the "time of evil" refers to the time of judgment, because of the great number of sinners and those whom terrible torments will overwhelm. It is, therefore, at the time of the resurrection, when all will rise: some to life eternal, others to eternal shame;[115] it is then, it says, that the just will not be ashamed, because nothing shameful will be found in their actions.

Moreover, it adds: *And in the days of famine, they will be filled.*[116] It must first be asked what these days of famine are. In a certain passage, God issues a warning through the prophet and says, "Behold, the days are coming, says the Lord, and I will send a famine upon the land, not a hunger for bread nor a thirst for water, but a famine of hearing the Word of God. And they will gather around from east to west to hear the word of the Lord, and they will not find it."[117] These, then, are the "days of famine," and this is the time of famine, when there are none who speak the word of God, just as even now there is

110. 1 Cor 2.9.

111. Cf. Mal 3.20. *Sol iustitiae* and *lumen* are functioning here as ἐπίνοιαι of the Word.

112. Cf. Rv 21.25; taking *qui ... nesciat ... sit* as a relative clause of characteristic.

113. Is 60.19–20; cf. Rv 22.5.

114. Ps 36.19.

115. Cf. Mt 25.46.

116. Ps 36.19.

117. Cf. Am 8.11–12.

a famine among the Jews. For nowhere are there prophets; the wise man is nowhere to be found; nowhere is there one who is considered prudent; nowhere the fifty-year-old; nowhere the wise counselor; nowhere is found a listener who understands; God has taken all these from Judea and from Jerusalem.[118]

But there also exists within us an immense fear that famine may perhaps threaten us as well. For just as those about whom we just spoke, by reading the Law but not carrying it out, met with this—namely, the clouds (that is, the prophets) were commanded not to shower down upon them the rain of God's Word,[119] they suffered a famine of God's Word, and all the gifts of God that we have spoken of earlier were taken from them—we too should be wary lest some kind of punishment such as this be brought upon us. Instead, we should become not only hearers of the Law, but also doers,[120] so that God will command his clouds—not one or two, but many—to shower rain upon us, so that in the Church "two or three prophets might speak and others might test them. And if it is revealed to the one seated, let the first one remain silent,"[121] that there might be many workers who correctly and unashamedly hand on the word of truth,[122] so that each teacher and those who preach the Word of God might say with Paul, "I planted," and another "watered, but God granted the growth."[123] Moreover, these things will happen if we who are watered by the clouds and who hear the Word of God produce those fruits that the Apostle describes, namely, "the fruits of the Spirit," which are "joy, love, peace, patience, forbearance,"[124] and others like these. If we delay in producing such fruits, we must fear that the clouds might be commanded to hold back their showers from us[125] and each one of the saints might begin to do what

118. Cf. Is 3.1–3.
119. Cf. Is 5.6.
120. Cf. Jas 1.22; Rom 2.13.
121. 1 Cor 14.29–30.
122. Cf. 2 Tm 2.15.
123. 1 Cor 3.6.
124. Gal 5.22.
125. Cf. Is 5.6.

is written: "But the one who has understanding will sit and be silent at that time, for the time is wicked."[126]

But we should also call to mind an account of our forebears concerning a time of famine, and how, during a time of famine, the just person is filled. I am thinking that the famine at the time of the prophet Elijah, when the sky was closed for three and a half years,[127] is applicable here. Then too, the people were indeed imperiled by a famine, yet Elijah did not experience hunger.[128] For in one instance, he was fed by an angel, and went forth on the strength of that food and survived for forty days and forty nights.[129] But at another time, he was fed through the assistance of ravens, when they brought bread to him in the morning and meat in the evening and he is also said to have drunk repeatedly from the stream of Cherith;[130] and when he encountered a widow during the time of famine in Zarephath in Sidon,[131] because he was a just man, he did not suffer starvation from the famine. But everywhere an abundance was available to him, while at the same time sinners were experiencing famine. But because Elijah was just, he did not know hunger.

So, then, even if famine should someday come—may the Lord protect his Church from this—nevertheless, if and when it happens,[132] the one who possesses understanding and who is trained in meditation upon God's word and continues to meditate on his Law day and night,[133] and who trains himself to grasp its spiritual meaning, this person will discover in these[134] the bread that comes down from heaven,[135] and the Word of God will become abundant food and flowing drink for him,

126. Cf. Am 5.13.

127. Cf. Lk 4.25.

128. *Non patiebatur famem:* playing on the two senses of *fames* as "hunger" and "famine."

129. Cf. 1 Kgs 19.8.

130. Cf. 1 Kgs 17.6.

131. Cf. 1 Kgs 17.10–24.

132. More literally, "if it ever happens."

133. Cf. Ps 1.2.

134. *In his;* the antecedent(s) could be either *lex* and *verbum Dei* or *intellectum* and *exercitium;* the former pair seems more likely.

135. Cf. Jn 6.41, 50.

and not food and drink only, but—if he is capable of examining thoroughly the deeper mysteries of spiritual understanding[136]—the words of God will be for him a delight.

Further, a deeper meaning can be uncovered in this passage in another way. The Lord and Savior stated: "Night will come, when no one is able to work."[137] He is speaking about that time which will come after this age, the time when each individual will receive punishments for his evil deeds. He then speaks about that night which is to come, when one can no longer do any work, but each individual will then be fed from the works which he accomplished while here in this life.[138] But when it is night, no one works at that evil time. While sinners are afflicted with punishments, there will doubtless be famine for those who gathered no fruits of good work. But in that time of famine, the just *will be filled,*[139] with the fruits, that is, of their justice.

For just as they gathered manna in the desert for six days, but on the sixth day, they gathered not one day's amount, but as much as would be enough for the next day and each one ate on the Sabbath day what had been gathered on the sixth,[140] so also now the coming of our Lord Jesus Christ and this time of his economy,[141] which he accomplished by his Passion in this age, must be considered a kind of "sixth day." And so while we are in the sixth day, let us gather double the manna, so that it might be enough for us when the authentic observance of the Sabbath arrives for the people of God. For if we fail to gather double the amount of food, to sustain us both in the present age and in the age to come, we will not be filled during the days of famine.

For while the just *will* thus *be filled in the days of famine, sinners*—it says—*will perish. But the enemies of the Lord, as quickly as they be honored and exalted, will pass away as smoke passes away.*[142]

136. *Profundiora sacramenta mysticae intellegentiae.*
137. Jn 9.4.
138. *Hic positus operatus est.*
139. Cf. Ps 36.19.
140. Cf. Ex 16.21–26.
141. *Dispensationis* = οἰκονομίας.
142. Ps 36.19–20.

The divine Scriptures teach us the value of this world's honors. When you see an individual swollen with the authority he has received over a particular province, or another who has become haughty with consulships, or another puffed up with various magistracies, when, then, you see all this haughtiness, consider that they *will pass away as smoke passes away.* Recall how many men you have seen in these positions of honor (even right up to your own day) and remember how great were the heights they reached, and see if nearly all of them have not, following their exaltation, passed away *as smoke,* thrown and cast down to where they had started. *But the enemies of the Lord, as quickly as they be honored and exalted, will pass away as smoke passes away.* On the other hand, the friends of the Lord, as quickly as they are rejected, despised, and humiliated by men, will be exalted and raised up by God, for "everyone who exalts himself will be humbled, and the one who humbles himself will be exalted."[143]

11. Following this, certain other things are added that require considerable explanation, for it says, *The sinner will borrow and not return, but the just one shows mercy and lends.*[144] This too, if we take it literally, will not seem true. For many sinners borrow money from one another and return it with interest, so that they themselves might also make a profit now and then from the money that they had invested.[145] The prophet clarifies this when he says, *The sinner will borrow and not repay.*[146] But if you understand who it is who loans at interest and who it is who receives the interest and if you ask who the sinner is who does not return the money he has borrowed, you will understand that what is written makes sense.[147]

For example, when Paul teaches and his hearers heed him, Paul is the one who lends the Lord's money at interest, while his hearers are those who receive from his mouth the money of the Word lent at interest. Indeed, if the person who receives

143. Lk 14.11.

144. Ps 36.21.

145. *Sumpserant;* taking the verb in a pregnant sense; cf. *OLD* s.v. § 9.

146. Ps 36.21; in this second occurrence of this verse Rufinus has *solvet* for *reddet.*

147. *Intelleges consequentiam* [= ἀκολουθίαν] *habere quod scriptum est.* Cf. *Hom in Ps* 38.2.6 [SC 411.388], where *ordo* perhaps renders ἀκολουθία.

money from him is just, he will pay the interest in full and say, "You gave me five coins;[148] see, I have made five more."[149] If he is just, he says, "You gave me five talents; see, you have ten"; or, "You gave me two talents; see, you have four."[150] But if he is a sinner, he fails to produce, on the basis of the Word of God he has received, the works entrusted[151] to him, and will return no interest, but he uses up everything he received in loan.

Now see that all of you, to whom I am speaking these things, are receiving my words as money on loan; this money belongs to the Lord. But if you doubt this, listen to the prophet who says, "The words of the Lord are pure words, silver tested by fire, purged of dross, and refined seven times."[152] If I teach badly, therefore, my money is counterfeit, just like those to whom it was said, "Your silver is counterfeit."[153] But if I teach well, the money or silver is not my own, but it belongs to the Lord, and it has been tested. So I am allowed to make a loan to you of the Lord's money, but not of money belonging to me, for the Word of the Lord prohibits making loans of human money at interest.[154]

What, then, is human money, and what is money belonging to the Lord? I think that the word of Valentinus is human money and that it is counterfeit; further, the word of Marcion and Basilides is human money and is counterfeit; the word of all the heretics is not tested money, nor does it have on itself the image of the Lord intact,[155] but rather an altered one,

148. *Quinque mnas;* the μνᾶ or *mina* is equivalent to 100 drachmas.

149. Cf. Lk 19.18.

150. Cf. Mt 25.20, 22.

151. *Opera mandati* [*ei*]; *OLD,* s.v. *mandatum* § 2, a legal meaning including a consensual contract, agreement, or commission.

152. Ps 11.7.

153. Cf. Jer 6.30.

154. Affirming the early Christian abhorrence of usury; cf. Lv 25.37; Dt 23.20.

155. *Nec dominicam integre in se habet figuram.* A similar metaphor is used by Irenaeus vis-à-vis faulty (Gnostic) readings of Scripture; cf. *Adversus haereses* 1.8.6 [SC 264.112–116]; because they lack the correct ὑπόθεσις of the Scriptures, the true image of the king is lost in the mosaic and hence misrepresented by the erroneous manipulation of the pieces. Cf. *Hom in Ps* 36.4.4 [SC 411.214–216] where the *haereticorum verba ... et doctrina* are juxtaposed to the Lord's "money":

which was fabricated, so to speak, outside the mint, since it was produced outside of the Church.[156] If, however, you see someone who is speaking openly not his own words, but God's words, one who is truly bold in saying, "Do you ask for proof of Christ who is speaking in me?"[157] know that this one indeed is lending not his own, but the Lord's money, and he is doing what is written, *All day long he shows mercy and lends*,[158] for he possesses the authority to make loans, which has been given to him by my God[159] Jesus Christ himself.

For he is the Lord who, in the parable, says to his servants to whom money had been entrusted, "Go, do business with it until I return."[160] And he says to that servant who had neglected to increase the money, "You should have given my money to bankers, and on my return I would have gotten it back with interest."[161] This, then, is the sinner who borrows and does not repay. The just person, however, will give back the money he received with interest, meaning that he gives back with works the Word of God he has received.

You hear a sermon on chastity, you warmly praise the teacher, you embrace the teaching, you admire the advice; through all these you have received the "money" of chastity. If you are a sinner, though, once you have left church, you put yourself right back into the business of this world: wantonness takes hold of you, drunkenness follows, and faithless conversations with cor-

---

Orate ergo ut haec nostra pecunia quam vobis feneramus tota inveniatur ex iustis laboribus, tota de dominica moneta procedens ut et vos fenus integrum consignetis et nos non audiamus quia "Oportuit te pecuniam meam dare nummulariis."

156. This theme recurs in *Hom in Ps* 36.4.4 [SC 411.214]. Ignatius of Antioch had used the imagery of two "coinages" to distinguish those belonging to God and those belonging to the world: νομίσματα δύο, ὁ μὲν θεοῦ, ὁ δὲ κόσμου τούτου; *Magnesians* 5.2 [SC 10bis.98].

157. 2 Cor 13.3.

158. Ps 36.26.

159. Origen is fond, in his preaching, of referring to Jesus as "my Lord Jesus" or even "my Jesus"; here the Munich Manuscript reads ὁ ἐμὸς κύριος Ἰησοῦς Χριστός [GCS n.f. 19.155], a formula found also in *Hom in Lev* 9.5 [SC 287.92]; cf. *Hom in Luc* 12.1 [SC 87.198] and 18.1 [SC 87.264] and see de Lubac, *History and Spirit*, 65–66.

160. Lk 19.13.

161. Mt 25.27.

rupt men. Having immediately forgotten all that you had received from the teacher, what you had praised, what you had admired, you fall headlong once again into lewd company[162] and have become the sinner who has borrowed the word of chastity[163] and does not return the works of chastity.

Similarly, if you hear a word of justice in church, and upon leaving, a neighbor whose field you had coveted meets you, and immediately forgetting what was said in church, in order to satisfy your avarice, you take possession of what is not your own, and so, having borrowed from justice, you do not return interest on the loan, while you do not carry out deeds of justice. And so in each of these cases, *The sinner borrows and does not repay, but the just one shows mercy and lends.*[164] Not only, it says, does the just person make loans, that is, not only does he preach the word, not only does he instruct the ignorant, but he also shows mercy toward the weak. For he follows the example of the Lord, who says, "I desire mercy more than sacrifice."[165]

12. *For those who bless him will inherit the land. But those who curse him will be wiped out.*[166] *Those who bless him,* that is, those who bless the just person, *will inherit the land.* What land? They will inherit that good land, that abundant land flowing with milk and honey,[167] where those good things are which are truly good; they will possess it, *those who bless* the just person, but *those who curse him will be wiped out.* Yet to you it seems like no serious matter to speak ill, from time to time, concerning the saints, and like a mere trifle for you to say about the servants of God: "That one is a such-and-such," and "That one is a fraud," and "That one loves the world," or "That one is a *poseur.*" Do you not hear that *those who curse* the just one *will be wiped out?*

But if this seems like something trivial to you, listen to God speaking in another place to the just person: "But I will be an enemy to your enemies, and I will oppose those who oppose

162. *Ad impudica rursum devolveris scorta.*
163. A descriptive genitive.
164. Ps 36.21.
165. Mt 9.13; cf. Hos 6.6.
166. Ps 36.22.
167. Cf. Ex 3.8, 17.

you."[168] You see how dangerous it is to be an enemy to the just or to speak ill of the saints. For if we really believe what the Lord said about every single one of his servants, namely, "I was hungry and you did not give me to eat," and what he adds, saying, "Who" did "this to one of these least of mine," did "it to me,"[169] it makes sense that he would also say, "It is you who were cursing me, who kept disparaging me and speaking falsely against me and making accusations against me." And if we should say, "Lord, when did we curse you or disparage you? When did we speak falsely against you?" then he will say to us, "Amen, I say to you, that when you did it to one of these least of mine, you did it to me."[170]

For just as in giving to eat to one of these, you have done so to me, and in giving to drink to one of these, you have given to me, and just as in clothing one of these, you have clothed me; so too in cursing one of these, you have cursed me; and if you have blessed or honored one of these, you have blessed and honored me, just as elsewhere he says nothing less: "The one who receives you, receives me,"[171] and, "The one who rejects you, rejects me."[172]

For this reason, then, let us curb our tongue, and let us regard the servants of the Lord with admiration; let us bless the just and never disparage them; let us not open our mouth to speak ill, lest perhaps we be wiped out; but let us bless, that we ourselves might obtain blessing through Christ our Lord, to whom are "glory and power for ever and ever."[173] Amen.

168. Ex 23.22.
169. Mt 25.40–42.
170. Mt 25.40.
171. Mt 10.40.
172. Lk 10.16.
173. Rv 5.13.

FOURTH HOMILY ON PSALM 36 [37]

HE STEPS OF MAN *are guided,* it says, *by the Lord.*[1] And at another point in this very Psalm it speaks about the steps of the just person in this way: *The law of his God is in his heart, and his steps will not be tripped up.*[2] But also in the seventy-second Psalm it is said: "My steps have almost been wasted."[3] Thus we use the noun "steps" (*gressus*) from the verb "to take steps" (*gradiendo*), just as it is written in Exodus that Moses saw a flame of fire and an angel when the bush was burning but was not consumed, and he said: "Stepping by it"—or passing by it—"I will take a look at this great sight."[4] Drawing on this passage, we have an opportunity to understand the matters at hand.[5]

So in terms of the passage in Exodus that we have just called to mind, namely, "Stepping by it, I will take a look at this great sight," I heard a certain individual from among the wise men who came before us, when explaining this passage, say that it is impossible at first for one who is fixed in the daily

1. Ps 36.23.
2. Ps 36.31.
3. Ps 72.2b.
4. Ex 3.2–3 [LXX]: ὤφθη δὲ αυτῷ ἄγγελος κυρίου ἐν φλογὶ πυρὸς ἐκ τοῦ βάτου ... εἶπεν δὲ Μωυσῆς Παρελθὼν ὄψομαι τὸ ὅραμα τὸ μέγα τοῦτο. In the Munich Manuscript, Origen's Greek has διαβάς where the LXX reads παρελθών [GCS n.f. 19.157]. The slightly awkward English "stepping by" is used here and following primarily because Origen wants his hearers to see the link between the verb "stepping" (διαβαίνειν /*gradior*) and the noun "steps" (διαβήματα/*gressus*), which is important for his exegesis of the Psalm text. The Latin of Rufinus replicates the etymological relation of διαβαίνειν and διαβήματα; the latter is used in the LXX text of Ps 36.31.
5. This is one of the foundational interpretive principles in Origen and in the Fathers generally: using Scripture to interpret Scripture.

life and activities of this world to look at a great sight—that is, to gaze upon and to examine closely great mysteries. Rather, it is necessary first to move beyond[6] all these things and to transcend all things of this world, and to have our understanding and our mind set free, and then to arrive at a view of great and spiritual realities and in this way at long last to see a great sight. He was speaking in explanation of this very passage that we have just called to mind. But we, who are eager in accord with the admonitions of the Scriptures to praise the words of wise men and to add to them,[7] are capable of adding something similar to what he said.

Every individual who makes his way toward virtue makes progress by walking, so that, through many stages of progress along the way, little by little he arrives at virtue.[8] Thus, making his way and, as it were, stepping along[9] by certain steps, he always steps past and goes beyond[10] those things that he has mastered,[11] and, letting go of the things that lie behind him, he stretches himself toward those things that lie before him.[12]

As he steps past, then, he moves first beyond the place of wickedness, and from there, making progress by steps or stages, he then passes other spiny thickets of sins, next the jagged rocks of iniquity, and the steep and slippery slopes of the vices. But when he has gone even beyond these, always stretching himself toward what lies before him, what remains is only a little wickedness, and all else bodes well for his journey, if, that

6. *Transire.*

7. Cf. Prv 1.5–6; 9.9. Note the impersonal construction: *Nos vero quibus stadium ... laudare et addere.*

8. Origen's lengthy treatment in *Hom in Num* 27 [SC 461.270–346] of the various *mansiones* of the Israelites on their way to the Promised Land is apposite to these "steps."

9. *Digreditur,* rendering διαβαίνων.

10. *Transit.*

11. *Ea quae explicuit:* literally, "which he has set in order"; Crouzel simply uses the French cognate and has (ambiguously) "il dépasse toujours et va au-delà de ce qu'il a expliqué ..." [SC 411.182–183]. The idea, of course, is that one making progress does not merely become complacent in his progress, but keeps moving.

12. Cf. Phil 3.13; we see here Origen's understanding of Paul's ἐπέκτασις.

is, while making his way, he keeps careful watch over his steps so as not to slip, bypassing every single place of wickedness so as not to dash his foot on it,[13] so that, as it is written in Exodus, he can see a great sight.[14] For no one who is still in the midst of wickedness and who has not stepped around or bypassed it will be able to gaze fully at that great sight of the hidden things of God, which is to say, of Knowledge and of Wisdom.[15] It is a great sight, when God is seen by a pure heart.[16] It is a great sight, when his Christ is recognized by a pure heart as the Word of God and the Wisdom of God.[17] It is a great sight to recognize and to believe in the Holy Spirit. This great sight, then, is the knowledge of the Trinity.

Nevertheless, in Exodus Moses too saw then a great sight, and it is said that it was an angel who was seen in the burning bush,[18] and he calls that "a great sight." For he understood who was in the angel. Indeed, he told him right away, "I am," he said, "the God of Abraham and the God of Isaac and the God of Jacob."[19] See, then, how great a sight this is, although it is itself a great thing to know that God "makes his angels spirits and his servants a burning fire."[20] And then, to be sure, this vision wherein an angel is said to appear to him was a great sight for Moses while still shepherding his father-in-law Jethro's sheep; but he even steps by or goes beyond these tasks.[21] But if he also crossed the Red Sea and the pillar of cloud covered him[22] and he worshiped the mysteries of what was to come,[23] then too will he be able to see an even greater sight. For he will enter the darkness and the cloud, where God himself is re-

13. Cf. Ps 90.2.
14. Cf. Ex 3.3.
15. Cf. Col 2.3; 1 Cor 1.24.
16. Cf. Mt 5.8.
17. Cf. 1 Cor 1.24.
18. *In rubo in igne;* cf. Ex 3.2.
19. Ex 3.6.
20. Ps 103.4.
21. *et digredienti vel transeunti ab his.* Origen seems to be playing on the words; Moses leaves these tasks behind as he moves forward following God's call.
22. Cf. Ex 14.20.
23. Cf. 1 Cor 10.3–11.

ported to be,[24] where it is written that Moses alone approached God, while the others stood far off.[25]

Moses makes such progress through these great sights that he says to God, "If," he said, "I have found grace in your sight, show yourself to me that I might see you clearly."[26] Then he hears this from God: "I will put you in the cleft of the rock"[27]—"but the rock was Christ"[28]—so that through the cleft "you might," for an instant, "see my back," that is, so that you might recognize the things that are to be fulfilled in the end times through the Incarnation,[29] "but my face you will be unable to see."[30]

But taking leave of so many sights,[31] let us turn now to what we set out to consider from the Psalm, namely, its saying that *the steps of man are guided by the Lord.*[32] We have explained earlier the path one is to travel toward virtue: that there are many things that the one who makes his way toward virtue should step around and bypass. So then, you too who are heading toward Christ,[33] who is the Power of God,[34] step around excess, lewd company, adultery; step around theft, false witness; next, step around both greed and all desire for money and other bad things; step around wrath; step around envy, because of which the earth first tasted human blood;[35] step around falsehood; step around the sadness of the world. Unless you step around all these things, you will not be able to see that great sight of the Lord.

There are, then, within us certain steps and feet by which we make this journey; there are steps of the inner man by which we can walk through that Way who says, "I am the Way,

24. Cf. Ex 19.16–25.
25. Cf. Ex 20.21.
26. Ex 33.13.
27. Ex 33.22.
28. 1 Cor 10.4.
29. *Per assumptionem carnis.*
30. Ex 33.23.
31. *Sed digressi quamplurimas visiones:* a pun on *digredior.*
32. Ps 36.23.
33. Cf. Phil 3.13.
34. Cf. 1 Cor 1.24.
35. Gn 4.11.

the Truth, and the Life."[36] We who make this journey must use many steps in order to bypass all those things we have just spoken of, for, *The steps of man are guided by the Lord.*[37]

The desire to carry this out is alone insufficient for the one who wishes to set out on this journey, if the Lord does not also guide his steps. For it frequently happens that those making their way do indeed walk, but they are incapable of keeping to the straight path, but fall into some kind of error, such as those who are engaged in philosophical study: they certainly seem to be setting out on the journey toward virtue, but because their steps are not guided by the Lord, they do not stay on the straight path. But this is no less true of the heretics, who also make their way, but since they understand the Scriptures in a fleshly, not a spiritual, way, they turn off to the left. If they do possess a spiritual understanding, but do not hold fast to the rule of apostolic truth in that very spiritual understanding, they fall off to the right, as the devil, so to speak, does not guide their steps but diverts them from the straight path.[38]

We, therefore, "turning off neither to the right nor to the left,"[39] advance along the middle Way, which is Christ the Lord,[40] because the Lord guides the steps of those who walk upon him. *By the Lord,* then, *are the steps of man guided, and he will long for his way,*[41] the Way, that is, of which we spoke before. For the one who is guided by God will long for Christ and will desire to remain always in Christ.

2. *When he falls,* it says, *he will not be thrown into confusion.*[42] Saying earlier that his *steps are guided by the Lord,*[43] here it

36. Jn 14.6; cf. *Hom in Ps* 36.5.1 [SC 411.226].

37. Ps 36.23.

38. The first type of heretic might be the Marcionites, who reject the Old Testament; the second, Gnostics who might allegorize but do not possess the rule of faith and thus are incapable of understanding correctly the "spiritual" sense of the Scriptures.

39. Nm 20.17.

40. Origen says something quite similar in his massive *Comm in Jn* 19.38: "Our Savior is the whole of the steps" to God; quoted in John Behr, *The Way to Nicaea* (Crestwood, NY: St Vladimir's Seminary Press, 2001), 183.

41. Ps 36.23.

42. Ps 36.24.

43. Ps 36.23.

speaks about his fall. Note, then, that even those who have set out on this journey sometimes happen to fall, even those who are guided by the Lord. But there is a significant difference between the fall of the just and the fall of the unjust.

When the just one falls, it says, he does not remain down. The unjust and the one who has not placed his hope in God, if he falls, remains down and does not get up; that is, if he sins, does not repent of his sin and is not capable of reform.[44] But the just person, even if he gives offense in some way, whether by word—for it is an apostle who says, "For we all give offense in many ways, and if someone does not give offense by word, he is a perfect man"[45]—even the just one, then, gives offense by word, but perhaps from time to time also by deed, but he knows his need for reform; he knows he needs to correct himself. He who had said, "I do not know the man,"[46] a short time later, having received a look from the Lord, knows he should weep most bitterly.[47] He who had spied a woman from the roof and had lusted after her also knows he should say, "I have sinned, I have sinned against you alone, and I have done evil in your sight."[48] If, then, the just one does not remain down when he falls, he will not remain in sin, but he will quickly spring back up, like a doe from a snare or a bird from a trap.[49] But the unjust individual will not only persist, but will also remain down, in his sins.

But what does the just one do? *The law of his God is in his heart, and his steps will not be tripped up* (*supplantabuntur*).[50] There it said, *The steps of man are guided by the Lord,*[51] but here it says, *the steps* of the just *will not be tripped up,* for *the Lord,* it says,

44. *Et peccatum suum emendare nescit,* taking *nescire* = *non posse* here; cf. *OLD* s.v. § 3a, and taking the following instances of *scit* to mean "knows the need for" more than "knows how to," especially in light of the play on *nescire* and *scit* when invoking Mt 26.72.

45. Jas 3.2.

46. Mt 26.72.

47. Cf. Lk 22.61–62.

48. Ps 50.6.

49. Cf. Is 13.14; Ps 123.7.

50. Ps 36.31.

51. Ps 36.23.

strengthens his hands.[52] In another Psalm, namely Psalm 72, it says, "My feet nearly slipped."[53] This, I think, should be understood in a similar fashion. For we who are making progress toward virtue make our way in a kind of ascent; if someone slips and falls in this ascent, he loses the progress he made on the way up. Thus his steps have been wasted.

This is, however, what occurs when one turns back after having made progress: just as it happened also to the wife of Lot, who was headed in the right direction in her departure from Sodom and who, in her escape from the punishments of the wicked, was making progress and going up to the mountain where she was headed under the guidance of an angel; but because she acted against the command of God—for she had been directed not to look back nor to stop in that region,[54] but to go up to the mountain and there be kept safe—when she turned and looked back at what was behind, there her steps were wasted, and she lost all progress gained before she had veered from her course.[55] She remained right there, having been turned into a statuette of salt.[56] This is what the Lord is talking about in the Gospel: "No one who puts his hand to the plow and looks back is fit for the Kingdom of God."[57]

Do you want me to show you others as well whose steps have been wasted? Remember those who passed through the Red Sea as if it were dry land but who, when they sinned, fell in the desert and it was there that their steps were wasted. But now, too, it could happen that one who has lived a celibate life for three or four years (or even more), or someone else who has

52. Ps 36.24.

53. Ps 72.2a: *mei autem pene moti sunt pedes* [SC 411.190]; initially, Rufinus had quoted Ps 72.2b, *paulominus effusi sunt gressus mei* [SC 411.180] (see above, p. 133 n. 3).

54. Cf. Gn 19.17.

55. *Digressa;* one wonders if this should not be conjecturally emended to *degressa* (while the apparatus offers no variants, the two words are frequently confused in the manuscripts), thus meaning "went off course" or "departed from the original plan."

56. Cf. Gn 19.26; this interpretation is less benign than that offered by Irenaeus, for whom Lot's wife becomes a type of the Church; cf. *Adversus haereses* 4.31.3 [SC 100.794]. (I am grateful to Robin Darling Young for this reference.)

57. Lk 9.62.

devoted himself to the study of the Word and of doctrine and to the works of wisdom, but if this one later on is overcome and crosses over to the lust of the flesh, or turns aside to other sins, or hands himself over to the life of the world or turns back around[58] to the business and riches of this corruptible life, you would not hesitate to say of him that his steps have been wasted.

Let us, then, pray the Lord to guide our steps and keep our ways, that our steps might not be tripped up, that our footsteps might be made strong on the Way upon which we set out—that is, upon Christ our Lord—as if upon firm rock, that we might be incapable of being tripped up in any way; tripped up, that is, by him whose head we watch for and who watches for our heel,[59] to whom we should never reveal our bare sole. Rather, we ought always to have our "feet shod in preparation for the Gospel of peace,"[60] so that, if the devil, the one who trips us up, comes and finds our feet protected and standing upon rock, he will be unable to trip us from there.

For although we said earlier that a kind of fall is possible and that a lapse can happen to those who follow the path of virtue, it should nevertheless be noted that in the passage where it said, *When he falls, he will not remain down,*[61] what it had asserted earlier was not so much about the just man as about "man" without any specification.[62] For it says: *The steps of man are guided by the*

58. *Transeat ... transferat ...* [*se*] *convertat:* an interesting series of verbs otherwise used positively above; perhaps this is "tongue-in-cheek."

59. Cf. Gn 3.15.

60. Eph 6.15.

61. Ps 36.24: *cum ceciderit, non prosternitur;* earlier, at the beginning of 2 [SC 411.188], he quotes *non conturbabitur* (= "he will not be thrown into confusion"); the Stuttgart Vulgate reads *non adlidetur* (*iuxta* Hebr) and *non conlidetur* (*iuxta* LXX), while both the Clementine and Neo-Vulgate read *non collidetur;* the LXX reads οὐ καταραχθήσεται (= "he will not be cast down completely"), also found in the Munich Manuscript; this gloss reveals that Origen understands "being tripped up" as equivalent to staying down once one falls, as will become clear below.

62. *De homine puro;* the Latin is ambiguous. Prinzivalli, *Origene, Omelie sui Salmi* (1991), 181, renders this "l'uomo puro e semplice"; Crouzel [SC 411.195], "l'homme en général." Cf. *OLD* s.v. *purus* § 10–11. The Munich Manuscript reads: περὶ ἀνθρώπου ὁ λόγος ἐστὶ τοῦ μήπω δικαίου, "this passage concerns the man

Lord, and he will long for his way; when he falls, he will not remain down.[63] In this it is shown that there are some falls that nevertheless do not necessarily indicate that the one who has fallen is overcome or downed.[64] For just as often happens in an athletic contest,[65] while two are engaged in a wrestling match, indeed one falls initially, but, although he has fallen, he gets up and wins, so also in our contest, which for us is against the prince of this world,[66] if it happens that one of us is overcome and falls into some sin, it is possible after the sin for one to come to his senses, get up, and recoil from the evil that he committed and not only restrain himself in the future but also make satisfaction to God, every night bathing his bed and moistening his covers with tears,[67] gaining confidence from the authority of the prophet where it is said: "Will the one who falls not go on to get up? Or the one who has turned away, will he not turn back? Woe to those who have turned away with a stubborn apostasy, says the Lord."[68] This is the one who was indeed capable of falling, but was not able to stay down.

But if you see someone who has fallen into a particular sin and who, after falling, loses hope of conversion and says, "How can I, who have fallen, now be saved? Now there is no hope, my sins hem me in, how can I dare to approach the Lord? How can I return to church?" And if someone like this should, out of this desperation, draw away even from God, then not only has he fallen, but in his fall he has been downed and is indeed overwhelmed.

It is certainly desirable that the athlete of piety and virtue[69]

---

who is not yet justified." It is possible that by the contrast of *purus* and *iustus* Rufinus is anticipating a distinction that Origen makes in a subsequent homily between one who is making progress (*qui proficit*) and one who has been made perfect (*perfectus*); cf. *Hom in Ps* 38.1.5 [SC 411.346], pp. 209–10 below.

63. Ps 36.23–24.

64. *Prostratum,* in an attempt to keep the perfect passive participle of *prosterno* of the Psalm verse.

65. *In agone.*

66. Cf. Eph 6.12 and Jn 12.31.

67. Cf. Ps 6.7.

68. Jer 8.4–5.

69. Origen elsewhere describes Job, in his grappling with Satan, as τῆς ἀρετῆς ἀθλητής; cf. *De oratione* 30.2 [GCS 3.394]; in *Hom in Luc* 9.2 [SC 87.176] he

remain always unyielding so that he lose not one match, so to speak, nor bend nor be tripped up. But if this does not happen and it turns out that he does fall, he should not lie prostrate after the fall (lest he stay down), but get up and correct his mistake, and by the satisfaction of his own penance make up for what he had done wrong, so that the Apostle should not say in his regard: "I mourn for many of those who have previously sinned and have not repented of the impurity and fornication and the shameful things they have done."[70] Moreover, why did the Apostle take up examples from a wrestling match when he says, "No one is crowned except the one who has competed lawfully,"[71] unless he wanted us to know the struggles and contests of the Law? He also said concerning himself, "I fight, though not as one striking the air."[72] And again, "I have fought the good fight."[73]

Because, then, a struggle and a contest have been set before us, we should also know the contest of the Law. There are athletes who conquer and win the crown in every contest. They win in the boys' class (παῖδας); they win when in the adolescents' class (ἀγενείους); they win when facing grown men (ἄνδρας).[74] Others are overcome when facing grown men, but they receive the crown in the adolescents' class, yet they sometimes also win in the grown men's class. Therefore, some always receive a crown, but others receive a crown on the second or third attempt.[75] It is certainly embarrassing and the worst of luck not to win even one crown in all these contests so various and diverse. So, then, the Christian too, for whom "the struggle is not against flesh and blood, but against principalities and powers and against the rulers of this world of dark-

describes the gestation of John the Baptist as exercise in anticipation of the contest.

70. 2 Cor 12.21.

71. 2 Tm 2.5.

72. 1 Cor 9.26.

73. 2 Tm 4.7.

74. Cf. *Hom in Lev* 16.1 [SC 287.262] and Ambrose, *Explanatio Psalmi* 36.52 [CSEL 64.110–111], where such "classes" of contestants are spoken of as relative to the Christian *agon*.

75. *Aliquanti secundo vel tertio coronantur;* alternately, "certain others receive a crown in the second or third class."

ness, against the spirits of wickedness in the heavens,"[76] in the face of so many adversaries such as these, should be vigilant, if he can, like a contestant, so that, as often as he competes, he might always win and immediately take first place[77] among the παῖδας, that is, among the children.

Do you want me to show you some who received the crown among the children, that is, at the very beginning of childhood?[78] Look at blessed Daniel, who from his childhood obtained the grace of prophecy, and in proving the wickedness of the old men, as a boy he won the crown of justice and chastity.[79] Do you want me to show you another who was crowned in the boys' class? Consider Jeremiah, who, when he excused himself from prophesying on account of his young age, heard from the Lord: "Do not say, 'I am a child,' for you will go to whomever I send you, and you will say whatever I tell you."[80]

But perhaps these seem to you as if they are already adults. I will give you an athlete who engaged in a contest and won a victory even before he uttered infant cries in the hearing of men.[81] Jacob, still within his mother's womb, wrestled with his brother, Esau, grasped his foot,[82] and won the victory;[83] because of this, he received from his parent the blessings of the firstborn, which belonged to the brother who was tripped up and overcome. Moreover, does it not seem to you that those children also, who "at the age of two and under" received the palm of martyrdom in Bethlehem for the sake of the Lord's name,[84] were also crowned in a children's contest? See how many examples we have of crowns in the boys' class!

76. Eph 6.12.

77. *Primas … coronas.*

78. *In primo statim lacte,* literally, "in the first milk"; cf. Lewis and Short, s.v., for similar uses of *lac.*

79. Cf. Dn 13.45–64; Daniel figures among the "athletes of piety" Origen adduces as examples in his *Ex ad Mart* 33 [GCS 2.28–29].

80. Jer 1.7.

81. *Inter homines,* the phrase rendered above as "when facing grown men" and "in the grown men's class." See p. 142.

82. *Supplantavit;* here the use of this verb is quite literal and most apposite in context.

83. Cf. Gn 25.22–24.

84. Cf. Mt 2.16.

We have returned to an explanation of that short verse which says *when he falls, he will not remain down.*[85] It goes on to state the reason why he does not remain down when it says, *because the Lord strengthens his hands.*[86] Notice how it speaks in sequence concerning each thing: so that he might not fall, it says, the Lord guides his steps, but if he should fall, he will not remain down: *The Lord*—it says—*strengthens his hand.*[87] You see, therefore, we are always in need of the Lord's help. First, so that we might not fall, but then, if we do fall, so that we might also get up.[88]

3. *I was young and have grown old, and I have not seen the just man abandoned, nor his offspring seeking bread. All day he is merciful and lends, and his offspring will be a blessing.*[89] Those who say without qualification[90] that the words of the divine Scriptures are to be taken literally[91] will doubtless say that in this passage David is confirming that, now that the time of his youth had passed (since he had already reached old age), in all that time he had never seen the just man abandoned to the extent that he was in need of bread.

What are we to make of the fact that the apostle Paul, while detailing and describing the lives of the prophets, says that they were in need, suffered trials, and wandered about in goatskins through rocky caverns and caves[92]—and, in regard to himself, recalls that he was often hungry and thirsty?[93] Since we realize from the scriptural accounts that the just frequently

85. Ps 36.24.

86. Ibid.

87. The text here employs the singular *manum.*

88. Cf. *Hom in Ps* 36.3.8 [SC 411.154], in explaining Ps 144.14: *Suffulcit Dominus omnes qui cadunt et erigit Dominus omnes elisos. Tantum est ut nos exspergiscamur aliquando et evigilemus, ut si quando per infirmitatem casus aliquis imminet, deprecemur Dominum ut mittat nobis verbum suum et sapientiam suam, quae suffulciat casuros et erigat.* See p. 122 above.

89. Ps 36.25–26.

90. *Simpliciter;* rendering ἁπλῶς, a reference to their reading of the text; see below, the next paragraph.

91. *Secundum historiam,* rendering κατὰ συντυχίαν.

92. Cf. Heb 11.36–38; cf. *Hom in Ps* 37.1.6 [SC 411.294].

93. Cf. 2 Cor 11.27.

suffer these things, how can it now be thought that David said these things according to the simple meaning?[94]

But let us see if there are not perhaps certain "ages" of our inner man like those of the outer, bodily man.[95] This is why from time to time it is said to men who are already mature that they are boys, and to others that they are young men, and to others that they are old men, and in any case it makes no sense that these things are said in terms of bodily age. Indeed, while many prior to Abraham lived six hundred or five hundred or at the least surely three hundred years, it was not said concerning any of these that he was older and full of days, except Abraham alone.[96] From this it must be understood that this is a designation not of bodily age, but of the maturity of the inner man. For this reason, we too should want to be called presbyters and elders not on the basis of bodily age, nor on the basis of the office of presbyter, but on the basis of the perfect understanding and seriousness of purpose of the inner man, just as Abraham, too, was called an elder, having reached an honorable old age.

In terms of the inner man, then, there is a kind of child's age, and also a young man's age and an old man's age, in reference to which the Apostle also said, "When I was a child, I spoke as a child, thought as a child, reasoned as a child; but when I became a man, I put away the things proper to a child."[97] It is my understanding, then, that these things were said by the Apostle not in reference to bodily age, but because when he first came to faith, he was a newborn child, desiring "spiritual milk without guile";[98] at that point he was understanding the Scriptures as a child, and thinking about the Gospel as a child, and reasoning as a child. But later, as he was growing in age

94. *Secundum simplicem intellectum* (= [*intellectus*] *secundum historiam* above; see notes 90 and 91). Since, on the basis of the historical testimony of the Scriptures, this passage of the Psalm is patently untrue, Origen wants his hearers to seek its deeper meaning.

95. Cf. Origen's comments in his *Comm in Cant,* pr. 2.7 [SC 375.94–96], where the "ages" of the inner man are discussed.

96. Cf. Gn 25.8.

97. 1 Cor 13.11; "child" here rendering *parvulus,* but of course "boy" would also be acceptable.

98. 1 Pt 2.2.

toward the likeness of Christ, about whom it was written that "he grew in age and wisdom and grace before God and men,"[99] he was putting away the things proper to a child; and it is for this reason that he said, "When I became a man, I put away the things proper to a child."[100] Therefore, when David said, "I was young and have grown old,"[101] it must be understood in this way: it is as if he were saying, "In terms of the inner man, at one time I was a child, but now I have grown old."

Indeed, if he had not grown old, he would not be a prophet. For it belongs to old men to prophesy. Even if you should sometime see a young man prophesying, do not hesitate to say about him that, in respect to the inner man, he has grown old, and for that reason he is a prophet. In fact, when Jeremiah had heard, "Before I formed you in the womb I knew you, and before you were born I sanctified you, and I made you a prophet among the nations,"[102] he answered, "I am a youth and do not know how to speak."[103] But the one who granted him the grace of being not a child but an elder in respect to the inner man, said to him, "Do not say, 'I am a youth.'"[104] Otherwise, if these words are not understood in this way, what reason would there be to tell a boy who is young and tender of age, "Do not say, 'I am a youth'"? That is to say, you would not be speaking the truth.

Therefore, he was young according to bodily age. But since the Lord had put his own words in his mouth, by which he was to uproot and overturn and destroy and then in return to build up and plant,[105] this power of words, which enlightened and sanctified his soul, did not permit his soul to remain childish; thus it was rightly said to him, "Do not say, 'I am a youth.'" Therefore, what David says—*I was young and have grown old, and I have not seen the just man abandoned, nor his offspring seeking bread*[106]—is likewise to be understood in terms of what we have

99. Lk 2.52.
100. 1 Cor 13.11.
101. Ps 36.25.
102. Jer 1.5.
103. Jer 1.6.
104. Jer 1.7.
105. Cf. Jer 1.10.
106. Ps 36.25.

said before concerning the youth or old age of the inner man.

Otherwise, in respect to the outer man, when bodily sickness comes or when trial or poverty or any of the troubles of this life occur, one would thus have to consider the just man to be abandoned by God. These things especially befall the just, for whom to suffer persecution for the sake of God's name is a regular occurrence, yet they are not abandoned as they suffer; and as they endure all these things, they say, "No one 'will separate us from the love of God, which is in Christ Jesus: neither trial, nor hunger, nor anguish, nor nakedness, nor the sword, nor height, nor depth, nor any other creature.'"[107] Indeed, the prophets, who wandered about the wilderness, through rocky hollows and caves, were in need, endured trials, were afflicted,[108] and although they were wandering about in the wilderness and were abandoned by men, nevertheless a multitude of angels surrounded them. Thus Elisha, when he had been abandoned by men, was surrounded by a heavenly army, as it is written: "'Open the eyes of this servant,[109] so that he might see that there are more on our side than on theirs.' And he saw the entire mountain filled with horsemen and chariots."[110] For the just man is never alone, but is bolstered by the support not just of one or even two or three angels, but the army of the heavenly host is present to him.

But if there is need for still more examples, take another. As long as Jacob was still in his parents' house with his brother, Esau, he was not accompanied by an army of angels. But when he had drawn apart to the solitude of the desert and was traveling alone to Mesopotamia, he slept in a certain place, and when he arose, he said that this place is called παρεμβολή, that is, "encampments," because he saw there not some single camp, but many camps of God.[111]

We have said these things because, so long as his goods are

107. Rom 8.35–39.

108. Cf. Heb 11.36–38.

109. *Pueri huius* = τοῦ παιδαρίου [LXX], the diminutive of παῖς, which can mean both "child" and "servant."

110. Cf. 2 Kgs 6.16–17.

111. Cf. Gn 28.11 and Gn 32.2–3; on Origen's confusion of the two episodes, cf. SC 411.208, n.1.

spiritual, the just man is said never to be abandoned. Now as to bodily goods, see what the just man says as he boasts of these as well: "Up to this hour"—he says—"we have hungered and thirsted, and we are naked, and we are struck with blows, and we toil as we work with our hands."[112] And again, "We are cursed and we give a blessing; we suffer persecution and we endure it; when blasphemed, we entreat."[113] But because one such as this was not abandoned by the Spirit, he said, "For this reason I am pleased in my weaknesses, in injuries, in needs, in persecutions, in distress for Christ."[114]

The one who is abandoned, then, is abandoned in two senses. He indeed is abandoned physically in the way we said earlier, in which all the saints suffer and yet are not harmed. But of those who are abandoned by the Spirit, it is said: "Since they did not choose to have God in knowledge, God handed them over to unsound judgment, so that they might do what is not suitable, filled with all iniquity, wickedness, greed, full of envy, murder, contention, sadness, deceit, grumblers, slanderers, hateful to God, insulting, proud, haughty,"[115] and other evils like this, for which also they were deservedly abandoned. But because such things are foreign to the just man, it says, *I have not seen the just man abandoned, nor his offspring seeking bread.*[116]

Further, if you hear "his offspring," are you to ascribe this to bodily offspring? But how will you find this to be true (that is, the offspring of the just not seeking for bread), when you see Ishmael, the one born of Abraham's seed, whom his mother, fleeing from Sarah her mistress, was carrying in the desert, and was surely seeking for both water and bread?[117] But Esau, also, when coming from the field, was starving and was brought so low by the madness of hunger that he squandered his birthright for a meal of lentils![118] Following what we have said earlier, then, we must understand "offspring of the just"

112. 1 Cor 4.11–12.
113. 1 Cor 4.12–13.
114. 2 Cor 12.10.
115. Rom 1.28–30.
116. Ps 36.25.
117. Cf. Gn 21.17–19.
118. Cf. Gn 25.29–34.

also spiritually. And what else are we to consider "offspring of the just" suitably to be, if not the disciple of the just, that is, one who, having received from the just person the seed of God's Word, is born to eternal life?

For example, if, through your prayers, I am counted worthy to be just, and to receive grace from the Lord in the word of Wisdom and in the word of Knowledge,[119] so that in accord with the grace that I myself obtained from the Lord, I might also minister the Word of God to you and plant it in your souls,[120] so that the Word of God, having entered your souls and being fixed in your hearts, might form your minds according to the image[121] of the Word itself, that is, that you might will and do that which the Word of God wills, and that, in this way, Christ himself might be formed in you,[122] then you will truly become the offspring of the just, who do not seek for bread, since you always have within yourselves the bread which comes down from heaven.[123]

But if in response you say to me, "How many people heard Peter and Paul, who were certainly the most just of teachers, yet sinned nevertheless—how will these be called 'the offspring of the just'?" But notice that, just as perhaps not all who are from Abraham are also called "offspring of Abraham"—those to whom it was said, "If you were sons of Abraham, you would certainly do the works of Abraham"[124]—so too those who heard Peter or Paul but did not do what Peter or Paul taught, were not their offspring, for they cast aside the Word from their soul and squandered by a kind of abuse the seeds[125] of the Word they received from them.

119. Cf. 1 Cor 12.8.

120. Cf. Mt 13.18.

121. *Speciem,* or alternately, "splendor."

122. Cf. Gal 4.19.

123. Cf. Jn 6.41.

124. Cf. Jn 8.39.

125. *Semen/semina* in this passage being rendered both as "seed" and as "offspring"; further, the use of *effuderunt* may allude to Onan, who quite literally prevented the seed from taking root: cf. Gn 38.9: *ille sciens non sibi nasci filios introiens ad uxorem fratris sui semen fundebat in terram ne liberi fratris nomine nascerentur.*

In fact, in this very Psalm in another place it also says, *The offspring of the impious will be wiped out.*[126] But it is certain that the bodily offspring of the impious are not wiped out. Indeed, Job was the offspring of the impious Esau, yet he was certainly not wiped out, but was revealed by the Lord as just and as a prophet and won praise from God above all the just.[127] But this is what we said before, that, just as the offspring of the just are his word and his teaching—a word that so nourishes and refreshes souls that they are said to have no need for bread, since Christ is their bread[128]—so, conversely, the teaching and the word of the impious are their offspring, which, it is said, are doomed to be wiped out,[129] because they are composed of falsehood; and when the light of truth comes, surely the darkness of lies will be put to flight.[130]

4. *All day long he shows mercy and lends.*[131] *All day long* the just man *shows mercy,* and *all day long* he is said to *lend.* He has time to do nothing else except lend from the money that he has in abundance. Yet surely this will not be the interpretation[132] proposed here also, that the just man sits all day long at a table[133] and has before him money to lend to those in need? Or perhaps this will be interpreted as referring to what was said through Moses: "And you will lend to many nations, but you yourself will seek nothing in return."[134] But clearly this should refer to the Master's money that is ordered to be invested with the money-lenders after it has been brought out of the treasuries of wisdom and of the knowledge of God,[135] so that we might make from five talents, ten, and from two, four.[136] More-

126. Ps 36.28.
127. Cf. Jb 2.3.
128. Cf. Jn 6.35.
129. Cf. Ps 36.28.
130. Cf. below, *Hom in Ps* 36.4.8.
131. Ps 36.26.
132. *Numquid et hic hoc putabitur,* here again rejecting a literal interpretation; an original meaning of *putare* is to "add up a balance, make up accounts" (quite apposite, given what follows); cf. *OLD* s.v. § 2.
133. *Ad mensam* [= τράπεζα], a money-changer's table.
134. Dt 15.6.
135. Cf. Col 2.3.
136. Cf. Mt 25.16–17; cf. *Hom in Ps* 36.3.11.

over, the more abundant the money we possess in our soul, the more we will lend all day long.

But, even now, although I am not a just man, nevertheless what I speak to you is the Lord's money that I am lending to you. But you are to pray that I may become a just man and that I might be able to lend you the money of justice, so that I might teach justice not by word only but also by being an example of justice.

This is why, just as there are unjust monies that are gathered wickedly and against the law through falsehood and lies and various, evil acts of greed, and conversely there are monies which are collected justly and in accord with the law, that is, from suitable and just labor, so also is it the case in word and teaching. There are words that are collected not well, neither justly nor lawfully, such as the words of the heretics and the teaching amassed in opposition to the law of God, which we should shun like wicked and pernicious funds derived from the Evil One.[137] Pray, then, that this money of ours that we are lending to you might be found to be entirely the product of just labor, wholly a product of the Lord's mint,[138] so that you might guarantee that the interest is paid in full and so I might not hear, "You should have given my money to the bankers."[139]

5. So then, *I was young and have grown old, and I have not seen the just man abandoned, nor his offspring seeking bread. All day long he shows mercy and lends.*[140] In an earlier place it is said that *the sinner borrows and does not pay back,*[141] and here that *all day long* the just man *shows mercy and lends.*[142] See how these are balanced in opposition: the sinner not only borrows, but, in

137. *De malo collectam;* or more abstractly, "from evildoing."

138. Cf. *Hom in Ps* 36.3.11 [SC 411.170], where the "money" produced outside the Church by heretics does not have the image of the Lord intact: *Ego puto Valentini sermo humana pecunia est et reproba et Marcionis et Basilidis pecunia humana est et reproba et omnium haereticorum sermo non est probata pecunia, nec dominicam integre in se habet figuram, sed adulteratam quae, ut ita dicam, extra monetam figurata est, quia extra ecclesiam composita est.*

139. Mt 25.27.

140. Ps 36.25–26.

141. Ps 36.21.

142. Ps 36.26.

addition, when he has borrowed, he does not pay back. But the just man not only does not borrow, but even lends, and lends not only once or twice, but all day long; that is, he shows mercy by lending his whole life long; and this is why *his offspring will be a blessing.*[143]

6. *Turn away from evil and do good, and dwell forever and ever.*[144] When you hear these things, it says, do what is good, and you will dwell forever; that is, if you do as you have been taught, your dwelling place will be eternal. For if you look "not to the things that are seen, but to those that are unseen—for the things that are seen are temporal, but those that are not seen are eternal"[145]—you will dwell forever.

7. *For the Lord loves judgment and does not abandon his holy ones.*[146] How is it that the Lord loves judgment? Since with him nothing is done without judgment, nothing is done without reason. And so, then, you, knowing that the Lord loves judgment, do all things with just and true judgment, listening to him who admonishes you when he says: Do all things with sound judgment, with sound judgment drink wine.[147]

8. *The Lord does not abandon his holy ones; they will be kept safe forever.*[148] Just as it says that he will dwell forever, so also *they will be kept safe forever.* Both certainly refer to the future time or age for which the holy ones will be kept safe, so that thereafter they live on in eternity.[149]

143. Ibid.
144. Ps 36.27.
145. 2 Cor 4.18.
146. Ps 36.28.
147. *Cum consilio omnia fac, cum consilio vinum bibe;* cf. Prv 31.4 (LXX): μετὰ βουλῆς πάντα ποίει, μετὰ βουλῆς οἰνοπότει. Cf. also Sir 32.24a, 31.32b, and 1 Tm 5.23: *vino modico utere.* Prv 31.4b (LXX) is quoted by Jerome: *Et in alio loco, Cum consilio vinum bibe; Commentarium in Ecclesiasten* 9.8 [CCL 72.326], where it is used as a gloss on 1 Cor 10.31. The entire verse is quoted by Ambrose: *Propheta dicit: et tu cum consilio omnia fac, cum consilio de factis tuis iudica, cum consilio vinum bibe, cum consilio loquere, ut effugias peccatum, ne incidas per multiloquium; Explanatio Psalmi* 36.66 [CSEL 64.124]. This use of Prv 31.4 is also found later in John Cassian as illustrative of *discretio* (διάκρισις); *Collatio* 2.4 [SC 42.115]. On the basis of an electronic database search, these are the only instances of this form of Prv 31.4 in Christian Latinity prior to Rupert of Deutz († c. 1130) [PL 168.1281].
148. Ps 36.28–29.
149. *Ut deinceps in aeternitate perdurent.*

The unjust will be punished, and the offspring of the impious will perish; but the just will inherit the land.[150] We have already spoken earlier regarding the nature of the offspring of the impious, when we related it to their word and their teaching, how they will be wiped out, when every lie is put to flight like the darkness from the light of truth.[151]

But the just will inherit the land. We have already spoken of this, how the just or meek will obtain the inheritance of that good and great land and how *they will dwell in it forever and ever;*[152] not only forever, but forever and ever. See how great the Lord's reward is. In return for the work of thirty or forty or as much as fifty years, a man will receive not only the reward of this age,[153] but forever and ever. But if one abides in the Word of God and cleaves to his Wisdom and is steadfast in the eternal Light, he will also reach the point where he may give glory to God forever and ever. Amen.

150. Ps 36.28–29.

151. Cf. above, *Hom in Ps* 36.2.4 [SC 411.106–108]; *Hom in Ps* 36.4.3 [SC 411.212].

152. Ps 36.29.

153. *Non solum saeculi huius retributionem; saeculum* is likely a rendering of αἰών, which can imply both the material and the temporal dimensions of the "age."

FIFTH HOMILY ON PSALM 36 [37]

HE LAW, indeed wanting us to open our mouth to the Word of God, gave this command: "You will speak these things," it says, "while seated at home and while you are on the way, when you are lying down and when you are rising."[1] But Solomon also makes the same point with a brief admonition in Proverbs, where he says, "Open your mouth to the Word of God."[2] The prophet now also teaches us in a similar manner when he says, *The mouth of the just will meditate wisdom.*[3] For truly nothing other than wisdom should come forth from the mouth of the just man. This is why, brothers, every one of you who is less experienced, on hearing the word of the prophet, should focus your efforts[4] and practice,[5] along with the works of justice, to bring forth from your mouths the word of wisdom as well. In order, then, that this command not seem difficult to you, I will offer to you a few words on wisdom.

The Apostle says that "Christ is the Power of God and the Wisdom of God."[6] Therefore, if you are always speaking Christ, if you are always meditating on his words, if you are keeping his commands in your mouth, your mouth will worthily meditate wisdom. For the meditation of wisdom does not

1. Dt 6.7; rendering *pergens in via* not merely as "on the road," but as "on the way," thus captures the allusion to Christ as Way implicit in Origen's preaching.

2. Prv 31.8.

3. Ps 36.30: στόμα δικαίου μελετήσει σοφίαν [LXX]; here taking "meditate" (*meditabitur*/μελετήσει) in its original sense of "to focus upon" or "rehearse."

4. *Date studium,* an explanatory gloss on the meaning of *meditabitur;* one can then infer that it is to be understood in the sense of "devote oneself to."

5. *Meditamini;* or alternately, "exercise yourselves"; so Crouzel [SC 411.225], "exercez-vous."

6. 1 Cor 1.24.

consist solely in one's capacity to teach or dispute, even extensively, in the Church and defeat his opponents; this, of course, is a work of wisdom, though for some more than others. In one individual, the very act of faith in God's wisdom is reckoned to be wisdom, and in another person the delight he experiences in the company of the wise and his love for their words is also called wisdom; so also for some others simply to ask questions about wisdom is reckoned to be wisdom.

But heed only this, brothers: let none of you be found not speaking or meditating wisdom, or worse, hating and opposing those who devote themselves to wisdom. Those who are ignorant[7] share with the others this most terrible vice, namely, that they think those who devote themselves to the word and to doctrine are wasting their time unnecessarily, and they embrace their own lack of learning rather than others' efforts and exertion. They alter the language, calling such exercises "verbosity," but their own ignorance or unwillingness to learn, "simplicity." Nevertheless, the most honorable is the one who proves his wisdom by his actions and who is acknowledged as wise because of the uprightness of his life. Blessed, then, is the one who opens his mouth to the Word of God[8] and who, growing in age as Christ did,[9] will grow also in wisdom. And assuredly, if we are unable to make further progress in wisdom, it should not bother us at least to comply by opening our mouth "in psalms, hymns, and spiritual songs,"[10] and more frequently to God in prayer. For even this kind of meditation of wisdom is no small thing, so that even in this way the mouth of the just man might be found always to be meditating wisdom.

Nevertheless, it seems to me that it was not without reason that it did not say, "The mouth of the just meditates wisdom," which could be seen as referring to the present, but said, *will meditate wisdom,* for without a doubt it has in view the future;

7. *Imperiti;* the comparative form (*imperitiores*) rendered above in the first paragraph more benignly as "less experienced."

8. Cf. Ps 80.11.

9. Cf. Lk 2.52; Eph 4.13.

10. Col 3.16.

on this point all other translators, except one, agree.[11] Might not, then, the use of this tense[12] perhaps represent something mystical, indicating a particular kind of hope, the promise of a future grace and an inheritance, such that the mouth of the just is to be filled, not with food or drink, not with delicacies and delights, not by feasting on sumptuous meals, but by meditating wisdom? No more will anyone be unpracticed[13] in the Kingdom of God, nor remain untaught;[14] no one will be estranged[15] from the knowledge of the way things are.[16] All of us—if deserving—will become disciples of Wisdom. If, here in this life,[17] one is educated and instructed in attaining the things possible to one still in the flesh, there he will then be enlightened by a more perfect training, and there, those things that are here pursued by effort and exertion will be part of the abbreviated course of the education to come. But the one who has not yet put aside the elementary subjects but still speaks as a child and thinks as a child,[18] there too he is taught as a child so that at a certain point, having become a grown man through progress in wisdom, he might put aside those things proper to a child.[19]

But does not the Law (if understood in a spiritual way) also indicate something like this, when it says, "You will speak re-

11. Crouzel, SC 411.228, n. 1, observes that it is not possible to determine which translator among many (Aquila, Theodotion, et al.) this might be.

12. *Hoc tempus;* on the significance of shifting tenses, cf. Quintilian, *Institutio Oratoria* 1.5.41, Loeb Classical Library 124, ed. and trans. Donald A. Russell (Cambridge, MA: Harvard University Press, 2001), 144, and 9.3.11, Loeb Classical Library 127, ed. and trans. Donald A. Russell (Cambridge, MA: Harvard University Press, 2001), 102.

13. *Imperitus;* here in the sense of "untrained" or "unpracticed," fitting given the sense of *meditare.*

14. Cf. Mt 13.52.

15. *Peregrinus;* literally, of course, "as a wanderer" or "pilgrim."

16. *Rerum* (possibly rendering τῶν πραγμάτων; alternately, "realities," understood as part of the schema: shadow–type/image–reality; cf. below in 2 and *Hom in Ps* 38.2.1 [SC 411.370–372].

17. *Hic positus.*

18. Cf. 1 Cor 13.11.

19. Cf. *De principiis* 2.11.5–7.

garding these things[20] while seated at home[21] and while you are on the way, when you are lying down and when you are rising"?[22] We can understand this in the following way: being "seated at home" and "lying down," means we speak the Word of God while in the Church (which is the "home" of God),[23] that is, while we are in this body; "on the way" means we speak the word of God while on that way who says, "I am the Way";[24] and "rising" means when we will have risen from the sleep of death in the resurrection; then, as we are rising from the sleep of death, we speak those things that are perfect, just as Solomon also says about the one who has made Wisdom his friend and intimate, "If you sit, you will be without fear, and if you sleep, you will gladly take your rest and you will fear no terror coming upon you nor the assaults of the wicked rushing upon you."[25] This should be enough concerning what is written, *The mouth of the just will meditate wisdom,* to which is added, *and his tongue will speak judgment.*[26]

2. The tongue of the just is understood to "speak judgment" in two ways: whether because everything he says is spoken with right judgment, with deliberation, and with counsel, and nothing is said out of wrath, nor in order to please men; nothing spoken out of sadness, nothing from fear; for each of these tends to perpetuate unsound judgment among men. Or because a just person surely speaks continually of the coming judgment, ever reminding himself, as well as those who listen to him, of fear of the judgment to come and the punishments in store for sinners,[27] of the future scrutiny[28] as well as the

20. *In eis;* above (the first sentence of this homily) simply has *haec.*

21. *In eis domi;* here the locative is used; above (first sentence), *in domo.*

22. Dt 6.7.

23. 1 Tm 3.15: *cum in ecclesia, quae est domus Dei;* the customary rendering as "house of God" does not capture the connection he intends to make here.

24. Jn 14.6; cf. *Hom in Ps* 36.4.1 [SC 411.186–188]; one wonders whether this is not to be understood sequentially: life in the Church—on "the way" [= *post mortem*]—resurrection; in any case, it is clear from what follows that the "instruction," begun in the Church in this life, is continued beyond death.

25. Prv 3.24–25.

26. Ps 36.30.

27. Cf. Mt 25.42.

28. *Futura examinatione.*

things promised to the saints and prepared for them by God,[29] he might save himself and those who listen to him.[30] This is how the saying *the tongue of the just will speak judgment*[31] will be fulfilled.

But further, if one must keep the future tense here also—for it said "will speak" not "speaks"—we can also understand it like this: however much we can in the present either speak or discern that which concerns the judgment of God, it is necessary for us to know what limits the Apostle is pointing out when he says, "How inscrutable his judgments and how unsearchable his ways!"[32] But if we will be able to attain that perfection of which he says, "But then face to face,"[33]—that is, when realities themselves[34] will become clearer to us—when we begin to recognize the meaning of every single thing in this world, whether they have happened or are happening, on the basis of what kind of judgment they have happened or what judgment God employs in each and every dispensation of his Providence; if one will be worthy to examine and see clearly how "the judgments of God are a great abyss"[35]—since we will be able to receive more fully the grace of that Spirit who "scrutinizes all things thoroughly, even the deep things of God"[36]—then truly and fully in accord with the difference in tense of the verb used by the prophet *will the tongue of the just speak* the judgments of God.[37]

3. *The law of his God is in his heart.*[38] Not only will the just *meditate wisdom in his mouth and will his tongue speak judgment,* but he also carries the law of God in his heart. For the law, like a kind of root planted deep in the heart, sprouts the words of

29. Cf. 1 Cor 2.9.
30. Cf. 1 Tm 4.16.
31. Ps 36.30.
32. Rom 11.33.
33. 1 Cor 13.12.
34. *Res ipsae,* likely rendering τὰ πράγματα αὐτά.
35. Ps 35.7.
36. 1 Cor 2.10.
37. Here taking *distinctio* and *verbum* as grammatical terms; cf. above regarding Paul and Rom 11.33: *necesse est nos illud scire quod definit apostolus.*
38. Ps 36.31.

justice, the words of holiness that the just person brings forth from his heart, and not only words, but also actions and deeds. The Jews, almost without ceasing,[39] meditate the law of God with their mouth and lips, but they do not have the words[40] firmly fixed in the depths of the heart, which is why it is said to them: "This people honors me with their lips, but their heart is far from me."[41] If we then, in accord with what we have read, meditate wisdom with our mouth, if our tongue speaks judgment, and if the law of God is in our hearts, we will obtain what comes next: *And his steps will not be tripped up.*[42]

I think you remember those things we discussed a short while ago[43] about steps, but we need to call to mind what was said so that we might see how some individuals are tripped up while walking and their steps wasted.[44] So if you keep this in mind and are diligent in remembering it, you should know that, if you meditate wisdom in your mouth and if your tongue speaks judgment and if the law of God is in your heart, your steps will never be tripped up.

4. Following this it says, *The sinner watches for the just.*[45] The sinner watches for the just and looks at him, and even to see him is, for the sinner, burdensome, and so he watches for an opportunity *to hand him over to death.*[46] Of course, this is what was done against the Savior by those who slew the prophets[47] and crucified God[48] and have persecuted us even to this day:[49]

39. Cf. Ps 1.2.

40. *Ea* [= *verba*].

41. Is 29.13; Mt 15.8.

42. Ps 36.31.

43. Cf. *Hom in Ps* 36.4.1–2 [SC 411.180–196].

44. Cf. *Hom in Ps* 36.4.2 [SC 411.192]: *istius ergo effusi sunt gressus.*

45. Ps 36.32.

46. Ibid.

47. Cf. Mt 23.31.

48. *Deum crucifixerunt:* this is an unusually bold claim and unlike anything in the extant works of Origen; there are no variants in the manuscript tradition, and the Greek for this passage is lacking; cf., however, Ignatius of Antioch, *Romans* 6.3 [SC 10bis.134], who was similarly bold: ἐπιτρέψατέ μοι μιμητὴν εἶναι τοῦ πάθους τοῦ θεοῦ μοῦ, "allow me to be an imitator of the suffering of my God"; a few lines later, *Romans* 7.2 [SC 10bis.134], the more ambiguous, ὁ ἐμὸς ἔρως ἐσταύρωται, "my love has been crucified."

49. *Etiam nunc;* cf. 1 Thes 2.15.

they watch for the people of God who belong to Christ, that is the disciples of Justice, and desire to hand them over to death and seek to kill them. But what does the just People of God and the disciple of Justice say? They use the Teacher's words and say, "You would have no power over me were it not granted you from above."[50] This can also apply to the time of persecution of the holy martyrs and confessors by the pagans. For impious persecutors watch for every just person and seek to kill him.

But an interpretation such as this should not make one feel safe in this time of peace.[51] Remember that every day the just has the devil as a persecutor and that he is the one watching for the just. For he is always lurking in ambush and "prowls like a lion seeking someone to devour."[52] But if you are faithful and rely upon the Lord, see what it promised you in return: *But the Lord will not abandon him into his* (that is, the sinner's) *hands nor condemn him when he will face judgment.*[53]

That "he will face judgment" is understood in two ways: that is, whether the just man is judged by God or whether God himself is judged along with the just man. For the divine Scripture often teaches that this happens when it says, "The Lord himself will come to trial."[54] Therefore, when the just man is judged with the Lord, he will not be condemned, and so it says, *Wait for the Lord,*[55] meaning that if you are troubled, if you are facing difficulties, if you are experiencing persecutions,[56] *wait for the Lord and keep to his way,* swerving neither to the right

50. Jn 19.11.

51. While his father, Leonides, was a victim of persecution and Origen certainly experienced the pressures of persecution during his youth, persecution was largely a localized and occasional phenomenon until the time of Decius (249–251 AD); one can infer that Origen is preaching at a time without active local persecution.

52. 1 Pt 5.8.

53. Ps 36.33.

54. *Ipse Dominus in iudicium veniet:* Is 3.14 (the Douay-Rheims translation of the Vulgate renders this "The Lord will enter into judgment"); cf. Is 41.1; Jer 2.9; Hos 4.1; Mal 3.5; what these texts say, however, is not quite the same thing as what Origen is saying (as Crouzel notes, cf. SC 411.236).

55. Ps 36.34.

56. Cf. Rom 8.35.

nor to the left.[57] For if you wait for the Lord unswervingly, you will obtain what follows: *And he will exalt you,* it says, *so that you will inherit the land.*[58]

We have spoken often of the "holy" land and of the land that is mentioned as the inheritance of the heavenly promises. The nature of its location is also made a little clearer in this verse. For this land in which we now live is said to be "below" in accord with what is written: "For God is in heaven above, but you on earth below."[59] But that land which is promised to the just as an inheritance is spoken of as being not below but above. This is why the promise made to the one who waits for the Lord and keeps to his way says, *he will exalt you so that you will inherit the land.*[60] For unless one is exalted and ascends on high and becomes heavenly, he cannot obtain the inheritance of that land. I think it is for this reason that, as this dry place on which we dwell, the lower support of this heaven (that is, of the firmament), is called its "land," so, too, of that higher realm that is called "heaven" in the proper sense, the lower support in which heavenly beings dwell and which is also, so to speak, the crest of this firmament is, as I have said, rightly called the "land" of that heaven,[61] but also the "good land,"[62] the "holy land,"[63] the "abundant land," the "land of the living,"[64] the "land flowing with milk and honey."[65] Therefore, now the divine Word says: *he will exalt you so that you will inherit the land.*[66]

57. Cf. Dt 5.32 and 17.11; cf. *Hom in Ps* 36.4.1 [SC 411.188].

58. Ps 36.34.

59. Eccl 5.1; *terra,* of course, being rendered both "land" and "earth."

60. Ps 36.34.

61. The challenge for the translator is that *terra* and *caelum* can be rendered in various ways; *terra* can be "earth," "land," and "ground," while *caelum* can mean, of course, both "heaven" and "sky." Here we see Origen's teaching on the "two heavens," i.e., the firmament of Gn 1.6–7 and the "heavens" of Gn 1.1. Cf. *Hom in Gen* 1.2 [SC 7bis.28] and *De principiis* 1.7.1 [GK 232–234].

62. Cf. Dt 1.25.

63. Cf. Ex 3.5.

64. Cf. Ps 26.13.

65. Cf. Ex 13.5.

66. Ps 36.34.

5. *You will see when the sinners perish.*[67] Perhaps this will happen first so that the just may see sinners and the wicked condemned. For the penalties and punishments for sinners are determined first, when the just see them and recognize the difference between a good life and a bad one, and when they understand that by their good life they have avoided evils so great that those who are being punished will, on seeing them in glory, say, "We fools thought that theirs was the foolish life."[68] Later, after they have seen how sinners perish, the just will themselves be exalted and taken to heaven to inherit the land.

Now, then, this prompts an explanation and offers consolation in regard to a question that not infrequently strikes at the heart of nearly every person. For very often those of us who are weak, when we see those who are wicked and impious living this life in complete happiness and flourishing with prosperity and success,[69] abounding in wealth and public honors,[70] rejoicing in an abundance of children, and basking in a sea of extravagance, we are scandalized, and in our hearts we say, "Where is God's justice? If things are governed by divine Providence, would God allow this wicked and impious individual to rise to such a high degree of happiness?" This is why the divine Word, when speaking in the person of the just man, says: *I have seen the impious* not only exalted but *exalted on high and lifted up,* above not just any trees, but *above the cedars of Lebanon:*[71] so that, even though the tree is quite high and the location of the pinnacle loftier than all others, yet, seeing all these things, *I passed by,* it says, *and behold, he was no longer.*[72] Just what is it, do you think, that the just one passes by so that this exaltation ceases? If you recall earlier we were speaking of Moses having passed by so that he might see a great sight; now you can realize too what it is that the just is said to pass by.[73]

67. Ibid.
68. Wis 5.4.
69. *Prosperis successibus.*
70. Quite probably a reference to public office.
71. Ps 36.35.
72. Ps 36.36.
73. Cf. Ex 3.3. The just, as part of his progress, passes by wickedness and sin

So when we see the wicked exalted and swelling with great pride, let us also, with both our mind and our understanding, pass from those things that are seen and are subject to time, and redirect our understanding to those things that are unseen and that are eternal.[74] Let us consider that the things that appear lofty are subject to time and last but a few days. Let us look to the Day of Judgment and so come to understand that the one who is *exalted on high and is lifted high like the cedars of Lebanon*[75] is nowhere to be found on the Day of Judgment. For he who is not a sharer in the One who eternally exists—the One who said, "I am who am"[76]—he is the one who is said not even to exist. In short, sinners are accounted as having no existence. This is why the Apostle said in relation to the call of the gentiles, "God chose the things that are not to destroy the things that are."[77] And in the book of Esther it is said, "Do not hand over your scepter, Lord, to those who are not."[78]

As long as someone marvels at the proud in their haughtiness, as long as he fawns over sinners and those who are proud, it is certain that this individual has not passed by and has not seen that these are as nothing, but is abiding in this present state, and that is why he marvels at their present glory. If, however, he passes by in the way we described earlier—that is, if, with his mind and understanding,[79] he passes from things of

---

as he makes his way toward virtue; cf. *Hom in Ps* 36.4.1 [SC 411.181–182]: *Igitur de his quae in Exodo scripta memoravimus, id est, "digrediens videbo visionem istam magnam".... quia non est possibile prius videre visum magnum, id est intueri atque perspicere magna mysteria stanti in conversatione et actibus mundi huius: sed transire oportet prius ab his et transcendere omnia saecularia et sensum nostrum ac mentem liberam fieri, et tunc ad magnarum et spiritualium rerum intuitum pervenire.... Unusquisque qui iter agit ad virtutem, proficit in ambulando, ut paulatim per multos profectus itineris perveniat ad eam.... Digrediens ergo transit primum locum malitiae et inde proficiens passibus et ingressibus transit alias peccatorum sudes, tum deinde scrupeas nequitiae cautes, et lubrica ac praerupta vitiorum.*

74. Cf. 2 Cor 4.18.

75. Ps 36.35.

76. Ex 3.14.

77. 1 Cor 1.28.

78. Est 14.11 (Vlg).

79. *Mente et sensu;* earlier, *mente et intellectu;* below, *in mente atque animo tuo* and *sensu et mente.*

the present that are subject to time to those which are to come and which abide forever—then he speaks the truth about the one whom he has seen lifted up like the cedars of Lebanon, *I passed by and behold, he was no longer,*[80] for "both heaven itself and earth will pass away."[81]

With the Lord, all things that are yet to be are regarded as already having taken place.[82] So when he was saying, "For food they gave me gall,"[83] without a doubt this was something yet to happen and yet it was spoken of as something already done. He did not say, "In my thirst they *will give* me vinegar to drink," but rather, "they *gave* me vinegar to drink."[84] So, then, with God, things that are yet to be are spoken of as already done. If, then, you are an imitator of God and if you imitate Christ, you do not wait for the sinner to pass away, you do not wait for the one who is haughty to be humbled and crushed, but you see for yourself with your mind and soul that these things have already transpired,[85] if you yourself pass, both in your understanding and in your mind, from things of the present to future realities.

Take this example in terms of what we are talking about. If you have been on a ship during a voyage, you have seen lands and promontories and mountains passing by—not because they are constantly moving, but because you are moving under the influence of a favorable wind—but they appear to withdraw and to be carried away; so also then in this case if you, by the prompting and inspiration of the Holy Spirit upon your mind,[86] set sail on a swift and favorable course, you will, with your understanding, pass by everything that is seen (because it is subject to time), and you will set your sight on those things

80. Ps 36.36.

81. Mt 24.35.

82. A direct assertion about divine knowledge as transcendent of the temporal order.

83. Ps 68.22.

84. Ibid.

85. *Transisse;* a pun, of course; literally, "passed."

86. *Si sancto Spiritu mentem tuam perflante et spirante* ... above, *vento prospero flante:* it is awkward in English to express the concept of "blowing," so I have settled on "under the influence of a favorable wind" and "by the prompting and inspiration of the Holy Spirit upon your mind."

that are eternal.[87] So certainly you are saying that all these things that are seen are as nothing now, for they will not exist in the future. Thus, *I saw the wicked exalted on high and lifted above the cedars of Lebanon, and I passed by, and behold, he was no longer.*

Something else in this passage strikes me even more. I see yet another impious one who is exalted and raised *above the cedars of Lebanon.* For when heretics fashion for themselves another kind of god above God the Creator, and they are exalted and raised by falsehood in their denial that God, the Creator of all, is a good God, by their impious assertions they are raised above the cedars of Lebanon, supporting themselves no doubt on opposing powers, by whose inspiration they fabricate stories in opposition to God the Creator of all things. And because they understand the Law only in a literal way and are unaware that it is spiritual,[88] they are deceived in their own thoughts.[89] If I see them, then, and pass by, they will be no longer. What should I "pass by"? If I pass by the literal level, if I pass beyond the surface of the story and I reach the spiritual meaning—for the Law is spiritual[90]—if I explain in terms of the spiritual meaning all those things in which they err and deceive themselves,[91] their impious and wicked dogmas will no longer exist. And so it will be fulfilled that the impious who is exalted and lifted up will no longer exist as I pass by.

But further, *when his place is sought, it will not be found.*[92] The "place" of impious teaching is the letter of the Law, and it is the letter that kills. Therefore, when we pass from the letter, which kills, to the Spirit, which gives life,[93] once the letter has been rejected, not even the "place" of the impious teaching can be found. But how are we to look for it? While we are disputing with our opponents and together investigating its meaning, then we are seeking the "place" of that teaching in

87. Cf. 2 Cor 4.18.
88. Cf. Rom 7.14.
89. Cf. Col 2.8.
90. Cf. Rom 7.14.
91. Taking *decipiuntur* as a medial passive.
92. Ps 36.36.
93. Cf. 2 Cor 3.6.

the letter of the Law. Yet when it is demonstrated that, insofar as the history is concerned—once the letter is taken away and rejected—it cannot stand; as we seek for it and argue about it, the "place" of that impious teaching is nowhere to be found.[94]

6. *Maintain innocence and see equity.*[95] The Word of God directs us to preserve innocence. Moral decay has made such inroads among humanity that in the minds of ever so many, innocence is considered folly. But Scripture judges it to be the work of highest virtue, for it considers innocence as that which injures no one, harms no one. So when it says, *Maintain innocence,* it has commanded that we keep ourselves from harming anyone, injuring anyone.[96] Moreover, we achieve this if we, with a mind ever attentive and vigilant, *see equity.* Thus, I understand Equity[97] in this passage to be like Truth, Justice, Life; that is, Christ.[98] For by seeing these in conjunction with one another,[99] we will see God.

Therefore, *maintain innocence and see equity, for there are remains for the peaceful man.*[100] I wonder what these remains that are kept for the peaceful man are? We usually speak of the "remains" when the spirit is separated from the body; just as the greater part of human nature is reckoned as spirit, so the part of the body that is left is referred to as "remains." If we therefore believe the words of the Apostle when he says that the

94. In this paragraph, Origen relates literal (*secundum historiam*) interpretation and spiritual interpretation, indicating that in engaging the heretics (*haeretici,* the antecedent of *eos,* translated here as "our opponents" in the previous paragraph) and accepting their presuppositions, one ends up being trapped at the level of the letter.

95. Ps 36.37; *aequitas* (in the LXX, εὐθύτης) serves here as one of the ἐπίνοιαι of Christ.

96. *Quae nemini noceat, neminem laedat ... ut neminem laedamus, nemini noceamus;* both a chiasmus and an instance of asyndeton.

97. In the *Comm in Cant* 1.6.11 [SC 375.254–256], Origen teaches that *aequitas* (playing on its opposite, *iniquitas*) should be (almost literally) the standard or *regula* for the Christian life: *Et ideo regulam quandam directam ponamus esse aequitatem, ut si quid in nobis iniquitatis est, hanc adhibentes et superducentes directoriam mandatorum Dei, si quid in nobis curvum, si quid tortuosum est, ad huius regulae lineam resecetur, ut possit et de nobis dici, "Aequitas dilexit te"* (Song 1.4).

98. A brief catalogue of some of the ἐπίνοιαι of Christ.

99. *Simul;* or more literally, "all at once."

100. Ps 36.37.

body "is sown in corruption" (meaning at the time of death) and "rises in incorruption" (when the time for resurrection comes), when even "this corruptible body will put on incorruption and this mortal body will put on immortality,"[101] then there will be *remains for the peaceful man.* Moreover, the remains of the peaceful man will be in peace and at rest there.[102] For the Lord further says, concerning those who are peaceful, that "they will" also "be called children of God";[103] "Father, I desire that where I am, these might be with me."[104] *The remains for the peaceful man,* then, are with Christ.

7. *But the wicked will be destroyed together;*[105] that is, all of them will be destroyed in equal measure, for their shared end is Gehenna. *The remains of the impious will perish*[106] then, when the One who has the power will cast into Gehenna, body and soul, the one who is lost.[107]

But the salvation of the just is from the Lord.[108] But it is better said in Greek: *But the salvation of the just is with the Lord.*[109] It did not say that the salvation of the just is in heaven, for this will pass away,[110] nor with any creature, for nothing [created] is steadfast or unchanging, but that *the salvation of the just is with the Lord,* who abides always, who is always the same, who is always steadfast, nor can man's salvation exist more securely anywhere than with the Lord. May he be my abode, may he be my house, may he be my mansion, may he be my rest, may he be my dwelling-place. So not only is the Kingdom of Heaven[111] proclaimed to us by holy Scripture, but also the Kingdom of

101. 1 Cor 15.42.
102. Cf. Wis 3.3.
103. Mt 5.9.
104. Jn 17.24.
105. Ps 36.38.
106. Ibid.
107. Cf. Lk 12.5.
108. Ps 36.39: *Salus autem iustorum a Domino.*
109. *Salus autem iustorum apud Dominum;* LXX = σωτηρία δὲ τῶν δικαίων παρὰ κυρίου. Ironically, *a Domino* may be closer in meaning to παρὰ κυρίου than *apud Dominum.*
110. Cf. Mt 24.35.
111. Cf. Mt 3.2; this, of course, is Matthew's preferred expression, vis-à-vis the other Gospels.

God.[112] As I recall, I have often said that the Kingdom of Heaven belongs to those who are still making progress, but the Kingdom of God belongs to those who already have reached the perfect end. This is why the salvation of the just is said to be with God even now, since certainly they have been counted worthy, by the perfection of their life, to reach all the way to the Lord himself.

And he is their protector in time of trouble.[113] What does this "time of trouble" mean, except our current state, when we journey through the tight and narrow way that leads to life?[114] This assumes, however, that we are journeying through the narrow way which leads to life and not through that spacious and broad way[115] that is widened by wealth and eased by luxury, that is smoothed by pleasures of the flesh, and that esteems the glory of the moment. Their protector is not God, but Mammon. The Protector, however, of those who are in trouble and who find themselves in a tight spot is God—for "many are the troubles of the just."[116] Indeed, they are troubled as they consider the time of judgment and examine themselves lest perhaps something be found in them that is a ground for accusation.[117] Therefore, because of this they are troubled and anxious, yet God will be *their protector in time of trouble,* at the time of judgment, when the impious are handed over for punishment. Then *the Lord will help them* in the time of trouble and *he will rescue them and take them away from sinners;*[118] and not only from sinful men, but also from opposing powers, certainly at the time when the soul is separated from the body and when sinful demons[119] hasten to meet it, those opposing powers, the

112. Cf. Mt 12.28; on the distinction between Kingdom of Heaven and Kingdom of God, cf. *De oratione* 25.1 [GCS 3.357].

113. Ps 36.39.

114. Cf. Mt 7.14.

115. Cf. Mt 7.13.

116. Ps 33.20.

117. *Ne forte aliquid inveniatur in eis quod vocetur ad culpam;* cf. *OLD* s.v. *culpa* § 4.c–d.

118. Ps 36.40.

119. *Peccatores daemones;* cf. below, recurring elliptically as *peccatores,* "sinful beings."

spirits of this air[120] who wish to detain the soul and call it back to themselves if they recognize something in it proper to their own works and activities.

For the prince of this world[121] and the powers of the air come to each individual soul as it leaves this world,[122] and look to see if they can find something of their own in it.[123] If they discover greed, it belongs to them; if they find wrath, or wantonness, or envy, or anything of the like, it belongs to them, they claim it for themselves, they draw it to themselves, and turn it[124] aside to the portion assigned to sinners. But if one has followed the example of him who said, "Behold, the prince of this world comes, and he does not find anything in me,"[125] if one will keep careful watch over himself in this way, these sinful beings indeed come, seeking what is their own in him, and, finding nothing, they will nonetheless assail him in an effort to divert him by force to their side.[126] But the Lord will rescue him *from sinners.* And perhaps this is why we are commanded—with a kind of mystery—also to pray for this, when we say, "And deliver us from the Evil One."[127]

120. Cf. Eph 2.2.

121. Cf. Jn 12.31.

122. Cf. Enrico Dal Covolo, "Note sulla dottrina origeniana della morte," in *Origeniana Quinta,* ed. Robert Daly (Leuven: Peeters, Leuven University Press, 1992), 430–37.

123. Cf. *Comm in Cant* 4.3.21 [SC 376.730]; *Hom in Luc* 23.5–7 [SC 87.316–320]; *Contra Celsum* 7.5 [SC 150.22–24]. At the very beginning of the second century, Ignatius of Antioch described the distinctive mark or "imprint" proper to each believer (ἴδιος χαράκτηρ); cf. *Magnesians* 5.2 [SC 10bis.98]. By the mid-fourth century, Cyril of Jerusalem would preach to those preparing for baptism that they were to be sealed or marked in a way that would make them recognizable to the Lord: προσέλθετε εἰς τὴν μυστικὴν σφραγῖδα, ἵνα εὔγνωατοι ἦτε τῷ Δεσπότῃ, *Catechesis* 1.2 [PG 33.372]. On the demonic efforts to impede the souls of the dead, see Jean Daniélou, *The Bible and the Liturgy* (Notre Dame: University of Notre Dame Press, 1966), 24 and 57–58, with particular reference to the baptismal σφραγίς.

124. *Eam* in each of these phrases refers to *unaquaeque anima* in the previous sentence.

125. Jn 14.30.

126. *Ad suam partem.*

127. *Et libera nos a malo;* cf. Mt 6.13. Taking *malus* (πονηρός) here as a personalized substantive; this accords both with Origen's argument above and with his interpretation in *De oratione* 30.2 [GCS 3.393–394].

It also adds the reason why the Lord rescues his just ones from sinners, whether at the end of our life or at the time of judgment, when that day, "the day," according to the prophet, of want and distress, the day of darkness and destruction, the day of judgment, comes:[128] the reason why they deserve to be rescued then is *because they hoped in him.*[129] Therefore, he will rescue both from trouble and from want those who hope in him.

But I want to show you, on the basis of the holy Scriptures, how you should hope. Just as "no one is able to serve two masters,"[130] so, too, no one is able to hope in two masters. No one is able to hope "in the uncertainty of riches"[131] and in the Lord. No one is able "to place their hope in princes"[132] and in God. No one can hope "in the power of a horse"[133] and in God. No one can have hope in the world and in God. For unless you hope in God alone, and God sees that your hope has been turned[134] toward eternal life and that you entertain absolutely no other hope except in him who gives life to the dead and who summons into being those things that have no existence,[135] you will not be able to be rescued from sinners. For he alone is the one who saves those who hope in him, through Christ our Lord, "to whom is glory and power forever and ever. Amen."[136]

128. Cf. Zep 1.15.
129. Ps 36.40.
130. Mt 6.24.
131. 1 Tm 6.17.
132. Ps 117.9.
133. Ps 146.10.
134. *Esse conversam;* literally, "has been converted."
135. Cf. Rom 4.17; *Hom in Ps* 38.2.12 [SC 411.402].
136. Rv 5.13.

FIRST HOMILY ON PSALM 37 [38]

GOD, THE Creator of human bodies, knew that the weakness of the human body was such that it would be susceptible to various illnesses and subject to injuries and other debilities. For this reason, making provision for the maladies to come, he produced remedies from the earth and imparted the science of medicine so that, should sickness afflict the body, there should be no want of a cure.[1]

Where are these introductory remarks taking us? No doubt these are references to the soul.[2] For when the Creator of all had made the soul, he was aware that it would be susceptible to vices and, for this reason, subject to and burdened by sins. So just as he prepared remedies for the body from plants combined by human craft and science, so too he prepared remedies for the soul in the words he has sown and scattered throughout the divine Scriptures, so that those who are brought low by some illness, as soon as they sense the first inkling of sickness or perceive the prick and pain of a wound—that is, when they see the soul doing something contrary to its nature—they might seek out an appropriate and fitting spiritual discipline for themselves, drawn from God's precepts, which might bring them healing. For he has also imparted the practice of a medicine whose chief Physician is the Savior, who said concerning himself, "Those who are healthy do not need

1. Cf. *De principiis* 2.11.5 [GK 450], where Origen suggests that, in the end, the characteristic potencies (*virtutes*) associated with various herbs and plants will be made fully known.

2. On this significant theme in Origen, see David G. Bostock, "Medical Theory and Theology in Origen," in *Origeniana Tertia,* ed. R. P. C. Hanson and Henri Crouzel (Rome: Edizioni dell'Ateneo, 1985), 191–99.

a doctor; but those who are sick do."[3] He indeed was the chief Physician who is able to cure every illness and infirmity.[4] But his disciples Peter and Paul and the prophets too are doctors, and so are all those who have taken the place of the apostles in the Church and to whom has been entrusted the practice of healing what is wounded. God has intended that these be the doctors of souls in his Church, because our God does not will the death of the sinner but awaits his repentance and prayer.[5]

And so this Psalm also, which has just now been read, shows us—should we at some point be hindered by our sins—in what way and with what feeling we ought to pray and beseech the Physician on account of our pains and frailties. If ever, therefore, the Enemy has taken possession of us and wounded our souls with his fiery darts,[6] this Psalm teaches us first of all that it is fitting, after sinning, to confess the sin and to keep the offense in mind so that the heart, prompted by recollection of the fault and pained because of its failure, will refrain and restrain itself so that it may not do any such thing again. And I think this is why the inscription of the Psalm is "A Psalm of David for Recollection."[7] Moreover, it tells what this "for recollection" means throughout the entire text of the Psalm itself.

Let us see what we, who are all sinners, are to say or do if we find that we have failed,[8] so that, when we have learned these things in the sacred Scriptures, we might also be found worthy to obtain a cure for our wound. For it was indeed good that our soul's "body," so to speak, should always be endowed with health[9] and, fully surrounded by the armor of God,[10]

3. Mt 9.12. On Christ the Physician, cf. *De principiis* 2.10.6 [GK 432–434]; *Hom in Sam* 5.6 [SC 328.191]; *Hom in Luc* 13.2 [SC 87.208]. On further medicinal metaphors regarding the prophets, see *Hom in Jer* 12.5 [SC 238.26 and 350]; *Hom in Lev* 7.1–2 [SC 286.302 and 310]; 8.1 [SC 287.10].

4. Cf. Mt 9.35.

5. Cf. Ezek 18.23.

6. Cf. Eph 6.16; cf. *Hom in Ps* 36.3.3.

7. Ps 37.1. Cf. Ronald Heine, *Gregory of Nyssa's Treatise on the Inscriptions of the Psalms* (Oxford: Clarendon, 1995).

8. *Si in aliquo delicto fuerimus inventi;* taking the verb as a medial passive.

9. *In sanitate donare.* A curious idiom.

10. Cf. Eph 6.13; cf. *Hom in Ps* 36.1.4 [SC 411.76] and 36.2.8 [SC 411.118].

remain invulnerable to all the fiery darts of the wicked devil,[11] experience no illness, no affliction, and that our inner man take on no vice or sickness. If, then, through neglect of itself or idleness of mind[12] it falls into sin, it should recognize what is coming upon it. It is a painful punishment to be rebuked or reprimanded, and a torment so severe that even those who appear faithful and devout, if by chance they slip into some fault (as people sometimes do) and face accusation, react with indignation and hate those who rebuke them. In fact, they are reprimanding them to make them better.[13]

This evil was also the cause of the prophets being hated by the people of old and assailed with persecutions. This caused Isaiah to be cut in two,[14] it forced Zechariah to be slain between the sanctuary and the altar,[15] and Jeremiah to be submerged in a muddy cistern.[16] And, in the end, this was what crucified our Lord Jesus Christ.[17] For all these vicious deeds and shameful acts that we mentioned above were committed for no other reason than this: that while all are unwilling to be punished[18] by curative discipline through the correction of those who are themselves delinquent, the people, unwilling to endure the remedy and the cure, were burning for the demise of the doctor!

They are therefore called "blessed" and "wise" by the sacred

11. Cf. Eph 6.16.

12. *Animi,* here probably equivalent to *mens,* maintaining a distinction in some sense from *anima;* the later pronoun, *eum,* makes it clear that *animus* is its antecedent.

13. Cf. *Hom in Jer* 14.1 [SC 238.66].

14. *Secari;* an apocryphal account of Isaiah's demise, found in the Talmud, Targum, and the *Ascension of Isaiah* 5.1–2;11.14. Justin, *Dial* 120 [*Iustini Martyris Dialogus cum Tryphone,* ed. Miroslav Marcovich (Berlin: De Gruyter, 1997), 276–78], had accused his Jewish opponents of having excised the account from the canonical Isaiah.

15. Cf. 2 Chr 24.21; Mt 23.35.

16. Cf. Jer 38.6.

17. *Et ad ultimum haec fuit causa quae Dominum nostrum Iesum Christum egit in crucem;* cf. Petronius, *Satyricon* 53.3, Loeb Classical Library 15, trans. W. H. D. Rouse (Cambridge, MA: Harvard University Press, 1987), 108: *Mithridates servus in crucem actus est, quia Gaii nostri genio male dixerat.*

18. *Resecari;* punning on the earlier use of *secari* in reference to Isaiah.

Scriptures who, if rebuked when they do wrong, do not hate those who rebuke them. For thus the Scripture says, "Do not rebuke the evildoers lest they hate you; rebuke the wise man and he will love you."[19] Do you see how the Scripture calls "wise" the one who is liable to reprimand, and who does not hate but instead loves the one who rebukes him? Such were those who were reprimanded by the Apostle and, having been reduced to silence, did not hate those who reprimanded them. And this is why I think that the one who had sinned so gravely in Corinth obtained mercy: namely, that having been criticized by the Apostle—and criticized so severely that he was cut off from the assembly of the Church—he did not harbor hatred toward the one who rebuked him, but patiently accepted the punishment and bore it valiantly. I even think that he came to have a greater affection for Paul and for all those who had obeyed the directives of Paul in regard to his punishment.[20] It is for this reason that Paul changes his decision and reunites to the Church the one who had been cast out and says in addition, "Strengthen your charity toward him."[21] For he saw that he had preserved charity after being punished. And therefore, in the wake of his sin, he did not so much say that charity should be shown toward him—for it was already in him—but that the charity that was in him should be confirmed by all.

It is therefore necessary that the one who sins be rebuked. But because this reprimand, though of benefit, is a burden to us who are weaker, we avoid enduring it in the presence of all. And what do I mean by "presence of all"? Sometimes, when rebuked, we do not tolerate the presence of even two witnesses,[22] but we criticize the one who makes the accusation, and we say: "You should have said what you wanted to me alone and not embarrassed me in the presence of many." We smart from the

19. Prv 9.8.

20. Here he connects 1 Cor 5.1–5 with what he understands as its resolution in 2 Cor 2.5–11. Cf. Claude Jenkins, "Origen on I Corinthians," in *Journal of Theological Studies* 9 (1908): 353–72, esp. 363–65.

21. 2 Cor 2.8.

22. Following the scriptural principle that an accusation of a capital offense be substantiated by the word of two or three witnesses; cf. Dt 17.6; Mt 18.16.

pain, we are upset, we seethe, and we experience an inner torment of soul.

If this, then, is what a reprimand is like when we are rebuked by others or in the presence of others, what do we do when God rebukes us, if God himself confronts and rebukes us in anger?[23] We who cannot endure the wrath of a bishop who speaks in rebuke but bristle as we receive it, how will we tolerate that anger (which is said to belong to God) when it accuses us? Thus the prophet, aware of how many different kinds of accusation there are, and—being human—though willing to be rebuked for his faults, yet apprehensive that the burden would be heavier (that is, that he be rebuked with the Lord's anger), also says here what he had already said in another, earlier Psalm: "Lord, do not rebuke me in your anger."[24] Moreover, he says what follows also in a similar way: *Nor reprimand me in your wrath.*[25]

Therefore, we must say something about being reprimanded, concerning which the Apostle teaches us in a more general way when he says, "Indeed, at the present moment every reprimand seems to be something not for joy but for sadness; yet later it will produce the most tranquil fruit of justice for those who have been exercised through it."[26] This can also be observed in children, how when they are reprimanded with lashes by the pedagogues or they are jolted awake by their teachers, they take it with great annoyance and reckon the pain, which is inflicted on them for the sake of their instruction, to be the greatest evil. And although they are not unaware that their progress depends on this kind of instruction and reprimand, nevertheless they bear it impatiently and with annoyance. But if the instruction of the young is like this, what should we think about ourselves who are old, what sort of instruction or reprimand do we suppose faces us, which is imposed neither by stewards nor by pedagogues?[27] Scripture

23. Cf. Ps 37.2.

24. Ps 6.2.

25. Ps 6.2; Ps 37.2.

26. Heb 12.11.

27. *Non a dispensatoribus neque a paedagogis;* probably a reference to the fact that household servants played a role in the education of the young in antiquity;

certainly knows the pedagogue[28] and the steward[29] and the tutor[30] of the child. What, I ask, should we think or feel, when our instruction and reprimand are carried out by the Head of the Household[31] himself?

Let us return to the analogy of children. If a child is reprimanded by a pedagogue, it will not be necessary for him to experience the severity of his father's punishment, which is provoked by more serious and shameful offenses. If a child is reprimanded by an instructor, his teacher will not be as harsh as his father is capable of being should he note serious failings in his son. For if the father reprimands for the greater and more serious sins and if the son's offense is so great as to incite his father's wrath, without a doubt after the torments, after the punishments, he must also fear the possibility of being disowned.[32]

If you have grasped this analogy, please pass from the example to the reality,[33] and understand what is being said about us humans. All bishops and all priests and even deacons instruct us, and, as they instruct us, they make use of reprimands and speak pointedly with rather stern words. Moreover, this is also the case when we are instructed by tutors and governors,[34] namely the angels to whom are entrusted the management and governance of our soul,[35] just as the Angel of Repentance is described in a certain passage as the one who

cf. H. I. Marrou, *A History of Education in Antiquity,* trans. George Lamb (New York: Sheed and Ward, 1956), and now Teresa Morgan, *Literate Education in the Hellenistic and Roman Worlds* (Cambridge: Cambridge University Press, 1998), esp. 17–19 on the various terms used for "teacher."

28. *Paedagogum;* cf. Gal 3.24.

29. *Dispensatorem* [= οἰκόνομος]; cf. Gal 4.2.

30. *Procuratorem* [= ἐπίτροπος]; cf. Gal 4.2.

31. *Paterfamilias* [= οἰκοδεσπότης].

32. *Abdicationis poena;* literally, "being disowned"; perhaps "being disinherited."

33. *Ab exemplo* [τύπος] *ad rem* [πρᾶγμα].

34. *Procuratoribus et actoribus* [= ἐπιτρόποις καὶ οἰκονόμοις]; throughout this passage, *dispensator* and *actor* appear to be synonyms; both render οἰκόνομος in the Vulgate.

35. Cf. *De principiis* 2.11.6 [GK 450–454], where this angelic care is exercised *post mortem.*

receives us in order to chastise us, as the *Shepherd* teaches—if, in fact, one considers that book worthy of acceptance.[36] Meanwhile, we who are human submit to various kinds of instruction, to those who chastise us and to those who punish us. Nevertheless, we are not as yet chastised by the Head of the Household, but by angels who are tutors, who divide the work of chastising and reforming each one of us, and it is easier to endure when we are reprimanded by one of these.

So too occasionally our correction has been entrusted also to the pedagogue. For whoever was under the Law—since "the Law was our pedagogue in Christ"[37]—was found wanting in the Law, they were being reprimanded by the pedagogue when they were punished on the basis of the Law. For they were punished either when they were stoned or when they endured one of the types of punishments which Moses had laid down in writing.[38] None of these about whom we have been speaking was punished by the Head of the Household himself. For neither the Law nor the Angel of Repentance was the Head of the Household.

But there are other sins for which the Head of the Household himself punishes the sinner, that is, one who, having gone past the boundaries of villainy, has extended the impiety of his evildoing beyond creaturely insolence. Nevertheless, no one but God alone knows when someone should be handed over to the tutors to be chastised; or when he should be turned over to the stewards to be rebuked; or even when he should be subjected to the pedagogue (in comparison to whom the reprimands of all these would be far lighter). And God alone

36. That is, as canonical—an acceptance that, in the late second and early third centuries, was often related to its use liturgically; cf. *Shepherd of Hermas,* Vision 5 (25) [SC 53bis.140–144], where the Shepherd reveals himself to Hermas as ὁ ἄγγελος τῆς μετανοίας. See Bruce Metzger, *The Canon of the New Testament: Its Origin, Development, and Significance* (Oxford: Clarendon, 1987), 140, where he notes that by the time Origen was composing his *Commentary on Romans,* c. 244–246 AD, he held the *Shepherd* to have been an inspired work (*Comm in Rom* 10.31).

37. Gal 3.24; cf. also Origen's comments on the Law as pedagogue in relation to the Gospel in his *Comm in Jn* 1.37–39 [SC 120bis.78].

38. Cf. Lv 20.1–21.

surely knows if such a one provokes the divine hand itself, so to speak, to punishment.

If you have understood what has been said, if you have followed the higher meaning,[39] look now at how the prophet follows this up when he says, "Although you reprimand me, God, do not reprimand me in anger."[40] But we do not wish to be reprimanded, nor do we tolerate the pedagogue bringing things to our attention, and we do not willingly accept the reprimands of tutors or stewards. And it is for this reason that it is necessary that correction be imposed on us by the very wrath of God. For the prophet says, *Lord, do not rebuke me in your anger nor reprimand me in your wrath.*[41]

2. But the one who says this should offer a reason why he does not wish to be rebuked in anger or reprimanded in wrath. And let us see what this reason is so that, should we fail, we too, by saying what this reason is and by doing what we are instructed, not incur the vengeance of the Lord, who rebukes with anger and who reprimands with wrath. *For,* it says, *your arrows have sunk into me, and you have strengthened your hand over me.*[42] The word of the Lord is like an arrow. In fact, the Savior spoke of it in this way: "he placed me like a chosen arrow and has hidden me in his quiver."[43] Therefore, the one who speaks the word of the Lord is shooting arrows. And when he speaks in reprimand or in chastisement, he pierces the heart of the hearer with a dart of reprimand.

In the case, then, of one who receives the words of the Lord in such a way that his heart is pierced by the words he hears and is goaded to repentance by them, it is certain that the dart of God's word has not glanced off him to no effect nor flown past him, but that all the arrows of God's words have been firmly fixed in him. And so in a certain place it also says, "Have you seen how Ahab has been struck through?"[44] Rightly now

39. *Altiorem ... intellectum.*

40. Jer 10.24.

41. Ps 37.2.

42. Ps 37.3.

43. Is 49.2; note here that it is Christ speaking through Isaiah; cf. *Hom in Ps* 36.2.8 [SC 411.120], p. 107 above.

44. 1 Kgs 21.29; see Marguerite Harl, "Les origines grecques du mot et de

the prophet also says, *Lord, do not rebuke me in your anger nor reprimand me in your wrath.*[45] The reason for this claim that follows is a sound one, and should serve to deflect from him the reprimand which stems from the Lord's anger: *for your arrows have sunk deep in me.*[46]

For example even now, if out of this entire gathering of listeners there are some who are aware that they are in some kind of sin—indeed, would that there were none!—nevertheless, it must be that there are some who are aware of it and if, upon hearing what we are saying, they listen in good faith,[47] their heart will be struck through by the darts of our words, and, pierced by such darts, they will be pained and turned to repentance, and will say, *Lord, do not rebuke me in your anger nor reprimand me in your wrath, for your arrows have sunk deep in me.* But if, on hearing these things, he is not struck through, but the arrow or dart finds in his soul, as in a body already dead, no awareness of pain, and he experiences no recollection of his sins, this man, indeed, is the kind who should be reprimanded with goads of the Lord's anger and rebuked by reproaches from his wrath.[48] For this one is unable to say to the Lord: *For your arrows have sunk deep in me.*

Would that all who hear me, struck through and so moved by the things that are said, might experience conversion and repentance and say to the Teacher, "*For your arrows have sunk deep in me,* and while you chastise us with God's word, while you beat us, while you strike us in the innermost parts of our conscience, *you have strengthened your hand over me.*"[49] For truly the pedagogue strengthens his hand over children while he beats and corrects them, and he strengthens his hands when stripes are inflicted not carelessly or lightly. And so one can say to the Lord when he has shot his arrows (but speaking to the

---

la notion de componction dans le Septante et ses commentateurs," in *Revue des études augustiniennes* 31 (1986): 3–21.

45. Ps 37.2.

46. Ps 37.3.

47. *recte et fideliter audiant.*

48. Striving to reproduce the chiasmus in the Latin of Rufinus: *arguas … corripias* [Psalm text]: *corripiatur … arguatur.*

49. Ps 37.3.

Lord through whomever the Lord wishes to send the arrows of his words) that *you have strengthened your hand over me.*[50]

For since the hand of the Lord is present to him who throws the darts of words and who fixes arrows in the soul of the hearer, with good reason he also says to the Lord: "*You have strengthened your hand over me, and there is no health in my flesh before the face of your wrath.*[51] For this reason I ask not to experience the power of your wrath itself, for receiving only an indication of it, and seeing somehow only its face as described through the words alone of the divine Scriptures, my entire body is already pained, and I am greatly troubled: *there is not* any *health in my flesh,* nor *is there peace in my bones,*[52] and that is so only because I imagine I feel or see the face of your wrath in the holy Scriptures, and not in fact your wrath itself. And if, because of this alone, I suffer such things, for this reason I pray that I will not suffer the wrath itself."

See, then, if these things are not clearly stated in the passage which says, *You have strengthened your hand over me, and there is no health in my flesh before the face of your wrath.* It could have said, "at your wrath," but now it says *before the face of your wrath.* For if it had said "at your wrath," what it said above—*do not reprimand me in your wrath*[53]—would surely be pointless. But now it says, *there is no health in my flesh before the face of your wrath.* For indeed the appearance alone of your wrath (that is, the very thought of your displeasure) has so thoroughly frightened and changed[54] me that there is no place for your wrath in me.

There is no health in my flesh.[55] The Apostle, in testimony against the one who had sinned at Corinth, offers this: "Hand over one such as this to Satan for the destruction of the flesh."[56] Is one to think that he was wishing that something evil would happen[57] to the man who, he was saying, should be

50. Ibid.
51. Ps 37.3–4.
52. Ps 37.4.
53. Ps 37.2.
54. *Convertit.*
55. Ps 37.4.
56. 1 Cor 5.5.
57. *Iniquum fieri.* Cf. Crouzel, SC 411.278, n. 2.

handed over to Satan for the destruction of the flesh? Rather, it is clear that it was for his own well-being[58] that he was handing over his flesh for destruction. For then he adds, "I have handed over one of this sort to Satan for the destruction of his flesh so that his spirit might be safe on the day of the Lord,"[59] showing that it is impossible for the spirit to be saved if the flesh is not handed over to destruction.

Listen to what this "destruction of the flesh" is. For that which is destroyed[60] is without doubt dead. The flesh is alive in a sinner; but in a just person, the flesh is dead. On account of this, the just person says, "We are always carrying about in our body the death of Jesus Christ so that the life of Jesus Christ might also be made manifest in our mortal flesh."[61] Likewise, we have received the command that says, "Put to death your members that are upon the earth."[62] And blessed is the one who is dead to sin, in accord with what is said: "The body indeed is dead on account of sin, but the spirit is alive on account of being made just."[63] So "to be handed over for the destruction of the flesh" means that the fleshly understanding[64] within us is to die off and the desire of the flesh is not to be alive in it.[65] Because of the fact that the understanding of the flesh is dead— that we might not think according to the flesh[66]—the spirit is made safe. Otherwise, as long as the understanding of the flesh[67] lives in us and the "flesh" is alive, we are unable to think in terms of spiritual realities. This, then, is how the Apostle handed over for the destruction of the flesh the one who had lived according to the flesh, so

58. *Pro salute eius;* it is difficult to reproduce in English the double meaning of *salus* in Christian Latin.

59. *Spiritus salvus fiat in die Domini;* 1 Cor 5.5.

60. *Interierit;* a cognate of *interitus.*

61. 2 Cor 4.10.

62. Col 3.5; here *mortificate,* cognate of *mortificatio* [νέκρωσις] of 2 Cor 4.10.

63. Rom 8.10; *justificatio* here rendering the Greek δικαιοσύνη.

64. *Sensus carnalis* [= τὸ φρόνημα τῆς σαρκός], literally, "the understanding of the flesh."

65. *In ea.* The antecedent is more likely *anima* than *caro.*

66. Cf. Rom 8.5.

67. *Sensus carnis ... sensus* [*in nobis*] *carnis;* in the preceding sentence, this is expressed adjectivally as *sensus carnalis.*

that, once the understanding of the flesh had died off, "the spirit might be safe on the day of the Lord."[68] If you have understood the words of the Apostle, let us return to the matter at hand.

Would that, when I sin in my body, the destruction of the flesh might be brought upon me, that the spirit might be saved (failure, moreover, always comes from the understanding of the flesh). For if the flesh is weak, its progressive weakening doubtless advances even to the death of the flesh, and at that point it is rightly said, *There is no health in my flesh.*[69] But if the flesh, once weakened, recovers its health, that is, it savors the things of the flesh and desires what is evil, then there is a "health" in the flesh that is certainly not good for the spirit.[70] The one, then, who is reluctant to be accused by God's wrath and to be rebuked by his anger offers the most legitimate reasons for his acquittal when he declares that he has been pierced through by the arrows of God's words and so unnerved and so thoroughly frightened by the appearance alone of the Lord's wrath, that there is absolutely no health in his flesh; that is, the desire for sin no longer remains in him.

I recall that once when I was speaking about that chapter in the Gospel where it is written: "The spirit is indeed ready, but the flesh is weak,"[71] I had thought along these lines: that before our Savior came to the cross and crucified the flesh and made it die off, before it was fully put to death, he first said that his flesh was weak. And, indeed, as long as the flesh was weak, he said that the spirit was ready. But when he hands the flesh over to the cross and finishes it off by means of a complete dying, he then no longer asserts that the spirit is ready,

68. 1 Cor 5.5.

69. Ps 37.4.

70. *Si vero* [*non*] *infirmatur quidem caro sed redit ad sanitatem suam, id est ut sapiat quae sunt carnis ac desideret malum, tunc sanitas est in carne, quod utique spiritui non est bonum.* Prinzivalli, *Omelie sui Salmi* (1991), 270, has seen fit to add the emendation (*non*), which seems unnecessary in the Latin, on the basis of Greek fragment 30 [SC 411.434]; the plain meaning, however, is clear enough.

71. Mt 26.41; here follows an idiosyncratic interpretation; cf. *Comm in Cant,* pr. 2.4 [SC 375.92], where Origen relates the "weakening" to the "outer man" of 2 Cor 4.6 viewed in light of Gn 2.

but that it has been placed in the Father's hands.[72] In describing these things as he experienced them, he was providing an example for our instruction. For it was for our sake that he was weak.

Let us, then, look at ourselves, to see if our flesh is weak, if it has not become lax from excess and pleasure, and whether this corrupted "health" is present in it. See if through daily self-denial the flesh is made weak, if through self-restraint desires are pruned away, lust is subdued, and vices cease. In that case, even if it has not yet died off, *there is* nevertheless *no health in* your *flesh,* so long as your earthly members are also being put to death.[73] But what causes the health in our flesh to cease to exist? When we consider the face of God's wrath. For when we recall the wrath of God and put his countenance before our eyes (drawing upon his own ordinance, which is why it is called the "face of wrath"),[74] the flesh, deeply dismayed and thoroughly frightened, becomes weak and languishes.

3. *There is no peace for my bones when faced with my sins.* One who has sinned should also say these words and keep in mind after he has sinned the fact that he has sinned, just as David himself used to say in the fiftieth Psalm: "And my sin is always before me."[75] There are certain individuals who, when they have sinned, are completely carefree: they neither think about their sin nor does the evil they have done occur to them, but they carry on with their lives as though they had done nothing at all. These, then, are incapable of saying, "For my sin is always before me." But when, after a sin, one is consumed with distress and afflicted on account of his sin and, prodded by the goadings of his conscience, experiences an incessant

72. In his *Dialogue with Heraclides* 7.1–8.17 [SC 67.70–73], in an attempt to undermine those who disparage the body, Origen discusses what occurred at the death of Christ: his spirit went to the Father, his soul to Hades, and his body to the tomb; the three were reunited at the Resurrection.

73. Cf. Col 3.5; *membra tua super terram* = τὰ μέλη τὰ ἐπὶ τῆς γῆς, in the Greek of Paul the prepositional phrase following the article serving adjectivally.

74. Cf. Ps 37.4.

75. Ps 50.5.

gnawing,[76] and is assailed by unseen accusations of guilt,[77] with good reason he says, *There is no peace for my bones when faced with my sins.*[78]

There is clearly a kind of "face" even of sins and, so to speak, a certain complexion and appearance with which those things done at one time are apt to be recalled and recognized. When, therefore, we have placed our sins before the eyes of our heart and, looking at each one of them, we blush in recognition of what we have done and repent of it, then, deeply troubled and quite frightened, with good reason we say that we have no peace in our bones when faced with our sins.

4. The one who repents of his sins should also add these words and say, *For my iniquities loom over my head; like a heavy burden they weigh down upon me.*[79] For those who are neither pained nor burdened on account of their sins but who are carefree and awash in extravagance cannot speak these words, nor do they sense that their iniquities are in fact rapidly growing higher and going up beyond their own head, while they themselves are shrinking and being brought to nothing;[80] for this reason they are incapable of saying, *For my iniquities loom over my head; like a heavy burden they weigh down upon me.* For how can they speak these words, those who not only take delight in their faults, but even, in their glee, prefer their own bad deeds? For them, their sin becomes not a burden, but actually a source of delight.

Therefore, to speak these words is not their part, but belongs to those for whom lust has grown cheap, to whom the vices are appalling, and those who have discovered that all delight in the charms of the present is for naught, because hereafter it has no future at all. These are the ones who can also say the words that follow: *Because my wounds have become foul and fetid.*[81]

76. *Mordetur sine intermissione.*

77. *Atque occultis confutationibus impugnatur.*

78. Ps 37.4.

79. Ps 37.5.

80. Cf. 2 Mc 6.12–17, where God's chastisement is viewed as a sign of his love for Israel, whereas he allows the sins of the non-Jews to accumulate to their destruction.

81. Ps 37.6.

"Do not," the Savior says, "cast your pearls before swine."[82] He calls "swine" those who take delight in the fetid stench of sins and who, like swine, seek out every fetid stench as if it were the sweetest smell. Consider the sinner as one who takes delight in his sins and who rejoices in his evil deeds: for he even wallows in its stinking dung, and, having no perception of the stench that is given off by the dung of sin, he finds delight in it as though they were the greatest pleasures and the sweetest delights. But if at some point it happens that he puts aside the sensibility and the sense of smell proper to swine and grasps the sensibility of the Word of God,[83] so that he might be able to smell the stench of his own sins, turned immediately to repentance and seeking reform, he becomes unable to endure his own stench, crying out for the Heavenly Physician[84] and showing him the sores from his fetid wounds, and says, *My wounds have become foul and fetid at the sight of my foolishness.*[85] Moreover, here he has correctly called sin "foolishness," for no one who is wise ever commits sin.[86]

5. *I was afflicted with miseries and bent low even to the end.*[87] If at some point you should see one who has sinned mourning and downcast by the sadness that is according to God—"for the sadness that is according to God accomplishes a repentance that is reliable for salvation"[88]—he truly says, *I was afflicted with miseries and bent low even to the end.* Perhaps this is why the holy Apostle himself too, aware that he had at one time sinned, says, "Miserable man that I am, who will liberate me from the body of this death?"[89] For he, too, had sinned when he persecuted the Church of God, which is why he says, "I am not wor-

82. Mt 7.6. Cf. *Hom in Gen* 11.1 [SC 7bis.280].

83. Another possibility is to render *sensus* as "mind" or "understanding," juxtaposing the "mind" of swine (like the "understanding of the flesh," τὸ φρόνημα τῆς σαρκός; cf. Rom 8.6–7) to the "mind" of Scripture. "Sensibility" is used here to capture the idea of sense perception, the metaphor being used by Origen.

84. Cf. Mt 9.12; cf. above at 1 [SC 411.258–260], on pp. 171–72.

85. Ps 37.6.

86. The contrast of *insipientia* and *sapiens* is lost in English.

87. Ps 37.7; cf. Ps 56.7 (*iuxta* LXX): *laqueum paraverunt pedibus meis et incurvaverunt animam meam.*

88. 2 Cor 7.10.

89. Rom 7.24.

thy to be called an apostle."[90] Therefore, he says, *I was afflicted with miseries.* He does not say, "I am still being afflicted." For if my sins have already passed, I was afflicted with miseries; but if they remain and I am engaged in them, I am still being afflicted with miseries. It therefore says, *I was afflicted with miseries and bent low even to the end.*

If you should see one who has sinned unable to look up to the sky but, with his body bent and his face—not only of his body but also of his soul—plunged downward toward the ground, twisting his neck around like a circle,[91] you understand how one is bent low even to the end. But if you want to understand by means of examples how each individual is bent low by his own sins so that he is incapable of looking up or raising his eyes to heaven, consider that tax collector who in the Gospel entered the Temple and, standing far off and not daring to raise his eyes to heaven, was striking his breast and confessing his sins as he said, "God be merciful to me, a sinner."[92] To be sure, it is fitting for this man to say, *I was bent low even to the end, and all day long I went about downcast.*[93] When it says this, it is as though it is expressing the heart and mind[94] of the repentant sinner who says, "Ever since I sinned, I have never laughed, I was never joyful, I never allowed myself anything pleasant, but was always in mourning, always engaged in penance, always in tears."

Such is the teaching of the Gospel, where the Lord says, "Blessed are those who mourn," and, "Blessed are those who weep."[95] But conversely, if one is a sinner and guilty of many evils and is struck with no sting from his shameful deeds, and even more, laughs and is joyful and well-pleased, and is in no way disturbed by the goads of his conscience, see if it is not fitting that what is written be said to him: "Woe to those who laugh now, for you will weep and mourn."[96]

90. 1 Cor 15.9.
91. Cf. Is 58.5.
92. Lk 18.13.
93. Ps 37.7.
94. *Affectum et animum.*
95. Cf. Mt 5.5 and Lk 6.21.
96. Lk 6.25.

6. *All day long I went about downcast, for my loins were filled with illusions.*[97] The receptacle for the human seed is said to be in the loins or genitals. It follows that the kind of sin being indicated here is that which stems from lust. For indeed the Apostle portrays lustful activity as among the worst violations when he says, "Am I to take the members that belong to Christ and make them members of a prostitute? Absolutely not!"[98] When, therefore, someone has sunk quite readily and without self-control into wanton behavior of this kind, then his loins or genitals are said to have been filled with illusions. For illusion belongs to the devil, who makes sport of the person[99] and prods him into the lack of self-control characteristic of this kind of sin.

It is no wonder, then, if the loins of sinful persons are filled with illusions, since Job also speaks this way about the dragon (who is understood to be the devil): "His whole power is in his loins, and his strength in the navel of his belly."[100] The devil's power, then, is found chiefly in the loins of a human being, from which fornication and adultery come forth, from which is begotten the corruption of the young and every kind of filth. So too is the sin of women clearly located in the navel of the belly, something he wished to express with language more suitable, as the power and strength of the dragon (the devil) are indeed found in both men and women.

And there is no health in my flesh.[101] In this verse he shows his progress and indicates that he is close to putting his flesh to death and bringing it to destruction. He repeats this here a second time[102] so that he might make clear that the cure for the annoying temptations has already been applied.

I have been afflicted and greatly humbled.[103] We are bidden to eat the bread of affliction on the feasts of the Lord,[104] and it

97. Ps 37.7–8.
98. 1 Cor 6.15.
99. *Illusio est enim diaboli illudentis hominem:* a pun lost in English.
100. Jb 40.16.
101. Ps 37.8.
102. Cf. Ps 37.4.
103. Ps 37.9.
104. Cf. Dt 16.3.

is said that during the same feasts a person should humble his soul. And when the feast of atonement is proclaimed, "Humble your souls" is said.[105] Therefore, since the one who repents of his sins afflicts himself and humbles himself like that tax collector we spoke of earlier, for this reason he then says that he acknowledges his heartfelt repentance, praying that he not be accused by the Lord's anger nor rebuked by his wrath.[106] For he says, *I have been afflicted and greatly humbled.*[107] He is saying, "Not only have I been afflicted and humbled, but I have been gravely afflicted and humbled greatly."

To give an example: say there is someone who is rich by worldly standards and is living quite affluently. He experiences a sudden collapse and is reduced to utter poverty; driven from house and homeland, relegated to islands and crags, he lives a meager and miserable life in solitude.[108] Then, recalling his homeland and his parents, remembering his noble status, his family, his goods and his property, his abundant riches and the entire life of luxury that he had enjoyed, with what laments and groans he will call to mind his former happiness. And so for this man, the recollection of what he lost is a greater punishment than the suffering he endures.[109]

In comparison with this example, consider for me also a person who has lived his life temperately, chastely, and justly, who is aware that he has acted uprightly. If this person experiences a collapse (falling away from his homeland, that is, from the Church), and is driven onto some island and its fearsome crags (which is the abode of sin), tumbling away from his resources and wealth (which for him were found in all his good deeds), he finds himself living in deep poverty. All the just deeds he performed will be forgotten on account of his sin. If, then, he finds himself in such straits, with what groans

105. Cf. Lv 23.27.

106. Cf. Ps 37.2.

107. Ps 37.9.

108. There are interesting verbal similarities here to the account of the conditions endured by the prophets found in Heb 11.36–38 and which recur more explicitly in *Hom in Ps* 36.4.3 [SC 411.202–206]; see above, p. 144.

109. Taking this last line, unlike Crouzel [SC 411.294], as a statement, not a question.

and cries will he call out and say, *"I cried out from the groaning of my heart, 'Lord, in your sight is all my desire and my groaning.'*[110] Everything I have done since I began to sin, whether the worldly desires I have pursued or whatever else I have done, I bring all this before you in my prayer and I place it in your sight. *And my groaning has not been hidden from you.*[111] For you know that I am always groaning over this."

My heart is deeply troubled, and my strength has abandoned me.[112] See my heart, O Lord, that it is deeply troubled on account of my sins. And so I pray that you do not accuse me in your anger nor rebuke me in your wrath.[113] But if *my strength has abandoned me,* doubtless I was at one time strong, and my manner of life was good, but I later fell, because *my strength has abandoned me, and the light of my eyes is no longer with me.*[114] This seems to be the voice of one who has fallen into darkness after being enlightened,[115] after the teaching has been handed on, and after coming to the knowledge of the truth. Therefore, that we will not also suffer the same fate, but rather that our light might always be in us and, as we carry out the works of light, we might, as sons of the light,[116] have confidence in Christ Jesus, let us ever and unceasingly entreat God the Father, "to whom are glory and power for ever and ever. Amen."[117]

110. Ps 37.9–10.
111. Ps 37.10.
112. Ps 37.11.
113. Cf. Ps 37.2.
114. Ps 37.11.
115. A clear reference to baptism, followed pleonastically by references to the accompanying catechesis, which enlightens.
116. Cf. Jn 12.36.
117. Rv 5.13.

SECOND HOMILY ON PSALM 37 [38]

ONE WHO confesses his sins to God and grieves in his soul[1] while he does penance—aware of the punishment that awaits the sinner after leaving this life—speaks these words, listing how many things he must endure upon turning to repentance and reform, how his friends are abandoning him and his neighbors also keep themselves at a distance because he has turned to confession of his sin and to sorrow for it. And so he says, *My friends and my neighbors have drawn near and stand opposed to me.*[2] Imagine for me a person who is indeed a believer (yet a weak one) who has allowed himself to be overcome by some sin and for this reason laments his failures and searches in every way for a remedy and for the healing of his wound; although he has been overwhelmed and has fallen, he nevertheless desires a cure to restore the health of his soul.

If, then, a person like this, aware of his sin, confesses what he has done and in the face of human shame gives little heed to those who censure, stigmatize, or ridicule him as he confesses, he nonetheless understands that, by means of this process, forgiveness will be granted to him and also that on the day of resurrection he will escape embarrassment and reproach before the angels of God[3] for the things on account of which he is now embarrassed before men. His understanding is such that he does not want to cover up or hide his stain, but he declares his failure, and does not want to be "a whitened sepul-

1. *In animo* (versus *in anima*); perhaps a reference to the higher activity of the soul, ordinarily rendered by Rufinus as *mens* (or occasionally as *principale cordis/principalis intellectus*).

2. Ps 37.12.

3. Cf. Lk 12.8.

cher, appearing beautiful to people on the outside, that is, to appear just to those who see him, but on the inside being full of every filth and the bones of the dead."[4] If, then, someone is so faithful that, on becoming aware of something, he steps forward and stands as his own accuser, upon hearing these things those who do not fear God's judgment to come would certainly not remain weak when in the company of those who are weak;[5] would not burn when in the company of those who cause scandal;[6] would not lie prostrate with those who have fallen, but would say, "Keep far away from me and do not come near me, for I am clean," and they would begin to despise him whom they were admiring only shortly before, and would withdraw their friendship from him who did not wish to conceal his failure. It is of these, then, that the one who is making confession says, *My friends and my neighbors have drawn near and stand opposed to me, and those close to me have stood far off.*[7]

But it is not necessary for one who desires to be saved after a failure to be afraid nor to be frightened at the criticism of those who give no thought to their own sins and who fail to remember the saying of the divine Scripture: "Do not reproach the one who turns himself from sin but remember that we are all guilty."[8] He should not spend time thinking about such persons, but rather give thought to his own soul, praying to God that he might be heard by him and lifted up after his fall so that he might be able to say what follows: "For I will declare my iniquity, and I will give thought to my own sin."[9] Although my friends and my neighbors are opposed to me and those close to me are drawing far away from me,[10] as long as I am my own accuser, as long as I confess my misdeeds without anyone rebuking me, as long as I refuse to imitate those who,

4. Mt 23.27.

5. Cf. 1 Cor 9.22.

6. Cf. 2 Cor 11.29: *Quis infirmatur et non infirmor, quis scandalizatur et ego non uror?* Note that in the scriptural text *scandalizatur* is passive; in Rufinus's translation of Origen's allusion it is an active participle (*cum scandalizantibus*).

7. Ps 37.12.

8. Sir 8.5.

9. Ibid.

10. Cf. Ps 37.12.

even when charged in court and convicted by witnesses, and even in the face of torturers' punishments, still cover up their evil deeds; for embarrassment at what they have done has a greater hold upon them than the penalty exacted by the torturer.[11] For surely I know that nothing is hidden from God but that everything is uncovered and manifest in his sight; so why do I hide and cover up what he knows? Why do I not rather accuse and convict myself? Why do I wait for an accuser, when my conscience (who is my accuser) is with me? Perhaps for this reason he too will spare me if I do not spare myself.

Therefore, *those close to me have stood far off, and those who were seeking my life used force. And those who were seeking evil for me spoke vanity.*[12] Once again, it is speaking about others. For there are certain persons who seek what is evil for the just and who do not rejoice in the same way when they hear something good about him as they delight when hearing bad things, and they exult when they see the just person in evil circumstances. And it is these who, when they see the just one confessing his sins, spew forth, as it were, a kind of foul poison, and it is for this reason that it says: *Those who were seeking my life used force. And those who were seeking evil for me spoke vanity.*[13]

It is really quite clear that those who seek evil for the just person are not the only ones who speak vanity, but so does everyone who strives to bring evil upon anyone else. For he who seeks to do evil is not speaking the things that are according to God. And this is why we ought rather to seek what is good. If we could only return good for evil even toward those who hate us, either persuading our enemies what the good is or working to call their defiant souls back to harmony and peace, we might then become children of the "Father who is in heaven, who commands his sun to rise upon the good and the bad and who rains upon the just and the unjust."[14]

2. *Those,* then, *who were seeking evil for me spoke vanity and were*

11. This actually appears to be a lengthy dependent clause without a genuine apodosis, so I have been forced to manipulate it a bit.

12. Ps 37.12–13.

13. Ps 37.13.

14. Mt 5.45.

plotting treachery all day long.[15] See the one who is waiting in ambush for the just.[16] For I already call him "just" who, first of all, becomes his own accuser, as the word of Scripture attests.[17] For Scripture calls him "wise" who, when accused, does not hate the one who brings the accusation but, even more, loves him.[18] So also he is called "just" who after sinning does not persist in his sins nor does he wait for the devil to become his accuser[19]—lest he bring his sins into full view—but accuses himself and convicts himself and, through his confession, is freed from death.

For *those who were seeking evil for me spoke vanity and were plotting treachery all day long. But I, like one who is deaf, did not listen to them.*[20] What more outstanding or excellent virtue is there than this: namely that an individual, upon hearing those who curse and disparage him speaking maliciously in criticism, detraction, and accusation, turns his ear away as if not listening and lowers his eye as if not looking so that he might not be roused by anger and lash out in vengeance, not seeking an eye for an eye[21] nor a word for a word, nor a curse for a curse, nor a lie for a lie, nor an accusation for an accusation.[22] Such, then, is the just one; as I have said already, I call that person "just" who, through his confession of his sins, will vomit out his passions.

3. *But I, like one who is deaf, did not listen to them, and like one who is mute, I did not open my mouth. And I became like one who does not hear.*[23] When I was being cursed, when I was being impugned, when people were bringing forward all kinds of charges against me,[24] I was *like one who is deaf* and *did not listen to*

15. Ps 37.13.
16. Cf. Wis 2.12.
17. Cf. Prv 18.17 (LXX); cf. also *Hom in Ps* 37.1.1 [SC 411.264]; *Hom in Ps* 37.2.1 [SC 411.304].
18. Cf. Prv 9.8.
19. Cf. *Hom in Ps* 38.2.4 [SC 411.386], where this theme is developed.
20. Ps 37.13–14.
21. Cf. Ex 21.24; Lv 24.20.
22. Cf. 1 Pt 3.9.
23. Ps 37.14–15.
24. Cf. Mt 5.11.

them, and like one who is mute, I did not open my mouth; in response to their curses I returned no curses. But what good is it for us to discuss these things? What good is it for us to explain these passages from the holy Scriptures if we do not remember them at the moment when the situation requires: when we are cursed by our brothers, when they disparage us, when we are insulted even to our face with charges and abuse, when everything that is happening arouses our fury and moves our soul to anger? It is then that we must remember these words; it is then that we should call to mind that it is written: *And I became like one who does not hear and who does not have a harsh word in his mouth.*[25]

There will be times when someone speaks against me and perhaps lies; and other times when what he says is even true. Nevertheless, I can say—and do so truthfully—much worse things about him. If indeed I am a sinner and recall none of these things of which we have now spoken, I will imitate the malice of that person, and I will become, not like God, but like him, returning curses for curses. But if I am a just person, *like one who is deaf,* I do not listen, *and like one who is mute, who does not have a harsh word in his mouth,*[26] I say nothing in reply, and though I have grounds to make an accusation, I do not accuse. For I understand that the correct way for one to make an accusation is to do so dispassionately, with a view toward the well-being[27] of the one being rebuked, not vengeance.

Therefore, if I rebuke someone when he speaks disparagingly about me or speaks ill of me, I am not acting properly. For I am rebuking him out of anger and indignation, desiring to inflict sadness upon him, not that sadness that is "according to God, the sadness that accomplishes a repentance that is reliable for salvation,"[28] but a sadness that harms rather than reforms the soul. If, then, we remember these things, we will not act this way; but when something like this happens to us, we say, *I became like one who does not hear and who does not have a harsh word in his mouth.*[29]

25. Ps 37.15.
26. Ibid.
27. *Salutem;* of course, "salvation," too.
28. 2 Cor 7.10.
29. Ps 37.15.

But why have I become like this? *For,* it says, *I have placed my hope in you.*[30] For if I had not placed my hope in you and had no faith in you who said, "'Vengeance is mine; I will give what is due,' says the Lord,"[31] I would indeed have avenged myself; but now I remember that precept whereby we are commanded not to avenge ourselves, but to leave that [to God].[32] And you will find these things in the divine Scriptures. You read: *I became like one who does not hear and who does not have a harsh word in his mouth. For I have placed my hope in you, Lord, and you will hear me, Lord, my God.*[33] I, like a deaf man, did not listen to those who were slandering me; but you [God], listen[34] to what they are saying.

If we were such as the divine Word desires us to be—like Elijah—we would indeed tell God to grant rain, and it would rain;[35] like Samuel at the time of harvest, we would ask that he grant from heaven an abundance of rain, and we would be heard. But how will God hear us now, when we do not listen to him? How will he do what we want, when we do not do what he wants? God wants us to be such that we speak to God like gods.[36] He wishes us to be children of God, so that we might become partakers[37] and, as God's children, co-heirs,[38] so that we might say (just as he did), "Father, I know that you always hear me."[39] We know that God has said to us, "I have said, you are all gods and children of the Most High."[40] But in return for our merits[41] we await rather that which follows (which we

30. Ps 37.16.

31. Dt 32.35.

32. Cf. Rom 12.19, itself a quotation of Dt 32.35.

33. Ps 37.15–16.

34. *Tu, audi;* an imperative.

35. 1 Kgs 18.45.

36. Cf. Ps 81.6.

37. *Consortes;* cf. 2 Pt 1.4. See Norman Russell, *The Doctrine of Divinization in Greek Patristic Thought* (Oxford: Oxford University Press, 2004), 151, on the importance of this text for Origen.

38. Cf. Rom 8.17.

39. Jn 11.42.

40. Ps 81.6.

41. *Pro meritis nostris;* here taken negatively ("on account of what we deserve").

deserve): "But you will die like mortals, and like one of the princes you will fall";[42] but *you will hear me, Lord my God.*[43]

4. *For I said: Do not let my enemies triumph over me.*[44] When I was slandered and did not respond in kind to those who were slandering me, I was saying these words: "'If,' in fact, 'I responded in kind to those who were repaying evils to me,'[45] I too would certainly be abandoned by God, and, once abandoned, I would necessarily fall. Moreover, when I fall, my enemies will triumph over me." But if I do not return evil for evil,[46] but leave[47] the judgment to God, with his help I will not fall down but will stand firm, and my enemies will not triumph over me. For I also said this: *While my feet were being moved, they were speaking great things against me.*[48] As long as I remain unafraid and steadfast, my enemies will not speak great things against me, for they have nothing to say. But as soon as I waver (not to say fall), they will at once begin to reproach me and say, "Do you see him? Look what he did. Though he teaches one thing, he does another, the opposite of what he teaches." Persons like this necessarily say, *While my feet were being moved, they were speaking great things against me.*[49]

But another voice, comparatively better than this last one, insofar as it relates to the speakers[50] introduced by the prophets, says this: "Yet my feet were not moved much,"[51] meaning, "The feet of that individual were certainly moved, but my feet were moved a little less." Perhaps there might be someone else

42. Ps 81.7.

43. Ps 37.16.

44. Ps 37.17.

45. Ps 7.5.

46. Cf. 1 Pt 3.9.

47. *Dereliquero;* a nice use of the verb from the line before (*derelinquar* ... *derelictus*).

48. Ps 37.17.

49. Ibid.

50. *Personas* [= πρόσωπα]; taken here in the technical sense of "role," "character," or "voice"; elsewhere in the homilies, Origen will refer to the "speaker" or "voice" (*vox*).

51. Ps 72.2. The text here substitutes the *paulominus* of 72.2b for the *paene* of 72.2a; therefore, this translation differs from what is found in *Hom* 36.4.1 (above, pp. 133 and 139 n. 53).

whose feet were moved either not a little or less to not a little extent; I think of the one who says: "He has set my feet upon rock."[52] This person attests absolutely no movement of his feet, but stability. Blessed are we, then, if absolutely no charge that we have moved our feet is raised against us, but we are found standing on rock, that is, upon the Lord Jesus Christ himself.[53] But if we are unable to remain so stable, at least this secondary and lesser position becomes ours, so that our steps are not moved much. But the third and last position is nearest to a fall, when our feet have been moved.

5. *For I am prepared for scourging.*[54] This, too, is the voice of the sinner—a good one, the best kind, so to speak—one who has indeed sinned, but who awaits scourging for his failures, by which he wishes to be reformed here and now, so that he might not be punished and perish in the future. Imagine a sinner who says to the Lord, "Since I have sinned, I am already right now *prepared for scourging;* do not keep me for the eternal fire,[55] do not keep me for the outer darkness.[56] While I am in this life, give me what is due for my sins, for you scourge every child you receive.[57] I beg you, scourge me too and do not keep me with those who are not scourged, 'who do not experience the labors of men and who will not be scourged like men,'[58] that is, who are completely abandoned by you, whose reform and correction you do not seek."

Therefore, he who knows the difference between the sinner who is scourged by him who "scourges every child he receives"[59] and the one who is not considered worthy of scourging, says to the Lord, "*I am prepared for scourging;*[60] that is, if you want to bring illness upon me, if you want to send sickness, I will endure them patiently. For I know that not only do I de-

52. Ps 39.3.
53. Cf. 1 Cor 10.4.
54. Ps 37.18.
55. *Noli me reservare igni aeterno;* cf. Mt 25.41.
56. Cf. Mt 8.12.
57. Cf. Heb 12.6.
58. Ps 72.5.
59. Heb 12.6.
60. Ps 37.18.

serve sicknesses for the forgiveness of my sins, but I desire all afflictions to be purgative, only so that I might not be kept for eternal punishments and tortures. If it pleases you to inflict penalties upon me, I endure them; if it pleases you that all my resources be destroyed, let them perish completely, only let my soul not perish before you. If you want me to be purified by the death of loved ones and those close to me, even let them die so that they too might be freed from the bonds of this kind; let children be taken away while they are yet children and who at their naïve age have not yet been tainted by the more serious stains of sins. I am prepared, therefore, to be reformed by scourging and to be flogged—I refuse none of these—only so that I might escape the punishments of eternal fire.[61] *I am prepared*, then, *for scourging, and my pain is before me always.*[62] I have pain before my eyes so that, by means of pain here and now, I can counterbalance the pain of punishments to come."

6. *For I declare my wickedness.*[63] We have spoken quite often of the declaration of wickedness, that is, the confession of sin.[64] See, then, what the divine Scripture teaches us, namely, that we should not conceal sin within. For perhaps like those who have undigested food stuffed within themselves (or heavy and annoying pressure of fluid or humor on the stomach), and once they vomit, they are relieved, so too those who have sinned, if indeed they hide or hold back their sin within themselves, are internally pressured and nearly suffocated by the humor and fluid of the sin. But if one becomes his own accuser, so long as he accuses himself and confesses, he vomits forth his fault and relieves every reason for sickness.

Only consider very carefully the one to whom you should confess your sin. First test the doctor to whom you are to expose the source of your sickness, one who knows how to be weak with those who are weak,[65] to weep with those who

61. *Supplicia aeterni ignis;* cf. Mt 25.41.

62. Ps 37.18.

63. Ps 37.19.

64. Cf. *Hom in Ps* 36.1.5 [SC 411.84]; *Hom in Ps* 36.2.1 [SC 411.98–100]; *Hom in Ps* 36.4.2 [SC 411.190]; *Hom in Ps* 37.2.1 [SC 411.300–302].

65. Cf. 1 Cor 9.22.

weep,[66] one who is versed in the practices of mercy and compassion. And so only when he has first demonstrated that he is a learned and merciful doctor, should you carry it out and follow his advice when he speaks or offers it. If he identifies your illness and anticipates that it is such that it should be exposed and cured in the assembly of the Church as a whole, after careful consultation and on the expert advice of that doctor, then this is the course of action to be taken; perhaps in this way others will be able to be edified and you yourself readily healed.

For I will declare my wickedness, and I will give thought to my own sin.[67] Whoever among you is aware that he is in some kind of sin and yet is as carefree as if he had done nothing wrong, such a one should be moved by this passage which says, *I will give thought to my own sin.* Is it in fact good for one who has sinned to remain tranquil[68] and, like one who has not sinned at all, to have no anxiety nor give thought to how he may wipe out his sin? If any blemish or sore appears on your body or if it is swollen from some injury, you are careful to seek out what type of cure should be applied and how the body's former health is to be restored. If some harsh liquid has been poured around your eyes, you are careful to seek out how you might heal it and prevent blindness.

When your soul is sick and burdened by weariness from its sins, are you free of anxiety? Do you have such little regard for Gehenna[69] that you scorn and mock the punishments[70] of eternal fire? Do you think so little of the judgment of God that you despise the Church when it cautions you? Do you not fear to share in the Body of Christ when you approach for the Eucharist, as if you were clean and pure, as if there were nothing unworthy in you? Do you think, in the midst of all this, you can escape God's judgment? Do you not remember that it is written: "Therefore, there are many among you who are sick and

66. Cf. Rom 12.15.

67. Ps 37.19; note the shift in tense (*pronuntio* above; *pronuntiabo* here).

68. Prinzivalli, *Origene, Omelie sui Salmi* (1991) has (unnecessarily) emended the text by adding [*non*].

69. Cf. Mt 10.28.

70. Cf. Mt 25.41.

weak and who sleep"?[71] Why are many weak? Because they neither exercise discernment regarding themselves nor examine themselves, nor do they understand the significance of what it means to share communion with the Church[72] nor what it means to approach these mysteries, so great and so sublime. They experience what those who are sick with fever usually experience: when they take the food of the healthy, they bring ruin upon themselves. These are the things about which it was said: *I will give thought to my own sin.*[73]

7. It follows: *But my enemies live and have been strengthened more than I.*[74] To all this, one should respond quietly[75] with: *I,* however, *will give thought to my own sin.* For often, if we who are sinners see our enemies living more prosperously, we are downcast and pour out complaints against divine Providence. But the one who wishes to be saved, when faced with all these things, should always answer himself with this: "Even though *my enemies live and have been strengthened more than I,* nevertheless *I will give thought to my own sin.* And although I see myself as a sinner, nevertheless when I also consider the fact that the sins of others are perhaps more serious, and seeing, too, that they show no concern for their sins, when I compare myself to those who give no thought whatsoever to their most serious offenses and I give thought to my own sin, I have hope in you."

8. *And those who hate me unjustly have multiplied.*[76] It is not possible in this life not to be hated.[77] Christ Jesus was hated.[78] And why do I say that it is not possible in this life not to be hated?

71. 1 Cor 11.30.

72. *Communicare ecclesiae* = *communicatio in sacris.*

73. Ps 37.19.

74. Ps 37.20.

75. *Ad quae omnia subsonare illud debet.* Souter, s.v. *subsonare,* offers this passage from Rufinus's translation as witnessing the meaning "explain secretly," which is clearly out of place here; Crouzel [SC 411.323] offers "doit faire écho," which perhaps does more for the term than is required; "respond quietly," in fact, is closer to the root meaning than Crouzel and more sensible than Souter.

76. Ps 37.20.

77. Cf. *Hom in Ps* 38.1.5 [SC 411.344] and the similar comments in the *Ex ad Mart* 41–42 [GCS 2.38–39].

78. Cf. Jn 15.18.

God himself,[79] who did not come into this life, was hated by some. For if he were not hated, the prophet would never have said, "Will I not hate those who hate you, Lord, and pine away over your enemies? I hated them with a perfect hatred."[80] Those who are followers of Marcion, Basilides, and Valentinus hate God and hate his words. Since, then, God is hated and Christ is considered anathema by the Jews even to the present day, since the Holy Spirit, who has spoken through the prophets, is hated by the heretics, do you want not to be hated but to be loved and spoken well of by all? Beware lest that judgment apply to you that says, "Woe to you when all people speak well of you"![81] Should we not rather take care that this alone should be what we say: *Those who hate me unjustly have multiplied?*[82]

I want to be hated, so that my conscience might know that I am enduring hatred unjustly. For the prophets were also hated, but unjustly. Christ was hated, but for no reason.[83] But if I am hated on account of my sin, I cannot say, *Those who hate me unjustly have multiplied,* for I am hated justly if I am hated because of my dishonorable and shameful actions. I cannot say, "For they hate me for no reason."[84] Would that we too could say with such great confidence, *Those who hate me unjustly have multiplied.*

9. *Those who repay me evil for good*—I was certainly doing good to them, but they, forgetting my good deeds, were repaying evil for good—*they were slandering me, for I was pursuing justice.*[85] My enemies slander and reproach me for sins that I may have done at one time, and they show no respect for[86] the fact that I am pursuing justice, nor do they grant forgiveness for my past misdeeds in light of my good deeds here and now.

79. *Deus ipse* [= ὁ θεός] here serving as the proper name of the Father.

80. Ps 138.21–22.

81. Lk 6.26.

82. Ps 37.20.

83. Cf. Jn 15.25.

84. Jn 15.25, itself alluding to Ps 24.19.

85. Ps 37.21.

86. *Erubescunt,* literally, "blush" (so Crouzel, SC 411.325, "ils n'en rougissent pas"), though taken here in a secondary, transferred sense, which makes more sense.

But you, Lord, *because I was pursuing justice, do not abandon me, O Lord my God.* Now this is the voice of one who is making confession and asking for mercy: *Do not abandon me, O Lord my God, and do not depart from me.*[87] In fact, in another Psalm it says, "Take not your Holy Spirit from me."[88] In this way it is saying to God himself, *do not depart from me.* This shows that God departs from some because of their merits and that he remains with others on account of their merits. Unhappy, then, is the person from whom God has departed, but blessed is the person with whom God remains.

Come to my help, Lord God of my salvation.[89] Let us therefore pray and say, *Come to my help,* for the battle is great and our enemies are strong. The enemy is treacherous; he is an unseen enemy who attacks through those who are seen. Come to our help, Lord our God, and assist us through your holy Son, our Lord Jesus Christ, through whom you have redeemed us all,[90] and through whom to you be "glory and power forever and ever. Amen."[91]

87. Ps 37.22.
88. Ps 50.13.
89. Ps 37.23.
90. Cf. Rv 5.9.
91. Rv 5.13.

FIRST HOMILY ON PSALM 38 [39]

JUST AS a single individual makes progress in following God, and, as he devotes himself to this endeavor, he continually betters himself,[1] so too this was the experience of an entire people. For this reason, while they were making progress, an enhancement of the Law was made on their behalf. Accordingly, as it is written in the Law, there are certain precepts for priests and Levites concerning sacrifices and the remaining rites. But since the people were making progress (at the time when they were still capable of making progress), the matter did not remain as first arranged, but certain, more prominent laws were made binding on them a second and a third time.[2]

If someone wishes to know what laws were added for priests and Levites, he should read the First Book of Chronicles and patiently examine that entire catalogue of names,[3] and he will discover there a remarkable ordering and division of the tribes; each, in keeping with its name and place, has obtained by lot something notable in that ritual order.[4] He will find also both the priests and the Levites arranged in distinct orders with different duties, so that some are appointed to open the doors of the temple,[5] others to whom the keys are entrusted,

1. *Melior seipso efficitur;* literally, "he is made better than himself"; I have chosen "continually" to express the same idea.

2. Cf. *De principiis* 2.11.5 [GK 446–450]. For Origen's understanding of the Law, see the helpful summary of Thomas Scheck, "Law," in *The Westminster Handbook to Origen,* ed. John McGuckin (Louisville, KY: Westminster John Knox, 2004), 138–40.

3. Cf. 1 Chr 9.10–33.

4. Cf. 1 Chr 24.5–31; 25.8–31; 26.13–32.

5. Cf. 1 Chr 9.17–27; 26.1–19.

and still others to whom care of the altars and the sacrifices is committed.[6] And, drawing on the account of that book, there are many things that we can say regarding the duties appointed to the priests.

If one, then, is able to see clearly how the Jewish people follow the pattern and shadow of the heavenly realities,[7] he should rise from the lower pedestal of the word to its peak and higher pediment and contemplate on the basis of these things the status and heavenly vocation of the priesthood to come, and therein he will contemplate what these priestly orders are, and what the duties of the Levites are which are carried out in the heavenly services, and he will form a mental picture in terms of heaven of all the things that he sees arranged here on earth.[8] For there, too, there will be the people, as well as Levites chosen from God's people; and in turn chosen from among these, outstanding priests, and, nonetheless, quite numerous varieties of priests; just as in the First Book of Chronicles it is revealed that there are twenty-four orders of priests, some indeed under Eleazar, but others under the leadership of Ithamar, to whom those who serve daily[9] are said to belong.[10]

2. But perhaps someone who hears this might ask: "What does this have to do with the Psalm?" A lot! For the inscription of this Psalm is: *Unto the end. A Psalm of David for Jeduthun.* We discover that this Jeduthun is one of those to whom was entrusted the study of and care for the hymns of God.[11] Once we discovered this name in the Psalm's inscription, it was necessary for us to show who this Jeduthun was and how, after the first law, a second ordinance was made concerning priestly duties.

6. 1 Chr 9.28–32.

7. Cf. Heb 8.5.

8. Cf. *De principiis* 2.11.5 [GK 448], where Origen suggests that the true meaning (*veritas*) and significance (*ratio*) of the various priestly orders and the festal cycle of Judaism will be made clear in the age to come.

9. *Ephemeri* = ἐφημερίαι, the division of priests appointed for daily service; cf. 1 Chr 9.33–34 and Lk 1.5.

10. Cf. 1 Chr 24.1–31.

11. Cf. 1 Chr 16.41–42.

Among the Greeks, whoever used to compose songs or musical pieces presented them for singing to those who seemed best to them in a contest.[12] And it used to be the case that one would be crowned in the competition, but another would write a song for the victor. Therefore, in the Psalms of the divine Scriptures, whichever ones are inscribed in the Septuagint as "Unto the End" are given the title "Victory Psalms"[13] by other translators, either in reference to a victory or for a victor, obviously because of what is introduced in them as a praise of victory. Therefore, David, filled with the divine Spirit, composed this Psalm and gave it to Jeduthun, to whom had been given the responsibility of singing songs to God, as to one who was quite gifted in this kind of art. It is therefore inscribed, *Unto the End. A Psalm of David for Jeduthun.*

3. But now let us see what the voice of the just one has brought forth. As if gazing at ourselves in a mirror, let us look to see if we are capable of being like this, or whether much is lacking in us, or if we are already quite close, although we have not yet fully attained [our goal].[14] Since, therefore, human speech is the beginning of many sins, and our mouth is at the service of many evils, and since it is extremely difficult for one to be found who keeps his mouth and his tongue from sin even for one hour, it says, *I have said: I will guard my ways so that I do not sin with my tongue.*[15] I have said to myself and have spoken inwardly, and I went on to say, "If I wish to preserve my ways from sin, this is how I can do so: if I guard my tongue." For, "On the basis of your words," it says, "you will be justified, and on the basis of your words you will be condemned."[16] And again, "Amen, I say to you, you will render an account on the day of judgment for every idle word."[17] It speaks not only of what you have spoken badly but what you have spoken idly, because a bad word is not idle, but accomplishes a bad work. But

12. *In agone,* itself a term applied also to the "contest" of the Christian life.
13. *Victoriales.*
14. Cf. *Comm in Cant* 2.5.9 [SC 375.358].
15. Ps 38.1.
16. Mt 12.37.
17. Cf. Mt 12.36.

an idle word is one that does not accomplish anything good or bad. If, therefore, on the day of judgment we will render an account not only for bad words but also for idle ones, who will boast that he has a chaste heart? Or who will say with confidence, "I am clean of sin"?[18]

Nevertheless, the just one speaks: *I have said: I will guard my ways so that I do not sin with my tongue. I have put a guard on my mouth.*[19] Elsewhere it is indeed written, "Guard your heart with all care,"[20] but here, *I have put a guard on my mouth.* And again, in another place it is written, "See that you surround your property with a hedge of thorns."[21] And again, "Secure your money and your gold, and make a door and a lock for your mouth, and a yoke and balance for your words."[22]

I think that keeping these mandates—the very observance of them, and not simply their resulting effects—makes the one who keeps them meek and blessed.[23] For as long as one always watches his mouth and guards his tongue, so that he does not speak before he reflects and considers within himself whether it ought to be said; if the statement is such that it should be uttered; if the person is such that he should or is able to listen; if the moment is right for speaking: as long as he carefully considers each of these things, all anger and pride are kept in check, and the strong impulse toward rage is calmed, and such a person brings all inward deliberation to a close. So at last a word comes forth that is marked by meekness, proceeding, as it were, from a mind both tranquil and calm, granting favor to those who speak and healing to those who hear.

4. But since we sin especially at that moment when the sinner stands against us, instigating and provoking us to blurt out something from our mouth for which we would be held accountable in the future judgment, the holy prophet describes

18. Jb 33.9.

19. Ps 38.2.

20. Prv 4.23.

21. Sir 28.24A [= Vulgate 28.28]; in the Vulgate τὸ κτῆμα is rendered as *aures*.

22. Sir 28.24B, 25B, 25A [= Vulgate 28.29].

23. Cf. Mt 5.5.

it in this way when he says, *While the sinner stood against me, I became quiet and humbled myself, and kept silent about what is good.*[24] If, therefore, when the sinner stood against me and was speaking evil of me and was slandering me, inciting me to respond to him in the same way and to utter from my own mouth similar words, at that moment I was contemplating silence, so that I might make no response at all.[25] This is why, then, it says: *While the sinner stood against me, I became quiet and humbled myself, and kept silent about what is good.*

But sometimes if we do not wish to be humbled, we think otherwise[26] and say to ourselves, "What is this? This person has held me in contempt and has dared to toss such insults in my face[27] and so to stir up words against me; should I too not respond to him in like manner or even more harshly, so that he hears something worse than what he said?" But the just person does not act this way, but rather humbles himself,[28] even if the one who slanders him and speaks abusively is a servant or a lower-class, sinful, nobody.[29]

He says: *While the sinner stood against me, I became quiet and humbled myself, and kept silent about what is good.* He did not say, "I was silent" only, but "I was silent about what is good." Here it shows that although there are good things within me and I have been educated and trained in good teachings and practices, and even if I am capable of instructing others also in what is good, nevertheless at that moment when the sinner stands against me and berates me with abusive and quarrelsome words, I restrain and repress even my good words so as neither to kindle the fire of his own destruction—since it is

24. Ps 38.2–3; *humiliatus sum,* understood here as a medial passive; cf. n. 28 below: *humiliat se.*

25. *Penitus;* cf. *OLD* s.v. § 5; this use is repeated twice more in this homily.

26. *Alia,* taken adverbially.

27. *Ausus est talia in os ingerere:* taking *os* here as an instance of metonymy; cf. *OLD* s.v. *os,* § 9b.

28. *Humiliat se;* see n. 24 above.

29. *Etiamsi servus sit ille ... aut si humilis et peccator sit et indignus.* On the *iniuria* resulting from insulting behavior, see Andrew Borkowski and Paul du Plessis, *Textbook on Roman Law,* 3rd ed. (Oxford: Oxford University Press, 2005), 340–42.

impossible to give in to evil and simultaneously to look upon the good—nor to cause damage by my own words.[30]

But why? Will the statement, *While the sinner stood against me, I became quiet and humbled myself, and kept silent about what is good,* appear as perfection, or at least progress, though not yet perfection? For I think there are three things to be inferred from this passage of the Scriptures, in which he says that the sinner stands against him and whispers[31] words intended to provoke him and rouse him to retribution. And, to be sure, if I am still young, I seek things like this, an eye for an eye, a tooth for a tooth,[32] and I return a curse for a curse.[33] But if I have already made some progress, though not yet perfect, I both keep silent and endure abusive words patiently and make no response whatsoever. But if I am perfect, I do not remain silent, but when cursed, I bless, just as Paul also said: "We are cursed and we bless; we suffer persecution and we endure; blasphemed, and we make supplication."[34] And because those who do these things (that is, who return blessings for curses and who make supplication in the face of blasphemy) seem to ordinary men to be like cattle and like refuse, like those who have no awareness of the injury inflicted on them, for this reason he goes on to say, "We have become like the scum of this world, the refuse of all."[35]

But we do not want to join the apostles and become the refuse of this world. We would rather be feared than scorned by others, and we are fixed on repaying those who injure us and anticipating the vengeance the Lord has reserved to himself when he says, "Vengeance is mine; I will repay, says the Lord."[36] But if we are unable to make such progress and to attain to the

30. *Sermonum meorum faciam detrimentum;* or, "nor to waste my own words."

31. *Loqui in auribus suis;* literally, "speak in his ears."

32. Cf. Ex 21.24.

33. Cf. 1 Pt 3.9; cf. *Hom in Ps* 37.2.2–4 [SC 411.306–314].

34. 1 Cor 4.12–13.

35. 1 Cor 4.13; cf. also Tb 5.19 (LXX); this term "refuse" (περίψημα) is also used by Ignatius of Antioch, *Ephesians* 8.1 [SC 10bis.64], in the context of martyrdom and sacrifice; cf. Allen Brent, *A Political History of Early Christianity* (London: T&T Clark, 2009), 200–201. The substantive *omnium* (πάντων) is ambiguous: "all things" or perhaps "all men."

36. Rom 12.19; Dt 32.35.

truth in its fullness so that, along with Paul, we can say, "We are cursed and we bless; we suffer persecution and we endure; blasphemed, and we make supplication," let us now at least say what we are taught through the prophet, *While the sinner stood against me, I became quiet and humbled myself, and kept silent about what is good.*[37]

5. And what further does it say? *And my pain,* it says, *has been renewed.*[38] Those who exchange blows in a match strive constantly to ready themselves by those very blows, so that they might endure bravely the blows inflicted by their opponents and not be conscious of the pain; and for them this is the highest achievement: to receive punches and kicks without pain. The one who is more accomplished among them, when struck a blow, is not stung by the pain. After him is the one who indeed feels pain but nevertheless does not succumb to it. Understand something like this also in regard to us: when we are cursed and the opponent stands against us, if we are indeed well trained and mentally fortified by means of lengthy practice[39] and if we are not saddened at all by curses or abusive words, but because of an abounding firmness of purpose and patience we are unaware, as it were, of pain and, through an abundant meekness,[40] we become in a certain way—should I dare say it—imitators of God.[41] For God is cursed by the heretics; he is blasphemed by those who deny his Providence; he is accused by those who are ignorant of the treasuries of his wisdom.[42] So tell me, can you think, then, that God is in fact grieved by all these injuries, but endures them as we do? Or does the divine nature, in virtue of its impassibility, experience no pain whatsoever and remain entirely unmoved by any injuries or abuses?

Every just and perfect person then will be like this, or rather will imitate such a person as the one who said, "We are cursed

37. Ps 38.2–3.

38. Ps 38.3.

39. *Longa meditatione;* this, of course, could also mean "meditation," but the context here suggests something else; cf. *Hom in Ps* 36.5.1 [SC 411.224].

40. *Et per multam mansuetudinem,* taken almost oxymoronically.

41. Cf. Eph 5.1.

42. Cf. Col 2.3; cf. *Hom in Ps* 37.2.8 [SC 411.322–324].

and we bless; we suffer persecution and we endure; blasphemed, and we make supplication."[43] But the one who is not yet perfect, who is nevertheless making progress, when cursed, becomes quiet and humbles himself[44] and is silent regarding the good. But one like this does suffer pain and says, *And my pain has been renewed.*[45]

Now imagine a wound that is being treated and, as its healing progresses, is nearly scarred over. Then, imagine another injury being inflicted upon that wound which had already begun to scar over, such that the wound is reopened by this second blow. This is the kind of thing that happens to the one who is making progress but who is not yet perfect and who has not as yet been fully healed.[46] If, then, while the skin is still quite tender, the blows of curses and abusive words are added to the injury,[47] his pain is renewed, and he is facing great pressures;[48] and it is then with good reason that he says: *While the sinner stood against me, I became quiet and humbled myself, and kept silent about what is good, and my pain has been renewed.*[49]

See, then, how one who is still engaged in the struggle, who seeks to restrain himself from wrath and rage, as long as he meditates upon these things internally,[50] when confronted with the sinner's instigation[51] (which indeed troubles and wearies him, but does not overcome him), and though aroused

43. 1 Cor 4.12–13.

44. Cf. *Hom in Ps* 37.1.6 [SC 411.292–94] and n. 24 above for *humiliatur* as middle voice.

45. Ps 38.3.

46. *Nec iam ad summam perductus est sanitatem,* literally, "nor has as yet been led to full health."

47. *Accedant ei maledictorum et conviciorum vulnera.* One is tempted to render this, "and insults are added to injury."

48. *Et parantur angustiae,* literally, "and difficulties are at hand."

49. Ps 38.2–3.

50. *Dum ipse haec apud se meditatur;* an example of the influence of Stoicism on Christianity; cf. Pierre Hadot, *What is Ancient Philosophy?* trans. Michael Chase (Cambridge, MA: Harvard University Press, 2002), 240–41, where Hadot cites Origen, *Comm in Cant* 2.5.7 [SC 375.358]; on this use of *meditari,* cf. *Hom in Ps* 36.5.1 [SC 411.224].

51. *Irritatio ei supervenit peccatoris.* I have turned the phrase around for the sake of flow.

and provoked to respond, nevertheless holding his pain in check,[52] he suppresses and curbs it. This person says, *My pain has been renewed,*[53] that is, "I was already making progress and believed that I had already arrived at health before I was aggravated and before I was provoked by abusive words; but now my wound is being torn open and the abuse is renewed with sharp pricks, while the pain of the injury is destroying my patience."

6. But in what follows, it describes still further the suffering[54] of the one who is making progress, when it says, *My heart has grown hot within me.*[55] For unlike one who has been made perfect, unlike one who by his longstanding firmness of purpose has already won happiness, when he hears the voice of someone speaking abusively and disparagingly, it is impossible for him to be without pain. He experiences pain and burns internally with a heart grown hot, and he is deeply troubled, but not to the point that he speaks from his troubled heart; but, disturbed by the insult he has received, he indeed grows hot internally, yet he reduces the flames of his heated passion through silence.

7. Let us also look at another saying of the just person, which we ought to imitate with the greatest zeal: *And in my meditation, a fire will blaze up.*[56] I too meditate on the words of the Lord and repeatedly train myself in them, but I do not know if I am the kind of person in the course of whose meditation fire comes forth from each and every word of God, setting my heart ablaze and inflaming my soul to keep those things upon which I am meditating.

I am now speaking the words of God, but I should want them to burn, first in my heart and then also in the minds of those who are listening, just like those words Jesus was speak-

52. *Remordens* [*se*]; cf. *OLD*, s.v. [*re*]*mordeo*, § 5. Jerome, commenting on Gal 5.17, seems to use *remordens* (with the reflexive) in a similar way: *Comm in Gal* 3 [PL 26.411B]: *quia fecerit, ut cum carni consenserit, et opera eius fecerit, rursum per paenitentiam se remordens, spiritui copuletur, et opera eius efficiat.*

53. Ps 38.3.

54. *Passionem;* perhaps more neutrally, "experience."

55. Ps 38.4.

56. Ps 38.4.

ing, which prompted those who had heard them to say, "Was not our heart burning in us when he opened the Scriptures for us along the way?"[57] If only now our heart would burn within us, as we open the divine Scriptures, and a fire be kindled in our meditation; if only we might be roused to put what we hear and read into action!

Such indeed were the words of Jeremiah, as it is written, when God says to him, "Behold, I have put my words like fire back into your mouth."[58] Why like fire? Because the words he spoke kindled those who listened and nothing lukewarm or cool remained in them. But just as fire consumes and destroys every material and admits of nothing unclean or polluted, so also those whose heart is kindled by the fire of the divine word will no longer endure being polluted by material or worldly dross, and they will retain nothing within them that is lukewarm and deserving to be vomited forth,[59] nor will they permit the charity within them to grow cold[60] from repeated acts of wickedness. But their lamps will always be lit and their torches burning, and they will be ready like servants awaiting their master on his return from a wedding.[61]

Or was it not this fire about which our Savior spoke: "I have come to send fire onto the earth, and what is it I desire except that it burn?"[62] Without any doubt this is the fire that drives away the chill of sin and invites the heat of the Spirit. This is assuredly what is also reported in the Acts of the

57. Lk 24.32; cf. *Hom in Ex* 12.4 [SC 321.364], where through this Lucan text the role of Christ as mediator of meaning and the importance of prayer receive emphasis: *Unde ostenditur non solum studium nobis adhibendum esse ad discendas litteras sacras, verum et supplicandum Domino et diebus ac noctibus obsecrandum, ut veniat Agnus ex tribu Iuda, et ipse accipiens librum signatum dignetur aperire. Ipse est enim qui scripturas adaperiens accendit corda discipulorum, ita ut dicant: Nonne cor nostrum erat ardens intra nos, cum adaperiret nobis scripturas.*

58. Jer 5.14; the text here adds the adverb *retrorsum,* absent from the Vlg and LXX.

59. Cf. Rv 3.16.

60. Cf. Mt 24.12; cf. *De principiis* 2.8.3 [GK 390–392], where Origen speculates on the "fall" of souls as resulting from their losing their heat or fervor.

61. Cf. Lk 12.35–36.

62. Lk 12.49.

Apostles,[63] when it says that there appeared to them separate tongues as of fire that rested upon the apostles, for it is clear that those who were to preach the word of the Gospel needed to be strengthened with the gift of fiery vigor, so that the souls of their hearers might catch fire through their handing-on of the word.

But how does it happen that a tongue's "fire" enters my heart and that I also speak from this fiery tongue in such a way that out of me a rapidly spreading fire is kindled by my words in the hearts of my hearers and accuses the sinner, and that my word becomes for him a punishment, so that, scorched and set on fire by these words, he comes to the repentance which achieves a reliable salvation from the sadness which is according to God,[64] which he received from the rebuke of God's word? If only I could kindle the soul of every listener[65] in this way, so that whoever possesses self-awareness, not enduring the fire of our words, but, set aflame with all that is in him, would destroy more quickly the filth of the vices hidden within and, after that, abolish everything whatsoever that belongs to the flesh and to the grosser matter belonging to it.[66] Then this fire would become in him a light and a burning lamp,[67] which should be placed "not under a bushel, but upon a lampstand so that it might give light to all who are in the house."[68]

Therefore, if the word, once heard, kindles a fire in you and you have understood what the Apostle said, "Who is the one who brings me joy, if not the one who is made sad by me?"[69]—for his words were fiery and the Apostle was joyful wherever he saw someone saddened upon hearing his words and made

63. Cf. Acts 2.3.

64. Cf. 2 Cor 7.10; the editors have treated this as a direct quotation; however, the inverted word order suggests more an allusion.

65. *Omnem animam auditorum;* I have, for the sake of the English, transferred the adjective.

66. *Omne quidquid carnis et materiae crassioris proprium est et amicum;* cf. *Hom in Ps* 38.2.8 [SC 411.394–396].

67. Cf. Jn 5.35.

68. Mt 5.15; for the role of this "fire" in teaching, see *Hom in Ex* 13.4 [SC 321.388–392].

69. 2 Cor 2.2.

remorseful by what he had heard and set ablaze by a fire in his conscience from recollection of his sin, and for this reason he said, "Who is the one who brings me joy, if not the one who is made sad by me?"—so we should also make every effort so that in our meditations a fire may be kindled,[70] which at first burns us by the recollection and consciousness of sin, but afterward illumines and brightens us once we have been purged from vice.[71]

8. *I have spoken*—it says—*with my tongue.*[72] Let us consider what he has said with his tongue, for through these words he seems to me to indicate something mystical.[73] He then says, *Make known to me, Lord, my end and what is the number of my days, so that I might know what is lacking in me.*[74] If, he says, you make known to me my end and how many days there are for me, I will be able by these means also to recognize what is lacking in me.

Or perhaps rather these words mean something like this: that just as there is some end proper to every art—for example, the end of construction is to build a house, the end of ship-building is to build a ship that can overcome the waves of the sea and sustain the force of the winds, and for every art there is some such end, on account of which the art itself seems to have been devised—so perhaps too there is some "end" for our life or even for the whole world, for the sake of which everything that occurs in our life happens or for the sake of which the world itself was founded or exists. This end the Apostle also mentions when he says, "Then comes the end, when he will have handed over the Kingdom to God and the Father."[75] To this end we should certainly make haste, so that our having been created by God might have meaning.[76]

Or, put another way, just as our bodily frame is small and,

70. Cf. Ps 38.4.

71. *Peccatorum ... vitiis* [SC 411.352].

72. Ps 38.4.

73. *Mysticum aliquid.*

74. Ps 38.5.

75. 1 Cor 15.24.

76. *Operae pretium,* literally, "might be something worthwhile"; cf. *OLD* s.v. *pretium* § 2.b.

as it were, tiny from our birth, nevertheless it quickly presses on and reaches toward an "end" to its growth through the increments of age; or again, just as our soul, in keeping with the fact that it exists in this body, hastens to speak, first in a stammering manner, and then more clearly, and finally achieves the capacity to speak in a full and complete way, so too in this way our entire life is customarily spent[77] stammering, as it were, now among men on earth, but is perfected and reaches completion with God in heaven.

It is for this reason, then, that the prophet desires to come to know his end—that for which he was made: that in envisioning his end and viewing all his days and considering what his perfection consists of, he might see how much is lacking in him in reference to that end toward which he is striving. For example, let us suppose an individual has been assigned to some craft and he says to his teacher, "I want to know what the perfection of this art is and who would be the perfect craftsman or builder." And when he has learned this, he could seek to find out how far short he is in reference to this perfection and how much progress he has made in his training in the art, so that when he knows the answer to each of these questions he would know what he has achieved and recognize what is lacking for perfection. So too the prophet now prays that he might learn from God, that his end and the number of his days might be made known to him.

But in this regard, it must not be thought that he is speaking in reference to bodily time or in terms of the years in this life, but he wants to know the entire number of days, those in the first life, those in the second dwelling, and those in the third.[78] "For my soul," he says, "has been a sojourner for a long time."[79] It is as though those who went out from Egypt were saying, *Make known to me, Lord, my end*—the land that is good[80] and a ground that is holy[81]—*and what is the number of my days*

77. *Imbuitur;* cf. Lewis and Short, s.v. § B.1.

78. Cf. *De principiis* 2.11.5–7 [GK 446–454]; *Hom in Ps* 36.5.1 [SC 411.228–230].

79. Ps 119.6.

80. Cf. Dt 1.25; 8.7.

81. Cf. Ex 3.5.

during which I walk, *so that I might know what is lacking in me*—how much remains until I reach the promised holy land—so, too, he wants to know the number of days during which he is journeying.

For we have certain days within this world, yet also certain days outside this world. For the course of our sun, bound by the space of this heaven,[82] makes one kind of day. But the one who is counted worthy to make an ascent to the second heaven has another kind of day. Moreover, the one who has been able to be taken up or reach to the third heaven[83] experiences a much brighter day, where he will not only find an ineffable light, but will also hear "words not permitted for a human to speak."[84]

I also know other "days,"[85] whose number the prophet perhaps with good reason seeks to know. Just as in this heaven, the sun, having risen and bringing light to the entire world, constitutes "a day," so also in the heart of the just person (which, due to the steadfastness and firmness of faith, is rightly called a "firmament"), if the Sun of Justice,[86] our Lord Jesus Christ, rises and illumines him with the light of knowledge and truth,[87] this constitutes "a day" in his heart; and the greater the frequency of his rising and his illumining, the greater the number of such "days" that will be reckoned for him. Fittingly, then, the prophet, aware of this kind of illumination, says, *Make known to me, Lord, my end and what is the number of my days, so that I might know what is lacking in me.*[88]

9. And he adds, *Behold, you have made my days old.*[89] In Greek

82. *Huius caeli spatiis terminatus; caelum,* of course, can mean both the English "sky" and "heaven."

83. Cf. 2 Cor 12.2.

84. 2 Cor 12.4.

85. Cf. *Hom in Jud* 1.1–3 [SC 389.50–60] and *Hom in Lev* [SC 286.370] on the significance of "day."

86. Cf. Mal 3.20.

87. Cf. Rom 2.20.

88. Ps 38.5.

89. Ps 38.6: *Ecce veteres posuisti dies meos.* The LXX has παλαιάς as a variant for παλαιστάς. *Vetus,* of course, is the Latin equivalent of παλαιός; however, παλαιστάς is more correctly παλαστάς and not etymologically related to παλαιός (old), but to παλάμη (hand). Jerome's two versions of this verse have *mensurabiles* (*iuxta* LXX) and *breves* (*iuxta* Hebr).

this is written as παλαιστάς, which indicates the measure of four fingers. With a desire to instruct us living now in this life and who pass days that are short and all too few, in this verse he has spoken of what we discussed earlier. From this it is understood that one person might be able to say (as if complaining about the shortness of time), "You have placed my days like one finger," but another, "two or three fingers." But I ask if any human is able to say, "My days are ten fingers," or "twenty," or even more.

Since we are encountering difficult passages, I would like to inquire if we find anything like this elsewhere in the Scriptures on the basis of which that which seems obscure might be revealed more clearly.[90] I recall that this is written in Isaiah: "Who," it says, "has measured water with his hand, and the heaven with his palm, and the whole earth with his fist?"[91] From these words, the wiser among those listening should consider the differences of the measurements in each individual passage: how among those who deserve to be called "heaven," the part of their life that is heavenly is said to be measured by the palm of God (whatever the "palm" of God is); and among those whose life is still earthly, their life is measured by the fist of God. But to ask now what is different about the divine "fist" probably goes beyond both our homily and your attention-span.[92]

Nevertheless, just as there he "has measured water with his hand, and the heaven with his palm, and the whole earth with his fist, and he has weighed the mountains on the scale and the hills in a balance,"[93] so here also, in following the same line of reasoning, this "measure" must be understood: there is nothing unmeasurable for God, nothing he cannot weigh, but

90. Here a fundamental hermeneutical principle of the Fathers is articulated: Scripture interprets Scripture, and the more obscure is to be interpreted in light of what is clearer.

91. Is 40.12.

92. *Sed pugilli divini differentiam nunc requirere et nostrum sermonem et auditum vestrum fortassis excedat;* perhaps alternately, "probably surpasses both our few words and your understanding."

93. Is 40.12.

all things exist for him in number and measure.[94] So, too, the life of the prophet has been numbered and measured out by God, since it is governed by the principles of his Providence.

10. He goes on in what follows to say, *My substance is as nothing before you.*[95] If he had not said, "before you," I would be quite sad indeed, because he would have been saying that the substance of his humanity is "nothing." But, as it is, because he said, "before you," it is as if he were saying, "certainly in comparison with angels or other created beings, my substance is not worthless nor of low esteem." Indeed, if we have lived a good life and kept the commandments of the Lord, we are invited to join the company of the angels. "They will be," he says, "like the angels of God in heaven."[96] But even if I am Peter—"against whom the gates of hell will not prevail"[97]—in comparison with God, my substance is nothing before him. It sufficiently expresses this with language appropriate to the nature. For everything whatsoever—great though it may be—that comes from nothing is nothing; for it is he alone "who is"[98] and who always "is." Our substance, however, is as nothing before him; for indeed it was created by him from nothing.[99]

11. But in what follows, in explaining what he said—*my substance is as nothing before you*—he adds, *nevertheless, complete vanity is every living person.*[100] How do you understand "living"? If indeed we think that true life is vanity, then why do we trouble ourselves? But see whether perhaps[101] the expression "every living" should not be understood as referring to this present life, as has been written and as we will establish by means of evidence. For everything that presents itself to man in this life

94. Cf. Wis 11.20.
95. Ps 38.6.
96. Mt 22.30.
97. Mt 16.18.
98. Cf. Ex 3.14.
99. Cf. 2 Mc 7.28.
100. Ps 37.6.
101. *Sed vide ne forte ... accipiendum sit* (taking *ne* as the negative of *utrum*); an odd construction, but the meaning is clear enough from what follows; cf. Albert Blaise, *A Handbook of Christian Latin: Style, Morphology, and Syntax,* trans. Grant C. Roti (Washington, DC: Georgetown University Press, 1994), § 272b.

is vain, even if we consider Moses in this life: for he too knows partially, and he prophesies partially[102] and sees through a mirror obscurely[103] and knows the shadow,[104] and he is taught the types,[105] and does not yet see the truth, and thus he is indeed living, but his life is vanity.

Do you wish to see that it is vanity? "When what is perfect comes, those things that are partial will be destroyed."[106] Now, everything that is destroyed is vanity. And if whatever is partial is destroyed, and if the prophets know partially, their life too is rightly called vanity. Moreover, the lesser things are destroyed when those which are better and perfect come and, by comparison with them,[107] they are proven to be vain; thus, being partial and imperfect, they are subject to destruction. *Complete vanity,* then, *is every living person.*[108]

But listen to Qoheleth, who bears witness to the fact that this line should be understood as referring to this life: he says, "I have praised all who have died more than all the living, as many as are alive up to now, and the one not yet born as better than these two."[109] He therefore praises the dead more than the living because they at least have the advantage of having been freed from the bonds of this world: they are no longer clothed in flesh and skin,[110] nor are they knitted together with bones and sinews,[111] and they are no longer subject to the necessities of the body. If you understand, then, what it means to be living in the flesh (even if it were Moses or anyone else), this life is a burden to him. For that[112] which is encompassed

102. Cf. 1 Cor 13.9.

103. Cf. 1 Cor 13.12.

104. Cf. Col 2.17.

105. *Figuras docetur,* a curious construction; cf. Heb 8.5; cf. also 1 Cor 10.6.

106. 1 Cor 13.10.

107. *Per haec;* the antecedent being the substantives *meliora sunt et perfecta.*

108. Ps 38.6.

109. Eccl 4.2–3; Rufinus, of course, here uses the title Ecclesiastes.

110. Cf. Gn 3.21; cf. Rufinus's metaphor in his *Preface* [SC 411.146]: *quia nec corpus humanum ex solis potuisset nervis ossibusque constare, nisi eis divina providentia vel mollitiem carnis intexuisset vel blandimenta pinguedinis.*

111. Cf. Jb 10.11.

112. *Quae* = *vita.*

by this mortal and earthly body is not liberated from corruption.[113]

See, then, that *complete vanity is every living person,*[114] and let us not esteem this vain life, but let us hasten to that holy and blessed and true life, and let us strive toward it with soul and mind once all vanity has been destroyed. Let us not call this light that we now employ "sweet"; for the ones who speak this way do not know the sweetness of true light; they have not even perceived any of the tokens of the true light, nor do they know that the object of their hope should be the angelic life of the soul once it escapes the vanity of this life.

For this reason, we who believe these things should already be transferred in mind and by faith to heaven, and, even as we walk the earth, we should maintain a heavenly manner of life,[115] so that our treasure might be there where our heart is[116] and that we might be counted worthy to attain the heavenly kingdom, through our Lord Jesus Christ, "to whom are glory and power forever and ever. Amen."[117]

113. Cf. Rom 8.21.

114. Ps 38.6.

115. *Conversationem* [= πολιτείαν]; cf. Phil 3.20; perhaps alternately, "we should maintain our citizenship in heaven."

116. Cf. Mt 6.21.

117. Cf. 1 Pt 4.11; Rv 5.13.

SECOND HOMILY ON PSALM 38 [39]

HOUGH MAN walks in an image.[1] An image is necessarily an image of something. For when holy Scripture says "image," it sometimes specifies and says whose image it is, but at other times it uses "image" without any specification. Further, when it says, in reference to the Savior, "who is the image," it is not silent regarding whose image he is, but says further, "who is the image of the invisible God, the first-born of all creation."[2] And what is more, when it teaches us about different images and that each and every individual bears some image, it says: "Just as we have borne the image of the earthly man, so let us bear the image of the heavenly man."[3] It named the image with the addition of either "of the earthly" or "of the heavenly." But elsewhere it speaks without any specification, as it even says here, *Though man walks in an image.* But in whose image? God's? Of the earthly man? Of the heavenly man? How am I to know what the divine Scripture intends to teach us in this passage, which says without any addition, *Though man walks in an* (I know not whose) *image?*

Indeed, if it were speaking exclusively of the just, it undoubtedly would have said, "Though man walks in the image of the heavenly man." Or, if it were referring only to sinners, it certainly would have said, "Man walks in the image of the earthly man." But since it is making a statement in a general way about all mortals, some of whom bear the image of the heavenly (those who live according to God's law), others of whom bear the image of the earthly (who live according to the

1. Ps 38.7.
2. Col 1.15.
3. 1 Cor 15.49.

flesh), it has then necessarily kept silent about the particular designation of the image and has offered a general statement about all men: every man walks in an image.

It is up to you to investigate and examine individuals on the basis of the faith and works, the conduct and actions, the thoughts and words of each, and to consider whether he walks in the image of the heavenly or in the image of the earthly. If you are merciful as your heavenly Father is merciful, then undoubtedly the image of the heavenly is in you. If you not only do good to your friends, but also return good for evil to your enemies, just as "the heavenly Father commands his sun to rise on the good and the evil, and he rains upon the just and the unjust,"[4] then the image in you is that of the heavenly. And if you are perfect in every way, just as your heavenly Father is perfect, the image in you is that of the heavenly. But, conversely, if you are not an imitator of Christ or the Apostle Paul, who says, "Be imitators of me, as I am of Christ," but an imitator of the works of the devil, who was a murderer from the beginning;[5] if you have a taste for earthly things and speak of them,[6] and if your treasure and your heart are on earth,[7] then you bear the image of the earthly.

But since we have found ourselves[8] in one of those passages in which the language of "image" is employed, it seems necessary to bring up as well the verse from that Psalm in which it is written concerning sinners, "Lord, in your city you will reduce their image to nothing."[9] It is therefore clear that, in his city, God reduces to nothing the image of sinners; but he undoubtedly keeps safe and preserves the image of the just. This, then, is the image of the earthly: the image of sinners, which God reduces to nothing in his city. That is, if one departs from this world[10] and carries with him the image of the earthly, he will,

4. Mt 5.45.

5. Cf. Jn 8.44.

6. *Si terrena sapias et terrena loquaris;* or, taking *sapere* in a secondary sense, "your wisdom and speech are earthly." Cf. also Jn 3.12.

7. Cf. Mt 6.21.

8. *Inventi sumus,* a medial passive.

9. Ps 72.20.

10. *Exierit de hoc mundo;* the ambiguity in the translation is intended, for it seems Origen means more than simply "dies."

on account of such an image, be reduced to nothing in that city of God; no one who does not bear the marks of the image of the heavenly will have a share among the citizens of that heavenly city.

2. But this verse seems to me to contain another mystery[11] as well: the life and activity of this world are something image-like and, indeed, are an image, but the life to come is not imaginary; it is real. The meaning of what is said here is that each individual possesses an image of virtue, but, strictly speaking, he does not live wholly in virtue itself. What I am saying is this: wisdom and knowledge are a significant part of the virtues. Yet in this present life, if one thinks that he has knowledge, he has not yet come to know as he is supposed to know, since the one who knows, knows in an obscure fashion.[12] Thus we walk in an image of knowledge and not in knowledge itself, through which there is "face-to-face" knowing.[13]

We walk no less in the very image of wisdom and not yet in wisdom itself, for we do not yet "behold the glory of the Lord with face unveiled."[14]

I venture to say the same for God's justice, that we walk in the image of justice and we do not yet make progress in that justice which is "face-to-face." For human nature, clothed in skin and flesh, and connected by muscle and bone,[15] was unable—according to the capacity and strength of its own nature—to understand, bear, and endure, uncovered and pure, the very truth of justice, since indeed Christ is himself the nature of the virtues.[16] For he is Justice, which did not come to

11. *Sacramentum.*

12. *In aenigmate;* cf. 1 Cor 13.12.

13. *Per quam facie ad faciem cognoscitur,* a continued allusion to 1 Cor 13.12. The verb is impersonal.

14. 2 Cor 3.18; cf. *De oratione* 9.2 [GCS 3.318–319].

15. *Neque enim capere poterat humana natura pellibus et carne vestita, ossibus et nervis inserta* [SC 411.374]; cf. the comment in Rufinus's Preface: *quia nec corpus humanum ex solis potuisset nervis ossibusque constare, nisi eis divina providentia vel mollitiem carnis intexuisset vel blandimenta pinguedinis* [SC 411.46].

16. *Si quidem ipse Christus est natura virtutum.* Justice is one of the ἐπίνοιαι of Christ. In his *Comm in Cant* 1.6.13 [SC 375.256], Origen refers to Christ as the "substance of the virtues": *Nec mireris sane, si dicimus virtutes esse quae diligunt Christum, cum in aliis ipsarum virtutum substantiam Christum soleamus accipere.*

the human race in its full splendor; for Jesus Christ emptied himself of the form of God, that he might take the form of a servant.[17]

If the words of Scripture were indeed speaking only about the Jews, it would perhaps have said, "though man walks in a shadow." But since, as I think, the words concern those who are superior to those who were living according to the shadow of the Law, it accordingly says, *Though man walks in an image.*

What this means will be more clearly understood from the words of the Apostle Paul,[18] who indicates that there are three distinct aspects to the Law,[19] calling them shadow and image and truth;[20] for he said, "The Law, while containing a shadow of the good things to come, not the image itself of the realities, is incapable, by means of the same sacrifices which they offer each year without ceasing, of making those who approach perfect."[21] Therefore, "the Law contains the shadow of the good things to come, not the image itself of the realities," demonstrating without a doubt that the image of the realities differs from what is called the Law's shadow. If there is someone capable of describing[22] the worship of the Jewish religion, he would realize that the Temple did not contain the image of the realities, but the shadow: he would see that the altar is also a shadow, that the goats and calves that are led to sacrifice are

17. Cf. Phil 2.7.

18. Origen generally ascribed Hebrews to Paul. It has become almost customary to cite Origen's reservations about Pauline authorship, as, e.g., Bruce Metzger, *The Canon of the New Testament: Its Origin, Development, and Significance* (Oxford: Clarendon, 1987), 138. This view, however, has been challenged, and Origen's basic confidence in the Pauline authorship of Hebrews has been deftly examined and articulated by Matthew Thomas, "Origen on Paul's Authorship of Hebrews," in *New Testament Studies* 65 (2019): 598–609.

19. *Tres quasdam species proprietatis designat in lege.*

20. This is a significant statement, both for Origen's epistemology and for his hermeneutics. The Old Testament is the shadow, Christ is the image, and the reality of what Christ images is understood anagogically. It would be tempting, though perhaps overly facile, to simplify this schema: Literal-historical/Christological/Anagogical.

21. Heb 10.1; cf. *Comm in Jn* 1.39 [SC 120bis.78].

22. *Describere;* perhaps alternately, "deconstructing," to use a term borrowed from modern literary theory and philosophy; this seems to be what Origen is suggesting.

all a shadow, just as it is written, "our life is but a shadow upon the earth."[23]

But if someone were able to pass from this shadow, he would come to the image of the realities, and would behold the coming of Christ in the flesh, and would see him as the priest, who even now offers sacrifices to the Father,[24] and will continue to offer them. Further, he would understand that all these things are images of spiritual realities and that heavenly things are signified by tangible rites. The term "image" thus refers to that which is grasped right now and which human nature is capable of seeing. If, with your mind and soul,[25] you are able to pass through the heavens and to follow "Jesus, who passed through the heavens"[26] and who now stands before the face of God on our behalf,[27] you will find there those good things whose shadow the Law contained and whose image Christ revealed in the flesh; these are the things prepared for the blessed, which "eye has not seen, nor has ear heard, nor has it arisen in the heart of man."[28] When you see these things, you will understand that he who walks in them and remains steadfast in his longing and desire for them already walks, not in the image, but in truth itself.

Nevertheless, *man walks in an image.* Let me repeat the words spoken by the Apostle, in which he points out two kinds of images, one earthly, the other heavenly, and let us compare them to this passage: *Though man walks in an image.* And let us distinguish the specifics of what is stated in a general way, so that when the passage is divided and broken up into its separate elements, what lies hidden within will become clear.

This is what we say: every hostile power as well as every single divine virtue[29] that gives help to those who desire to at-

23. Cf. 1 Chr 29.15; Jb 8.9.

24. Cf. 1 Pt 2.5; Heb 10.12.

25. *Mente et animo.*

26. Heb 4.14.

27. *Assistit nunc vultui Dei pro nobis.* Cf. Heb 9.24.

28. 1 Cor 2.9.

29. *Unaquaeque virtus* [= δύναμις] *divina,* clearly juxtaposed to *omnis potestas inimica;* perhaps a reference to angelic assistance. Cf. 1 Cor 15.24; Eph 1.21; Jean Daniélou, *The Angels and their Mission according to the Fathers of the Church,* trans. David Heimann (Westminster, MD: The Newman Press, 1957; repr., Allen, TX: Christian Classics, 1987), esp. 83–94. Without the modifiers *omnis* and

tain salvation produces certain images in the soul of those who show their receptivity to them by their various inclinations. For example, as I have said before, all of us who are human certainly bear an image, whether of the heavenly or of the earthly, yet there is also a considerable diversity among these. Every sinner, for instance, bears the image of the earthly, but not each in the same way. For the murderer and the liar do not bear the image of the earthly in an equal manner, nor do the adulterer and the slanderer, the seducer of children and the thief. Although all of these bear the image of the earthly, there is a considerable diversity among them according to the differences among their sins.

Having then considered the differences in the image of the earthly, consider also the differences in the image of the heavenly; take Paul, who bore the image of the heavenly, and Timothy also. What do we see? Do we think that the image of the heavenly was found in the same way in Paul as it was in Timothy? Was there nothing greater, nothing more admirable in Paul's image than in Timothy's image? As far as I am concerned, Paul was greater than[30] Timothy in the merit of his life, the power of his speech, and the grandeur of his mission, so much so that in him a greater and more splendid image of the heavenly shone forth, that image which Christ formed in him, since Christ spoke in him.[31] Christ formed another, and, in my opinion, lesser image in him who said: "The angel said who spoke in me."[32] As you ponder each of these for yourself, you will discover differences in the image, whether the earthly among sinners or the heavenly among the holy.

Everything that we do at each hour or moment forms some image; and for this reason we should examine each and every one of our actions and evaluate ourselves, in this action or in that statement, and determine whether a heavenly or an earthly

---

unaquaeque, one might see this as the juxtaposition of "the power of the Enemy" with "divine strength."

30. *Secundum hoc quod praecedebat;* perhaps also a reference to Paul's greater age.

31. Cf. 2 Cor 13.3.

32. Zec 1.14.

image is being painted[33] in our soul. But it will not seem unhelpful as well to warn you that many in this world have perished on account of the images of wicked kings—or, rather, tyrants—for this reason alone: that tyrannical images were detected in them, and this alone was enough to bring a charge against them. Now then, let each one of you diligently examine himself, review the hidden recesses of his heart, and discern carefully what images he is bearing there. If you discover there the devil's portrait and the image of Satan, what escape will there be for your life, who will have mercy upon you, when from the secret chamber of your heart emerges the image of the tyrant?

But if you want me to be more specific in indicating images of this sort, listen: anger is an image of the tyrant, as are greed, deceit, pride, arrogance, worldly boasting, envy, drunkenness, gluttony,[34] and the like. If you fail to expel these from your house very quickly, if you do not remove and scrape away every taint of this most wicked painting from your mind,[35] and wipe away every trace of its poisonous color, the very images will cause you to perish. This is what is to be said about the passage: *man walks in an image.*

3. It continues: *He stores up and knows not for whom he gathers.*[36] If we were to do a thorough job of explaining this passage, it would have been necessary to inquire what are the things that are being stored up without knowing for whom they are being gathered, as well as what are the things that are being gathered without knowing for whom they are left.[37]

33. *Depingitur;* alternately, "is being represented" or "formed"; cf. *OLD* s.v. § 4. Given the reference to the "painting" (*huius picturae)* of the images which follows, "being painted" seems preferable.

34. *comessationes;* cf. the etymology found in Pseudo-Jerome, *In Ep ad Rom* 13 [PL 30.706] (probably the work of John the Deacon; cf. CPL 952), a gloss on Rom 13.13: *non in comessationibus et ebrietatibus, non in cubilibus et impudicitiis; comessatio est mensae collatio.*

35. *A sensibus tuis;* literally, "from your thoughts"; cf. *OLD s.v. sensus* § 9; so Crouzel [SC 411.382]: "de tes pensées"; Prinzivalli, ed., *Origene, Omelie sui Salmi* (1991), 379, more literally, "dai tuoi sensi"; the former seems more likely as the *mens* or higher activity of the soul would seem to be the locus of these *imagines.*

36. Ps 38.7b.

37. *Permanent:* "remain" in the sense of "be left for"; cf. *OLD* s.v. § 2b; cf. also Mt 19.21; Mk 10.21; Lk 18.22.

And next: *And now what is my hope? Is it not the Lord?*[38] Just as Christ is our Wisdom and Christ is our Justice, according to what is written: "he who became for us Wisdom from God and Justice and Holiness and Redemption,"[39] so also our Hope, that is, our Patience, is Christ. For this reason, "the wise man should not glory in his own wisdom nor the strong man in his own strength,"[40] because in Christ we possess all things. Now, then, what is my hope, that is, my patience? It is the Lord.

And my substance is from you.[41] If I have a substance that consists of spiritual wealth, it is from God. For "God breathed into the face of man the spirit of life, and man became a living soul."[42]

4. *Rescue me from all my iniquities.*[43] It is necessary that *from all* be added, to make it clear that no iniquity should constrain or hinder us. But let us consider how God rescues us from iniquities. If we repent of our wicked deeds and are turned back to God, God accepts our conversion and grants forgiveness of our iniquities according to the degree of our conversion. For the one who is forgiven more loves more; that is why it is said that "much has been forgiven that woman, because she has loved much."[44] Thus the measure of forgiveness is determined by the degree of repentance. But we should not deceive ourselves and think that these are granted without regard for standards or judgments.

For I think that he who has fulfilled all righteousness[45] is the one who washes away all his iniquities. But the one who has done a few deeds of righteousness or accomplished only a portion of it, would cancel only a certain portion of his iniquities. Now the one who has undertaken perfect and complete penance for all his wickedness in such a way that he can then offer

38. Ps 38.8.
39. 1 Cor 1.30.
40. Jer 9.23.
41. Ps 38.8.
42. Gn 2.7.
43. Ps 38.9.
44. Lk 7.47.
45. *Omnes iustitias;* in most cases I have rendered *iustitia* and its cognates as "justice," but here the context clearly calls for "righteousness"; cf. Mt 3.15.

a pure heart to God, that person at the same time has washed away every stain of his sins. But if his repentance was partial, he then deserved only partial forgiveness. Since the prophet knew all this and was aware that God indeed rescues some individuals from all their iniquities and frees others from some of their iniquities, I think this is why he is confident that he has acted in a way worthy of rescue from all his iniquities and says boldly to the Lord: *Rescue me from all my iniquities.*[46]

5. *You have offered me as an object of scorn to the fool.*[47] As long as we have sins, it is necessary for us to be reproached by the fool, the devil, who is our accuser.[48] If our sins are found not to be wiped away but inscribed in us by the devil's pen, the enemy will reproach us for the very deeds we have done. For just as every good deed is said to be "written not by ink, but by the Spirit of the Living God,"[49] so every wicked deed is written with the ink and pen[50] of the devil. It is for this reason that our Lord and Savior has erased the bond[51] of our sins, which had been written against us with the devil as witness, just as he had foretold through the prophet who said, "Behold, I will blot out your iniquities like a cloud and your sins like the mist,"[52] and "I will remember them no more."[53]

So that we may not be reproached by the Fool, let us turn

46. Ps 38.9.

47. Ibid.

48. *Ab insipiente et accusatore* [= ὑπὸ τοῦ κατηγόρου] *nostro diabolo;* cf. Rv 12.10; cf. *Hom in Ps* 37.2.2 [SC 411.306].

49. 2 Cor 3.3.

50. He uses the terms *stylus* ([reed] pen) and *calamus* (quill), apparently without much difference in meaning, though, of course, *stylus* lends itself to the metaphor of impressions made in or on the soul (like a tablet). In *De principiis* 2.11.4 [GK 446], Origen discusses the innate desire for God implanted in the human person and how, much as in preparing a painting (the same metaphor applied above in terms of the devil's image), an outline of the truth is "sketched" on the heart with the "pen" of Christ: *Cum aliquis velit imaginem pingere, si ante futurae formae lineamenta tenuis stili adumbratione designet et superponendis vultibus capaces praeparet notas, sine dubio per adumbrationem iam inposita praeformatio ad suscipiendos veros illos colores paratior invenitur, si modo adumbratio ipsa ac deformatio stilo Domini nostri Iesu Christi "in cordis nostri tabulis" perscribatur.*

51. *Chirographum,* certificate of debt. Cf. Col 2.14.

52. Is 44.22.

53. Jer 31.34.

ourselves from all our iniquities, lest, detecting in us the stains of sins, that is, the marks of his will, he reproach us and say, "Look, this one was called a Christian and was marked on the forehead with the sign of Christ, but he carried in his heart my will[54] marked with my signature![55] See, this one renounced me and my works in baptism, and yet he was an accomplice in my works and obeyed my laws!" Freed, therefore, from all iniquities, let us make every effort that, on the Day of Judgment, we may not succumb to such reproaches of the fool, the devil.

6. *I was silent and did not open my mouth; for it was you who did this.*[56] We have already explained this earlier, when we treated the verse that said, *While the sinner stood against me, I became quiet and humbled myself, and kept silent about what is good.*[57] Indeed, it is good when the barbs of detraction, slander, and abuse are hurled at us to keep in mind this verse: *I was silent and did not open my mouth; for it was you who did this.*

It seems reasonable, however, to ask what *it was you who did this* means, for the Psalm did not add what he had done. Yet the Psalm's logical sequence[58] is itself instructive for us, since it describes, as it were, a kind of struggle between us and the sinner who stands in opposition to us; for it indicates that God himself has done this, that is, that God caused these struggles as an exercise for us and for the sake of our progress.[59]

I will therefore keep in mind that you have caused these struggles and that it is you who have prepared these exercises in patience for us. For when I was incited to anger, when I was

54. *Meas autem voluntates;* perhaps, since plural, alternately, "my purposes" or "my designs."

55. *Meas autem voluntates et mea chirographa gerebat in corde;* clearly juxtaposed to the "sign" or "seal" of baptism borne on the forehead.

56. Ps 38.10.

57. Ps 38.2–3; cf. *Hom in Ps* 38.1.4 [SC 411.340].

58. *Ordo* [perhaps = ἀκολουθία], a technical term of exegesis meaning "coherence." Cf. Bernhard Neuschäfer, *Origenes als Philologe* (Basel: Friedrich Reinhardt, 1987), 244–46; and D. Dawson, "Allegorical Reading and the Embodiment of the Soul in Origen," in *Christian Origins: Theology, Rhetoric, and Community,* ed. Lewis Ayres and Gareth Jones (London: Routledge, 1998), 26–43. Cf. *Hom in Ps* 36.3.11 [SC 411.168], where *consequentia* likely renders ἀκολουθία.

59. This is a clear expression of Origen's understanding of struggle as educative or remedial.

provoked by abusive language, in order that I not transgress the bounds of patience nor permit any word displeasing to you to pass from my lips: *I was silent and did not open my mouth.* But if I am able to advance even further,[60] following the principles established by Paul, I will not only keep silent and not open my mouth, but further, when cursed, I will bless, and when blasphemed, I will entreat.[61]

7. *Take away your blows from me; I have been worn down from the strength of your hand.*[62] What the Latin translators have called blows (*plagas*) is written in the Greek texts as scourges (*flagella*),[63] so that it is: *Take away your scourges from me.* This seems to be what someone in the position of being corrected by scourges says, since he is rebuked as a human being for his sins, or scourged that he might be made better.

This is how many understand the passage that says: "Son, do not be offended by God's discipline nor grow weary when you are rebuked by him. For God chides the one whom he loves; he scourges every son he receives."[64] So if one is ever chided with rebukes of this kind, it seems quite appropriate for him to say, *Take away your scourges from me; I have been worn down from the strength of your hand.* This seems to be quite fittingly related to what is written: *You have chided*—or disciplined[65]—*man with rebukes on account of his iniquity.*[66]

But I also am aware of other scourges with which we are more violently tormented, those very ones that Wisdom describes through the prophet (for indeed I call him a prophet): "Who will give scourges to my thinking and wisdom's rebuke to my heart, so that they may not spare my thoughtless deeds[67]

60. *Amplius aliquid ... valuero profligare,* taking *amplius aliquid* as an accusative of extent; literally, "If I will have been able to accomplish something more," perhaps an echo of Rom 8.37: ἐν τούτοις πᾶσιν ὑπερνικῶμεν. The context is certainly similar to 1 Cor 4.12, the allusion that immediately follows it.

61. Cf. 1 Cor 4.12–13.

62. Ps 38.11.

63. = μαστίγας.

64. Prv 3.11–12.

65. *Vel erudisti;* Origen's gloss on the text reveals his understanding of punishment as medicinal or educative.

66. Ps 38.12.

67. *Ignorationibus* (ἀγνοήμασιν in LXX).

nor ignore my sins?"[68] Do you see how he prays for his heart to be scourged for his sins and for his thoughts to be beaten? If you ever find yourself afflicted after sin and tormented in your heart and accused by your thoughts, if you ever observe yourself reprimanded[69] by your conscience and scourged by its blows, take hope for yourself of improvement and salvation. For the path to conversion is nearer to you than to those who do not even realize that they have sinned and who are neither saddened by their sins nor endure the scourging of their conscience. If, then, you see yourself scourged and tormented in your thoughts[70] and recognizing the hope of salvation near at hand, say concerning those who have sinned in the same way, but who have not repented in like manner for their sins: "They are not among the labors of men, and they will not be scourged with men, since pride held them."[71] So if you are tormented and distressed in your heart, say to the Lord: "Many indeed are the scourges of sinners, but mercy will surround those who hope in the Lord."[72]

Thus we have shown that scourges are prepared for men in two ways: either externally in a manner we can feel, when we are scourged with weariness, injuries, and various kinds of afflictions, or also when from the recollection of an oppressive sin, we are pierced in the heart by the sting of our conscience. It will therefore fittingly be said in respect to either: *Take away your blows from me.*

But perhaps someone says, "Granted that this kind of prayer, which asks that external torments cease, seems helpful, but will it also be seen to constrain the corrective sting of the heart and mind?"

Due measure is sought in everything; even more is due measure most appropriate in regard to scourges. For if they exceed due measure, they will harm you, even though they are them-

68. Sir 23.2; this text differs significantly from that found in the LXX and later in the Vlg.

69. *Notari;* perhaps even "indict"; the sense is arguably legal.

70. *Flagellari ... in cogitationibus tuis;* the text parallels Sir 23.2, *in cogitatu meo flagella.*

71. Ps 72.5–6.

72. Ps 31.10.

selves good. What am I saying about scourges? It says, "You will find honey. Eat what suffices for you, lest perhaps having eaten too much, you vomit."[73] For if due measure is beneficial in honey, how much more rightly is it to be sought and maintained in scourges? This is why the Apostle, too, fearing the excessive scourging of the heart of one who had sinned and was greatly saddened, said: "Lest perchance one like this be overwhelmed with even greater sadness."[74]

8. *You have disciplined man with rebukes for his iniquity and have made his soul waste away like a spider's web.*[75] The soul that sins becomes heavier.[76] For such is the nature of sin, and for this reason it is written: "This people's heart has become heavy."[77] For just as sin makes it heavy, so, conversely, virtue renders the soul light; so (to stretch in a way the novelty of this expression)[78] virtue wipes out and eliminates everything in the soul that is corporeal and renders the soul more purely incorporeal.[79] That, however, the soul of one who sins grows heavy and

73. Prv 25.16.

74. 2 Cor 2.7.

75. Ps 38.12.

76. *Crassior;* among the meanings for *crassus* is "dull or undisciplined," and it would fit Origen's "educational" motif. The dialectic (heavy-light) that is employed here might also be rendered as thick-refined. While a case might be made for the latter, the former was chosen to make it clear that Origen is not speaking here of a double creation (the ethereal body prior to the fall—the embodied existence after the fall; see Henri Crouzel, *Origen,* trans. A. S. Worrall [San Francisco: Harper and Row, 1989], 94–98), but rather of the condition of the believer's soul in this life. On this, see *De principiis* 2.2.2 [GK 298]: *materialis ista substantia huius modi habens naturam, quae ex omnibus ad omnia transformetur, cum ad inferiores quosque trahitur, in crassiorem corporis statum solidioremque formatur, ita ut visibiles istas mundi species variasque distinguat.*

77. Mt 13.15, quoting Is 6.10; *incrassatum* is the rendering of the scriptural ἐπαχύνθη.

78. *Ut extorqueam quodammodo vocabuli novitatem;* a curious, but clearly parenthetical, remark; Origen knows it is obviously metaphorical to assign weight to souls, hence the remark.

79. *Corporeum ... incorpoream* [probably = σωματικόν ... ἀσώματον]. On this important distinction in Origen, see Lawrence Hennessey, "A Philosophical Issue in Origen's Eschatology: The Three Senses of Incorporeality," in *Origeniana Quinta,* ed. Robert Daly (Leuven: Peeters, Leuven University Press, 1992), 373–80; on this notion of incorporeality as critical for understanding Origen's hermeneutic, see Brian Daley, "Origen's *De Principiis:* A Guide to the Principles

becomes, so to speak, fleshly, is indicated by what is written: "My Spirit will not remain in these men, for they are flesh."[80] For "flesh" is undoubtedly its term for sinful and heavier souls.

If, therefore, the soul should grow heavy and become "flesh," it teaches what kind of remedy God has prepared: *You have disciplined man with rebukes for his iniquity,* it says, *and have made his soul waste away like a spider's web.* It is thus God's work to effect this wasting away and to destroy everything whatsoever of the heavier matter that surrounds the soul, in order to reduce and file away the "wisdom of the flesh"[81] and thus at long last to call the soul back to the refined[82] understanding of heavenly and unseen realities.

In the prophet Ezekiel, we find such realities indicated with considerable mystery, where meats are said to be placed into the cauldron or stockpot and boiled, and it is said that they are cooked down and reduced, or that the meats are boiled until the stock is thoroughly cooked down.[83] This was written in these very words, because cauldrons or stockpots, heated by fire, will receive us, and we who have made our souls fleshly or heavy will be thrown into them, unless we first take the initiative while in this world to "reduce" our flesh through penance, so that the heaviness of our soul will be reduced to the lightness of a spider's web.[84] If after this we still walk in the flesh, we will be cast into those stockpots that are heated with wood or hay or stubble, that is, with our own works that we have preferred to[85] the foundation of Christ.[86]

---

of Christian Scriptural Interpretation," in *Vetera et Nova: Patristic Studies in Honor of Thomas Patrick Halton,* ed. John Petruccione (Washington, DC: The Catholic University of America Press, 1998), 3–21.

80. Gn 6.3.

81. *Prudentiam carnis;* cf. Rom 8.7 [probably = τὸ φρόνημα τῆς σαρκός], which in the Vlg is rendered *sapientia carnis.* Cf. *Hom in Ps* 36.1.2 [SC 411.68]; *Hom in Ps* 37.1.2 [SC 411.280].

82. *Subtilem;* a pun, earlier rendered "light."

83. Cf. Ezek 24.3–5.

84. Here Origen is mixing the metaphors found in Ps 38.12 and Ezek 24.3–5, to which he has just alluded.

85. *Superposuerimus;* cf. *OLD* s.v. § 3.c; another possible, but less likely, meaning is "which we have built upon the foundation of Christ"; cf. 1 Cor 3.11.

86. Cf. 1 Cor 3.11–12.

Jeremiah, in my opinion, says just this: "I have seen," he says, "the cauldron or stockpot seething, facing from the north."[87] Or again, when he saw a rod of nut wood.[88] Let us inquire into this passage, for he is showing the rod as well as the heated stockpot at the same time for this reason, that if you were to receive disciplines with the rod and become better, you would not need the heated stockpot. But if you remain undisciplined and are not made better by the rod, that is to say if you fail to repent when verbally reprimanded or checked[89] and when rebuked by such a rod as Paul speaks of—"What do you want? Should I come to you with a rod or in charity of spirit and gentleness?"[90]—if therefore you are not made better with such a rod, you will be cast into the stockpot, and the stockpot will be heated. Jeremiah saw each of these at the same time—both the rod and the stockpot; while we look at them both, we should distinguish between them. This is why it is written: *You have made his soul waste away like a spider's web.*[91]

9. If, then, we relate the text to this creature, which by its nature accomplishes a very subtle work and one that the eye can barely see,[92] the interpretation given above will seem appropriate. But if someone makes reference to what Isaiah writes in his book, namely, "They have woven a spider's web,"[93] it must

87. Jer 1.13; Crouzel, SC 411.398, n. 1, observes that Ambrose reproduces the citations of Ezekiel and Jeremiah in his *Enarr in Ps* 38.34 [CSEL 64.208–209].

88. *Virgam vidit nuceam.* Cf. Jer 1.11. Origen's text (as translated by Rufinus) differs significantly from the later Vulgate, which offers the sole reading *vigilantem.* Cf. Jerome, who, in *Ep* 53.8 [CSEL 54.460] to Paulinus, dated between 386 and 400 AD, has *virgam nuceam et ollam succensam a facie aquilonis.*

89. *Confutatus;* an original meaning of *confutare* is "to check or stop the boiling of a liquid," quite à propos of the metaphor being used.

90. 1 Cor 4.21.

91. For a brief summary of Origen's ideas about the afterlife, see the instructive article of Lawrence Hennessey, "Origen of Alexandria: The Fate of the Soul and Body After Death," *Second Century* 8 (1991): 163–78.

92. *Si ergo sermonem ad naturam animalis istius retorquemus, ex illa parte qua opus subtilissimum et quod vix oculus comprehendere potest expleat, apta videbitur expositio ista quam superius explanavimus* [SC 411.398]; this odd sentence seems to allude to the contrast between the beauty of the spider's web and its tenuous character, as he is about to make clear.

93. Is 59.5.

be understood in another way: for you should know that everything which the sinner has "woven" and accomplishes is like everything the spider weaves: it amounts to nothing, though it seems varied and structured, and though carried out with a subtle skill.

How numerous the webs woven by those rich who have gone before us, who accumulated wealth with various kinds of craftiness and clever contrivances, who sought magistracies, offices, and consulships in diverse ways,[94] whether through ambition or cruelty: all of these wove spider's webs. All their deeds were as empty and worthless as the webs of a spider, and for that reason their souls have wasted away like a spider's web. *Nevertheless, every man is vanity.*[95] We have already explained this earlier.[96]

10. *God, hear my prayer and my appeal; turn your ear to my tears.*[97] Again, one should offer prayer to God with tears and be moved to appeal to the Lord from one's inmost being, so that the mind, with faith in the judgment to come, might recollect its own sins, and not without tears and weeping, since the one who is distraught and in tears says to the Lord: "I pour out my prayer in your sight."[98]

Therefore, *Turn your ears to my tears and do not be silent,* he says, *from me.*[99] That is, do not remain silent when I pray. And what else? Even now, as I speak, say, "I am here."[100]

11. *For I am a foreigner before you and a sojourner like all my ancestors.*[101] Because I am a sojourner, I must also be a foreigner, for I am unlike you. For you alone are eternal, and we have a beginning (inasmuch as one can be discovered). Yet however worthy I may become in your sight, I nevertheless remain a foreigner and sojourner before you: for all my ancestors were foreigners and sojourners before you; Abraham, too, is a sojourner before

94. *Diversa;* here adverbial.
95. Ps 38.12.
96. Cf. *Hom in Ps* 38.1.11, treating Ps 38.6 [SC 411.362–366]. See pp. 219–20.
97. Ps 38.13.
98. Ps 141.3.
99. Ps 38.13.
100. Cf. Is 58.9.
101. Ps 38.13.

you,[102] for he did not always exist, but he began to exist when you willed it; this is true, as well, for Isaac, Jacob, and all the just.

12. *Forgive me, that I may be restored before I depart and no longer exist,*[103] for I am a foreigner. As long as I am with you, I have existence. But should I depart from you, I would lose even my very being, and I will be as one who does not exist. So for this reason it says about those who sin: "And they will be as though they do not exist."[104] And elsewhere: he summoned into being those things that do not exist.[105] *Forgive me, that I may be restored before I depart and no longer exist.*[106] Nevertheless, it must be understood that our existence—whether to exist or not—is within our power.[107] For as long as we cling to God[108] and attach ourselves to him who truly exists, we also have existence. If, however, we should depart from him and cling not to our God, we decline through vice in the opposite direction. This is not meant to indicate the annihilation of the soul's substance; but the individual is called "non-existent" when he does not abide in the One who truly exists and who always exists; for his existence comes from Him.

For this reason, the prophet's word also exhorts us, when it says: "We will follow the Lord our God, and we will cling to him."[109] But may we ourselves also say: "My soul has clung to you,"[110] in Christ Jesus our Lord, to whom are honor and glory, forever and ever. Amen.

102. Cf. Gn 23.4.

103. Ps 38.14.

104. Ob 16.

105. Cf. Rom 4.17; *Hom in Ps* 36.5.7 [SC 411.254].

106. Ps 38.14.

107. Taking *in nobis* as the likely equivalent of ἐφ' ἡμῖν, a term in ancient philosophy employed by the Stoics to express freedom. This is a bold statement, if construed in this way, but the context (the following lines) seems to demand it. On this, see Charlotte Stough, "Stoic Determinism and Moral Responsibility," in *The Stoics,* ed. John M. Rist (Berkeley: University of California Press, 1978), 203–30; the standard study is Albrecht Dihle, *The Theory of Will in Classical Antiquity* (Berkeley: University of California Press, 1982), but see now the posthumously published lectures of Michael Frede, *A Free Will: Origins of the Notion in Ancient Thought* (Berkeley: University of California Press, 2011).

108. Cf. Ps 72.28.

109. Jos 24.24.

110. Ps 62.9.

GENERAL INDEX

INDEX OF HOLY SCRIPTURE

Old Testament

New Testament

RECENT VOLUMES IN THE FATHERS OF THE CHURCH SERIES

ST. EPHREM THE SYRIAN, *Songs for the Fast and Pascha,* translated by Joshua Falconer, Blake Hartung, and J. Edward Walters, Volume 145 (2022)

CASSIODORUS, ST. GREGORY THE GREAT, AND ANONYMOUS GREEK SCHOLIA, *Writings on the Apocalypse,* translated by Francis X. Gumerlock, Mark DelCogliano, and T. C. Schmidt, Volume 144 (2022)

MORALIA ET ASCETICA ARMENIACA: THE OFT-REPEATED DISCOURSES, translated by Abraham Terian, Volume 143 (2021)

ORIGEN, *Homilies on Isaiah,* translated by Elizabeth Ann Dively Lauro, Volume 142 (2021)

ORIGEN, *Homilies on the Psalms: Codex Monacensis Graecus 314,* translated by Joseph W. Trigg, Volume 141 (2020)

ST. AMBROSE, *Treatises on Noah and David,* translated by Brian P. Dunkle, SJ, Volume 140 (2020)

RUFINUS OF AQUILEIA, *Inquiry about the Monks in Egypt,* translated by Andrew Cain, Volume 139 (2019)

ST. CYRIL OF ALEXANDRIA, *Glaphyra on the Pentateuch, Volume 2: Exodus through Deuteronomy,* translated by Nicholas P. Lunn, Volume 138 (2019)

ST. CYRIL OF ALEXANDRIA, *Glaphyra on the Pentateuch, Volume 1: Genesis,* translated by Nicholas P. Lunn, with introduction by Gregory K. Hillis, Volume 137 (2018)

ST. MAXIMOS THE CONFESSOR, *On Difficulties in Sacred Scripture: The Responses to Thalassios,* translated by Fr. Maximos Constas, Volume 136 (2018)

WORKS OF ORIGEN IN THIS SERIES

Homilies on Genesis and Exodus, translated by Ronald E. Heine, Fathers of the Church 71 (1982)

Commentary on the Gospel according to John, Books 1–10, translated by Ronald E. Heine, Fathers of the Church 80 (1989)

Homilies on Leviticus, translated by Gary Wayne Barkley, Fathers of the Church 83 (1990)

Commentary on the Gospel according to John, Books 13–32, translated by Ronald Heine, Fathers of the Church 89 (1993)

Homilies on Luke, translated by Joseph T. Lienhard, SJ, Fathers of the Church 94 (1996)

Homilies on Jeremiah; Homily on 1 Kings 28, translated by John Clark Smith, Fathers of the Church 97 (1998)

Commentary on the Epistle to the Romans, Books 1–5, translated by Thomas P. Scheck, Fathers of the Church 103 (2001)

Commentary on the Epistle to the Romans, Books 6–10, translated by Thomas P. Scheck, Fathers of the Church 104 (2002)

Homilies on Joshua, translated by Barbara J. Bruce, edited by Cynthia White, Fathers of the Church 105 (2002)

Homilies on Judges, translated by Elizabeth Ann Dively Lauro, Fathers of the Church 119 (2010)

Homilies on the Psalms: Codex Monacensis Graecus 314, translated by Joseph W. Trigg, Fathers of the Church 141 (2020)

Homilies on Isaiah, translated by Elizabeth Ann Dively Lauro, Fathers of the Church 142 (2021)

Homilies on Psalms 36–38, translated by Michael Heintz, Fathers of the Church 146 (2023)